Self-Constitution

Self-Constitution

Agency, Identity, and Integrity

Christine M. Korsgaard

OXFORD
UNIVERSITY PRESS

OXFORD
UNIVERSITY PRESS

Great Clarendon Street, Oxford OX2 6DP

Oxford University Press is a department of the University of Oxford.
It furthers the University's objective of excellence in research, scholarship,
and education by publishing worldwide in

Oxford New York

Auckland Cape Town Dar es Salaam Hong Kong Karachi
Kuala Lumpur Madrid Melbourne Mexico City Nairobi
New Delhi Shanghai Taipei Toronto
With offices in
Argentina Austria Brazil Chile Czech Republic France Greece
Guatemala Hungary Italy Japan South Korea Poland Portugal
Singapore Switzerland Thailand Turkey Ukraine Vietnam

ISBN 978-0-19-955280-1

Printed in the United Kingdom by
the MPG Books Group Ltd

In Memory

Marion (Maren) Hangaard Kortbek Korsgaard

1919—1999

Perfect Mother, Best Friend

Contents

Abbreviations for Frequently Cited Works

References to and citations of frequently cited works are given parenthetically in the text, using the abbreviations cited below. For the editions and translations quoted, please see the Bibliography.

1. Aristotle

References to Aristotle's works will be given by the standard Bekker page, column, and line numbers, using the following abbreviations.

NE	*Nicomachean Ethics*
M	*Metaphysics*
MA	*Movement of Animals*
OS	*On the Soul*
POL	*Politics*

2. Hume

T   *A Treatise of Human Nature* (cited by book, section, and page number)

3. Kant

References to Kant's works will be given by the page numbers of the relevant volume of *Kants gesammelte Schriften*, which appear in the margins of most translations. The *Critique of Pure Reason*, however, is cited in its own standard way, by the page numbers of both the first (A) and second (B) editions. The abbreviations used follow:

ANTH	*Anthropology from a Pragmatic Point of View*
C₁	*Critique of Pure Reason*
C₂	*Critique of Practical Reason*
CBHH	"Conjectures on the Beginning of Human History"
G	*Groundwork of the Metaphysics of Morals*
IUH	"Idea for a Universal History with a Cosmopolitan Purpose"
LE	*Lectures on Ethics*

MM   *The Metaphysics of Morals*
PP   *Perpetual Peace*
REL   *Religion within the Limits of Reason Alone*

4. Nietzsche

GM   *The Genealogy of Morals*

5. Plato

References to Plato's works are inserted into the text, using the standard Stephanus numbers inserted into the margins of most editions and translations of Plato's works. Other works are indicated by title.

R   *Republic*

6. My own works

CA   *The Constitution of Agency*
CKE   *Creating the Kingdom of Ends*
SN   *The Sources of Normativity* (cited by section and page number)

Preface

One who is just does not allow any part of himself to do the work of another part or allow the various classes within him to meddle with each other. He regulates well what is really his own and rules himself. He puts himself in order, is his own friend, and harmonizes the three parts of himself like three limiting notes in a musical scale—high, low, and middle. He binds together those parts and any others there may be in between, and from having been many things he becomes entirely one, moderate and harmonious. Only then does he act.

(Plato, *Republic* 443d–e)

Both human beings and the other animals act, but human actions can be morally right or wrong, while the actions of the other animals cannot. This must be because of something distinctive about the nature of human action, about the way in which we human beings make choices. In this book, I try to explain what that distinctive feature is, and how it is connected to some of the other things that make human life different from the lives of the other animals. The name I give to the distinctive feature is the traditional one—rationality. As I understand it, reason is a power we have in virtue of a certain type of self-consciousness—consciousness of the grounds of our own beliefs and actions. This form of self-consciousness gives us a capacity to control and direct our beliefs and actions that the other animals lack, and makes us active in a way that they are not. But it also gives us a problem that the other animals do not face—the problem of deciding what to count as a reason for belief or action. To put the point another way, this form of self-consciousness makes it necessary to *take control* of our beliefs and actions, but we must then work out how to do that: we must find normative principles, laws, to govern what we believe and do. The distinctive feature of human beings, reason, is therefore the capacity for normative self-government.

The capacity for normative self-government brings with it another distinctively human attribute, normative self-conception, perhaps more than anything else the thing that makes being human both an adventure and a curse. For an action is a movement attributable to an agent as its author, and that means that whenever you choose an action—whenever you take control of your own movements—you are constituting yourself as the author of that action, and so you are deciding who to be. Human beings therefore have a distinct form of identity, a norm-governed or practical form of identity, for which we are ourselves responsible. As a rational being, as a rational agent, you are faced with the task of *making something* of yourself, and you must regard yourself as a success or a failure insofar as you succeed or fail at this task.

If, when we act, we are trying to constitute ourselves as the authors of our own movements, and at the same time, we are making ourselves into the particular people who we are, then we may say that the function of action is *self-constitution*. This conception of action opens up the possibility that the specific form of goodness or badness that applies to human actions—rightness or wrongness—is goodness or badness *of their kind*, goodness or badness *as actions*. A good action is one that constitutes its agent as the autonomous and efficacious cause of her own movements. These properties correspond, respectively, to Kant's two imperatives of practical reason. Conformity to the categorical imperative renders us autonomous, and conformity to the hypothetical imperative renders us efficacious. These imperatives are therefore constitutive principles of action, principles to which we necessarily are trying to conform insofar as we are acting at all.

That way of putting it will make it clear that the conception of morality and practical reason that I defend in this book is the Kantian one. But I also draw on the work of Aristotle, to explain the sense in which an intentional movement can be attributed to an agent as its author, and on Plato, to explain the kind of unity that a person must have in order to be regarded as the author of her movements. For it is essential to the concept of an action that it is attributable to the person as a whole, as a unit, not to some force that is working in her or on her. And it was Plato who taught us, in the *Republic*, that the kind of unity required for agency is the kind of unity that a city has in virtue of having a just constitution.

Following Plato's lead, in this book I argue that the kind of unity that is necessary for action cannot be achieved without a commitment to morality. The task of self-constitution, which is simply the task of living a human life, places us in a relationship with ourselves—it means that we interact with ourselves. We make laws for ourselves, and those laws determine whether we constitute ourselves well or badly. And I argue that the only way in which you can constitute yourself well is by governing yourself in accordance with universal principles which you can will as laws for every rational being. It follows that you can't maintain the integrity you need in order to be an agent with your own identity on any terms short of morality itself. That doesn't mean that we have a reason for being moral that is selfish, that morality gets us something *else*, the integrity needed for agency and identity. Rather, it means that a commitment to the moral law is built right into the activity that, by virtue of being human, we are necessarily engaged in: the activity of making something of ourselves. The moral law is the law of self-constitution, and as such, it is a constitutive principle of human life itself.

In this book I argue that thinking is just talking to yourself, and talking is just thinking in the company of others (9.4.12). I have been working on this book for a long time, and have had the benefit of thinking in the company of many others. It was as a result of reading Derek Parfit's work that I first began to think of identity as a problem that human beings have to solve (see my "Personal Identity and the Unity of Agency: A Kantian Response to Parfit," CKE essay 13). I am grateful to Derek for that, and I apologize to him for kidnapping his Russian nobleman for my own purposes (see Chapter 9). Jay Schleusener once remarked to me that Socrates was "good at being a person," and anyone who reads this book will see what I have made of that thought. I first published a short version of the ideas found here as an essay, "Self-Constitution in the Ethics of Plato and Kant," in 1999 (*Journal of Ethics*, 3: 1–29; now CA essay 3), after delivering it in various places as a talk. I would like to thank audiences at the inaugural meeting of the Society for Ethics at the Eastern Division Meetings of the American Philosophical Association, the University of Amsterdam, the University of Constance, the Humboldt University of Berlin, the University of Pittsburgh, the University of Virginia, the University of Salzburg, the University of Toronto, York University of Toronto, and the University of Zurich for discussions of that paper.

I presented some of the other ideas found here as a talk, "Human Action and the Kantian Imperatives," to audiences at a joint session of the University of Adelaide and Flinders University, at the University of Auckland, as the Simone Weil Lecture at Australian Catholic University, at the Autonomous University of Mexico, the University of Canterbury, the University of Dunedin, the Research School of Social Sciences in Canberra, and Stanford University. I am grateful to all of these audiences for helpful and stimulating discussion.

I expanded the longer manuscript from which those essays were drawn into a set of lectures, which I delivered as the Locke Lectures at Oxford in 2002. I am deeply grateful to members of the Department of Philosophy at the University of Oxford for that opportunity and for their hospitality while I was there. I also delivered those lectures as the Hägerström Lectures at Uppsala in 2002, and individual lectures from the set, over the next few years, at the Scots Philosophical Society at the University of Aberdeen, as the Paton Lecture at St Andrews University, at the University of California at Berkeley, at Brandeis University, as keynote speaker at a Brown University Graduate

Student Conference, at a conference at the Center for Subjectivity Research at the University of Copenhagen, as the Royal Institute of Philosophy Lecture at Durham University, at the University of Glasgow, at the Central States Philosophical Association at the University of Missouri at Columbia, at Ohio University, at the University of Reykjavik, at the University of Stirling, and at Union College. I am grateful to the audiences on all of these occasions.

I also had very helpful discussions of the manuscript with the faculty of the Department of Philosophy at Lehigh University, and with the Colloquium on Ethics, Politics, and Society at LUISS University in Rome. I am especially grateful to Susan Wolf and the members of her seminar in 2004 for their extremely helpful and thought-provoking questions. I had the benefit of a great deal of commentary at a conference devoted to my work in Madrid in 2004. I would especially like to thank Mary Clayton Coleman, Ana Marta González, and David Dick for their comments on that occasion.

For individual comments on the manuscript at various stages of its evolution I would like to thank Melissa Barry, Alyssa Bernstein, Charlotte Brown, Sarah Buss, Douglas Edwards, Barbara Herman, Govert den Hartogh, Peter Hylton, Arthur Kuflik, Anthony Laden, Jonathan Lear, Anton Leist, Richard Moran, Julius Moravcsik, Herlinde Pauer-Studer, David Plunkett, Andrews Reath, Miles Rind, Arthur Ripstein, Amélie Rorty, Tamar Schapiro, and Theo van Willigenburg. I am sure that this list is radically incomplete—indeed I know that it is, for I have in my files an extremely helpful set of written comments, unsigned, the author of which I am unable to identify. I can only apologize to everyone who I have left out.

The book was completed under the auspices of a grant from the Mellon Foundation, to whom I am profoundly grateful. I would also like to thank Eylem Özaltun, Nataliya Palatnik, and Paul Schofield for proofreading the manuscript, saving it from many errors, and suggesting many helpful changes. And finally I would like to thank Douglas Edwards for help selecting the cover, and Peter Momtchiloff for his apparently boundless patience during the many years it took me to get ready to publish the book.

Christine M. Korsgaard
May 2008

1

Agency and Identity

1.1 Necessitation

1.1.1

Human beings are *condemned* to choice and action. Maybe you think you can avoid it, by resolutely standing still, refusing to act, refusing to move. But it's no use, for that will be something you have chosen to do, and then you will have acted after all. Choosing not to act makes not acting a kind of action, makes it something that you do.

This is not to say that you cannot fail to act. Of course you can. You can fall asleep at the wheel, you can faint dead away, you can be paralyzed with terror, you can be helpless with pain, or grief can turn you to stone. And then you will fail to act. But you can't *undertake* to be in those conditions—if you did, you'd be faking, and what's more, you'd be acting, in a wonderfully double sense of that word.[1] So as long as you're in charge, so long as nothing happens to derail you, you must act. You have no choice but to choose, and to act on your choice.

So action is necessary. What kind of necessity is this? Philosophers like to distinguish between *logical* and *causal* necessity. But the necessity of action isn't either of those. There's no logical contradiction in the idea of a person not acting, at least on any particular occasion. You could not fail to act, in all the ways I've just described, if there were. And although particular actions, or anyway particular movements, may have causes, the general necessity of action is not an event that is caused. I'm not talking about something that works *on* you, whether you know it or not, like a cause: I am talking about a necessity you are *faced* with.

Now sometimes we also talk about *rational* necessity, the necessity of following the principles of reason. If you believe the premises, then you *must* draw the conclusion. If you will the end, then you *must* will the means. That's rational necessity, and it's a necessity you are faced with, so that comes closer.

---

[1] Later I will argue that, for essentially the same reason, you cannot undertake to be an unjust person (9.1.5).

But the necessity of action isn't quite like that either, for in those cases we have an if-clause, and the necessity of action is, by contrast, as Kant would say, unconditional. The necessity of choosing and acting is not causal, logical, or rational necessity. It is our *plight*: the simple inexorable fact of the human condition.

1.1.2

But once inside that fact, once we face the necessity of acting, we are confronted with a different kind of necessity. We live under the pressure of a vast assortment of laws, duties, obligations, expectations, demands, and rules, all telling us what to do. Some of these demands are no doubt illicit or imaginary—just social pressure, as we say (as if we knew what that was). But there are many laws and demands that we feel we really are bound to obey. And yet in many cases we would be hard pressed to identify the source of what I call the *normativity* of a law or a demand—the grounds of its authority and the psychological mechanisms of its enforcement, the way that it binds you. In philosophy we raise questions about the normativity of highbrow laws like those of moral obligation or theoretical and practical reason. But it is worth remembering that in everyday life the same sort of questions can be raised about the normativity of the laws and demands of professional obligation, filial obedience, sexual fidelity, personal loyalty, and everyday etiquette.[2] And just as we may find ourselves rebelling against, say, the sacrifice of our happiness to the demands of justice, so also, in a smaller, more everyday way, we may find ourselves *bucking* against doing our chores or returning unwanted phone calls or politely thanking a despised host for a dull party.

The surprising thing is not that we resist such demands, but that our resistance so often fails. Sometimes to our own pleasant surprise, sometimes merely with bewilderment or bemusement, we find ourselves doing what we think we ought to do, in the teeth of our own reluctance, and even though

---

[2] Some philosophers think this is not a separate point: they think that insofar as we are bound by the laws and demands listed here it is because they are morally obligatory. That view in turn can take several forms: (1) they are derivable from moral considerations; (2) although not derivable from moral considerations, all of their normativity (if they really have any) is derived from morality; (3) they are independent sources of normativity, but morality backs and reinforces them. The first of those options founders over the obvious cultural relativity and situational nature of the obligations in question: universal reason does not tell us, say, when to bring gifts. On the second view, there is something like a moral obligation to be polite, whose details are filled in by cultural practice. My own view, spelled out in *The Sources of Normativity*, is a version of the third option: they are independent sources of normativity, yet may require moral backing if they are to maintain their normative force in the face of reflection. (SN 3.4.7–3.6.1, pp. 120–30, and section 5 of the Reply, pp. 251–8.) I believe we should prefer the third view, since people in whose lives morality has only a tenuous footing may nevertheless experience and take seriously these lower-order demands.

nothing obvious forces us to do it. We toil out to vote in unpleasant weather, telephone relatives to whom we would prefer not to speak, attend suffocatingly boring meetings at work, and do all sorts of irksome things at the behest of our families and friends. Part of the lawless charm of a character like W. C. Fields springs from the fact that most of us are almost incapable of ignoring the requests of children, and yet we chafe under the enthrallment. It is a fact worthy of philosophical attention that the wanton disregard of life's little rules makes the people who would never break them laugh. To be sure, there is no question that in what Joseph Butler called "a cool hour," most of us would unhesitatingly choose to be the kinds of people who generally do what they ought.[3] As Aristotle observes:

> no one would maintain that he is happy who has not in him a particle of courage or temperance or justice or practical wisdom, who is afraid of every insect which flutters past him, and will commit any crime, however great, in order to gratify his lust for meat or drink, who will sacrifice his dearest friend for the sake of half a farthing, and is as feeble and false in mind as a child or a madman. (POL 7.1 1323a26–34)

But there is also no question that in those warmer hours when we actually choose the particular actions demanded of us, we often manifestly do not *want* to do them. And yet we do them, all the same: the normativity of obligation is, among other things, a psychological force. Let me give this phenomenon a name, borrowed from Immanuel Kant. Since normativity is a form of necessity, Kant calls its operation within us—its manifestation as a psychological force—*necessitation*.[4]

1.1.3

In recent years, it has become rather unfashionable to focus on the phenomenon of necessitation. It seems to evoke the lugubrious image of the good human being as a Miserable Sinner in a state of eternal reform, who must constantly repress his unruly desires in order to conform to the demands of duty. Necessitation is thus conceived as *repression*. In opposition to this, some recent virtue theorists have offered us the (to my mind) equally rebarbative picture of the virtuous human being as a sort of Good Dog, whose desires and inclinations have been so perfectly trained that he always does what he ought to do spontaneously and with tail-wagging cheerfulness and enthusiasm. The opposition between these two pictures is shallow, for they share the basic

---

[3] See Joseph Butler, *Five Sermons*, ed. Stephen Darwall. The quotation is from Sermon 4 (Sermon 11 of the original *Fifteen Sermons Preached at the Rolls Chapel* from which these five are selected), paragraph 20, p. 56.

[4] *Nötigung* (G 4:413).

intuition that the experience of necessitation is a sign that there is something wrong with the person who undergoes it.[5] The disagreement is only about how inevitable the evil is. It may be natural to think of necessitation as a sign that something is wrong, since necessitation can be painful, and it is natural to interpret pain as a sign that something is wrong. But necessitation is so characteristic, so utterly commonplace a feature of human experience, that we should not be in a hurry to jump to that conclusion. In the *Republic*, Socrates says that the phrases we use to describe necessitation, phrases like "self-control" or "self-mastery" or "self-command," seem absurd on their surface, since the stronger self who imposes the necessity is the same person as the weaker self on whom it is imposed. But Socrates also suggests that these phrases are like "tracks or clues" that virtue has left in the language (R 430e). Necessitation, he thinks, reveals something important about human nature, about the constitution of the human soul. What it reveals—that the source of normativity lies in the human project of self-constitution—is my subject in this book.

1.1.4

The trouble with those two images of virtue—the Reformed Miserable Sinner and the Good Dog—and with the philosophical theories behind them, is not merely that they denigrate the experience of necessitation. It is also (and relatedly) that they do not give an adequate explanation of how we are necessitated. This is a somewhat complicated point, but let me try to explain what I have in mind.

Although there is reason to doubt whether David Hume would have accepted the characterization of normativity as a kind of necessity and its operation as a kind of necessitation, his theory of the natural virtues will serve my purposes well here, so I'm going to ask you to set those doubts aside. Just think about the question how normativity operates *in* us on the Humean view. Hume believes that moral concepts are generated from the point of view of a spectator, moved by sympathy to form sentiments of impartial love or hatred, inspired by people's dispositions and motives, which we accordingly deem "virtues" or "vices." For example, if I see that you pay your employees less than they need to live on, and reason that your desire for profit is the motive, then sympathy with your employees may lead me to condemn your desire for profit, and to call it the vice of greed. The person

---

[5] Kant himself seems to fall into this error in the *Groundwork*, when he suggests that necessitation is only experienced by an imperfectly rational will (G 4:414). I argue that this should not be Kant's considered view in "The Normativity of Instrumental Reason" (CA essay 1), pp. 51–2.

Hume calls "naturally virtuous" is simply someone whose dispositions and motives are those that, from this spectator point of view, strike us as lovable. She is, for example, beneficent, and the spectator, sympathizing with those whom she benefits, finds her beneficence lovable and so judges it to be a virtue.[6] Although this standard of virtue is a human standard derived from a human point of view, and not an external standard imposed by God or Objective Values, it is nevertheless external to the operative dispositions and motives of the naturally virtuous person herself. The naturally virtuous person as such isn't necessitated or even motivated by the standard of virtue: she is good, but not because the standard of virtue is a force that operates within her.[7] Nor is the goodness of her dispositions and motives in any essential way the result of her own possession of that standard; she might have cultivated her dispositions on purpose to meet the standard, but then again, she might not—she might just be *naturally* good. If we ask why the good person does *virtuous* actions *as such*, there is no real answer. Hume can only say: "well, that's just what it *means* to be naturally good: it is to be the sort of person who has the sorts of dispositions and desires that spectators call 'virtuous'." Like Francis Hutcheson before him, Hume allows the standard of virtue to operate as a psychological force only in a second-best case.[8] He says:

When any virtuous motive or principle is common in human nature, a person, who feels his heart devoid of that principle, may hate himself upon that account, and may perform the action without the motive, from a certain sense of duty, in order to acquire by practice, that virtuous principle, or at least, to disguise to himself, as much as possible, his want of it. (T 3.2.1, 479)

So in the naturally virtuous person, the normative standard does not operate as a psychological force; and in this second-best case, it does so only through the medium of self-hatred. Normative standards are not, in and of themselves, psychological forces at all.[9]

Sentimentalist theories of this kind originally developed (and still usually situate themselves) in opposition to dogmatic rationalist theories, according

---

[6] Here I am summarizing Hume's views as they appear in *A Treatise of Human Nature*, Book 3, part 3. The two examples I've given may seem different, since in the second the character trait in question (beneficence) seems to be identifiable prior to moral judgment, while in the first (greed), it does not. Strictly speaking I think Hume's view should be that the character trait in question is not identifiable prior to moral judgment, although that makes the examples a bit cumbersome to spell out. On this see my "The General Point of View: Love and Moral Approval in Hume's Ethics" (CA essay 9), pp. 295–6.

[7] It is somewhat different in the case of what Hume calls the "artificial" virtues, such as justice. The just person is motivated by thoughts about what is required by justice. But, as I mention below, it is arguable that those thoughts do not move him directly, but only because he has a desire to avoid his own self-hatred or self-disapproval.

[8] For Hutcheson's view on this point, see his *Illustrations on the Moral Sense*, section 1.

[9] See Charlotte Brown, "Is Hume an Internalist?"

to which normativity—in particular, rightness—is an objective property grasped by reason. On such views, the rightness of an action, or for that matter the logical force of an argument, is an objective fact about the external world, which the rational mind as such grasps, and to which it then conforms its beliefs and actions. Dogmatic rationalists do suppose that normative standards operate within us as psychological forces, for reason may have to exert its force against unruly desires. But on reflection we can see that dogmatic rationalists transfer to *reason itself* the same bland—and seemingly blind—conformity to external standards that sentimentalists attribute to the dispositions of the naturally virtuous person. Dogmatic rationalists believe that norms exist outside of human reason—they arise from Objective Values or Moral Facts or some sort of rational structure that exists "out there" in the universe. But if reflection on that fact prompts us to ask *why* human reason finds it necessary to conform to these standards, there is no real answer. The dogmatic rationalist can only reply: "well, that's just what it *means* to be rational, to have a mind (or a will) that conforms to the standards that we call 'rational'." In fact in theories of this kind "human reason" is really nothing more than the name of that faculty within us, whatever it might be, that conforms to rational standards. It is not identified in any other way.[10] Reason as envisaged by these theories is like a normative module that has been inserted into you, for the purpose of making the laws of reason, which are essentially outside of you, also be a force within you. Human reason is Objective Reason's little representative within. And if we ask what gives rise to the psychological necessity of conforming to the laws of reason, the answer is in effect just to *point* at the module: human beings have a representative of reason within them and *that* makes it necessary. But, really, why should *we* conform to the demands of this little representative within us, or for that matter, why does *it* conform so readily to the demands of Objective Reason outside? Like other homuncular theories, dogmatic rationalism does not give an explanation of reason's capacity to bind us, but merely points with premature satisfaction at the place where the explanation must go.

So there's a parallel here: if we ask Hume why the good person conforms to the standard of virtue, there is no answer: we can only say, "that's just what it means to be a good person." And if we ask the dogmatic rationalist why human reason conforms to the standards of reason, there is again no answer: we can only say, "that's just what it means to be reason." It is certainly

---

[10] For other discussions of this point see my Introduction to *The Constitution of Agency*, pp. 2–3; "The Normativity of Instrumental Reason" (CA essay 1), pp. 55–6; and "Acting for a Reason" (CA essay 7), pp. 212–15.

true that from a third-personal point of view, when we call people vicious or irrational, we mean that they fail to conform to certain standards. But that failure is the outward manifestation of an inner condition, and these theories do not tell us what that inner condition is. They don't tell us how we are necessitated.

1.1.5

Let me try to phrase my complaint in a slightly different way. According to the dogmatic rationalist theories I've just described, when we do experience necessitation, it is the necessitation involved in the struggle *to act rationally.* The *goal* of acting rationally itself is taken for granted: but there are forces within us, unruly desires, which sometimes interfere with our capacity to meet that goal. It is only then that we must exercise self-command, and that we experience necessitation. Otherwise, being rational would be effortless. In the same way, in Hume's account of natural virtue, necessitation (or something like it) only occurs in the second-best agent who is explicitly trying *to be good.* In the best case, in the naturally virtuous person, goodness is effortless. So according to these theories, insofar as the standards of goodness or rationality operate within us as psychological forces, they operate as unachieved or endangered *goals.*

I believe that these theories both underestimate and misplace the role of necessitation in our psychic lives. There is work and effort—a kind of struggle—involved in the moral life, and those who struggle successfully are the ones whom we call "rational" or "good." But it is not the struggle *to be rational* or *to be good.* It is, instead, the ongoing struggle for integrity, the struggle for psychic unity, the struggle to be, in the face of psychic complexity, a single unified agent. Normative standards—as I am about to argue—are the principles by which we achieve the psychic unity that makes agency possible. The work of achieving psychic unity, the work that we experience as necessitation, is what I am going to call *self-constitution.*

1.1.6

More specifically, in this book I will be dealing with three topics that I take to be intimately related. The topics are the nature of action, the constitution of personal or practical identity, and the normativity of the principles of practical reason.[11] For the sake of orientation I am going to begin by laying out the

---

[11] For an argument in favor of seeing the issue of personal identity in practical terms, see my "Personal Identity and the Unity of Agency: A Kantian Response to Parfit" (CKE essay 13).

basic elements of the conception that I believe relates these topics. Necessarily, what I say at this early stage will seem mysterious and cryptic, or at the very least dogmatic. So I ask you to keep in mind that this is a summary of a view to be defended in detail in the rest of the book and that nothing that follows is meant to be uncontroversial or obvious.

1.2 Acts and Actions[12]

1.2.1

Let me begin with the nature of action. If we want to learn what it is that makes actions right or wrong, we must start by asking what actions are, what their function is (2.1.1). John Stuart Mill thought he knew the answer to both of these questions. In the opening remarks of *Utilitarianism*, he says:

All action is for the sake of some end, and rules of action, it seems natural to suppose, must take their whole character and color from the end to which they are subservient.[13]

According to Mill, action is essentially production, and accordingly its function is to bring something about. Whether an action is good depends on whether *what* it brings about is good, or as good as it can be.

The influence of this conception of action on contemporary Anglo-American moral philosophy has been profound. Nowadays even moral philosophers who are not utilitarians appear to be comfortable only if they can explain moral value in terms of the production of various goods and harms. Deontological considerations are sometimes characterized as "side-constraints," as if they were essentially restrictions on ways to realize ends.[14] As such, they have been found mysterious by many philosophers.[15] If the whole point of action is to produce the good, how then can it be good to restrict that production? A standard move in utilitarian arguments, a move that Jeremy Bentham made right from the start, is to insist that productive success—effectiveness for good—is an obvious, unquestionable standard for actions. The burden of proof, he argues, is on his opponents to show that there is any other standard that actions have to meet.[16] And while many moral

---

[12] Some of the material in this section has appeared in "From Duty and for the Sake of the Noble: Kant and Aristotle on Morally Good Action" (CA essay 6), where I first worked it out, and in "Acting for a Reason" (CA essay 7).

[13] John Stuart Mill, *Utilitarianism*, p. 2.

[14] The term is used and the idea explained by Robert Nozick in *Anarchy, State, and Utopia*, pp. 28–33.

[15] This perplexity is expressed, for example, by Samuel Scheffler in *The Rejection of Consequentialism*, p. 82, and by Thomas Nagel in *The View from Nowhere*, p. 178, though neither of them ultimately endorses the idea that deontological restrictions are paradoxical.

[16] Jeremy Bentham, *An Introduction to the Principles of Morals and Legislation*, chapter 1, pp. 125–31.

philosophers have been prepared to try to pick up that burden, by showing that there are deontological constraints on the use of our productive capacity, hardly anyone has thought to challenge this assessment of where the burden of proof really lies.

1.2.2

But it has not always seemed obvious to philosophers that action is production. In Book 6 of the *Nicomachean Ethics*, when trying to work out what art or craft is, Aristotle says:

> Among things that can be otherwise are included both things made and things done; making and acting are different . . . ; so that the reasoned state of capacity to act is different from the reasoned state of capacity to make . . . Making and acting being different, art must be a matter of making, not of acting. (NE 6.4 1140a1–16)

According to Aristotle, action and production are two different things. And in the following section, Aristotle remarks on one of the most important differences between the two, namely that:

> while making has an end other than itself, action cannot; for good action itself is its end. (NE 6.5 1140b6–7)

Actions, or at least good actions, are chosen for their own sake, not for something they produce.

1.2.3

Actually, this is one of three different things Aristotle tells us about why good actions are done by virtuous agents. First of all, in at least some cases an act is done for some specific purpose or end. For instance, Aristotle tells us that the courageous person who dies in battle lays down his life for the sake of his country or for his friends (NE 9.8 1169a17–31). In the same way, it seems natural to say that the liberal person who makes a donation aims to help somebody out (NE 4.1 1120b3), the magnificent person who puts on a play aims to give the city a treat (NE 4.2 1122b23), the magnanimous man aims to reap honors (NE 4.3 1123b20–21), the ready-witted man aims to amuse his audience in a tactful way (NE 4.8 1128a24–27), and so on. At the same time, as I've just mentioned, Aristotle says that virtuous actions are done for their own sake. And finally, Aristotle also tells us that virtuous actions are done for the sake of the noble (e.g. NE 3.7 1115b12; 3.8 1116b3; 3.9 1117b9, 1117b13–14; 3.11 1119b15; 4.1 1120a23; 4.2 1122b6–7).

On an oversimplified conception of moral psychology these will look like three inconsistent accounts of the purpose or aim of virtuous action. But a

little reflection will show why there is no inconsistency here, and at the same
time, will throw light on Aristotle's conception of action. What corresponds
in Aristotle's theory to the description of an action is what he calls a *logos*—as
I will render it, a principle. A good action is one that embodies the *orthos logos*
or right principle—it is done at the right time, in the right way, to the right
object, and—importantly for my purposes—with the right aim. To cite one
of many such passages, Aristotle says:

> anyone can get angry—that is easy—or give or spend money; but to do this to the
> right person, to the right extent, at the right time, with the right aim, and in the right
> way, *that* is not for everyone, nor is it easy; that is why goodness is both rare and
> laudable and noble. (NE 2.9 1109a26–29)

The key to understanding Aristotle's view is that the *aim* is included in the
description of the action, and that it is the action as a whole, *including the aim*,
that the agent chooses.

Let us say that our agent is a citizen-soldier, who chooses to sacrifice his life
for the sake of a victory for his *polis* or city. The Greeks seem to think that is
usually a good *aim*. Let's also assume that our soldier sacrifices himself at the
right time—not before it is necessary, perhaps, or when something especially
good, say cutting off the enemy's access to reinforcements, may be achieved
by it. And he does it in the right way, efficiently and unflinchingly, perhaps
even with style, and so on. Then he has done something courageous, a good
action. Why has he done it? His *purpose* is to secure a victory for his city. But
the object of his choice is the whole action—sacrificing his life in a certain
way at a certain time in order to secure a victory for the city. He chooses this
whole package, that is, to-do-this-act-for-the-sake-of-this-end—he chooses
that, the whole package, as a thing worth doing for its own sake, and without
any further end. "Noble" describes the kind of value that the whole package
has, the value that he sees in it when he chooses it.

1.2.4

Now this means that Aristotle's view of the nature of action is precisely the
same as Kant's. Kant thinks that an action is described by a maxim, and
a maxim is also normally of the "to-do-this-act-for-the-sake-of-this-end"
structure. Kant is not always careful in the way he formulates the maxims of
actions, and that fact can obscure the present point, but on the best reading
of the categorical imperative test, the maxim of an action which is tested by it
includes both the act done and the end for the sake of which that act is done. It
has to include both, because the question raised by the categorical imperative
test is whether there could be a universal policy of pursuing *this sort of* end

by *these sorts of* means.[17] For instance in Kant's own *Groundwork* examples, the maxims of action tested are things like "I will commit suicide in order to avoid the personal troubles that I foresee ahead" and "I will make a false promise in order to get some ready cash" (G 4:422). What the rejection of these maxims identifies as wrong is the whole package—committing suicide in order to avoid personal troubles, and making a false promise in order to get some ready cash. The question of the rightness or wrongness of, say, committing suicide in order to save someone else's life, is left open, as a separate case to be tested separately. Indeed, Kant makes this clear himself, for in the *Metaphysics of Morals* he raises it as an interesting question whether a man bitten by a rabid dog who commits suicide, in order to avoid harming others when he inevitably goes mad from the rabies, does something wrong or not (MM 6:423–424). Committing suicide in order to save someone else's life is a different action from committing suicide in order to avoid the personal troubles that you foresee ahead.

And "moral worth" or being done "from duty" functions in Kant's theory in the same way that nobility does in Aristotle's. It is not an alternative purpose that we have in our actions, but the characterization of a specific kind of value that a certain act performed for the sake of a certain end may have. When an agent finds that she *must* will a certain maxim as a universal law, she supposes that the action it describes has this kind of value. Many of the standard criticisms of the idea of acting from duty are based on confusion about this point. The idea that acting from duty is something cold, impersonal, or even egoistic is based on the thought that the agent's purpose is "in order to do my duty" *rather than* "in order to help my friend" or "in order to save my country" or whatever it might be. But that is just wrong. Sacrificing your life in order to save your country might be your duty in a certain case, but the duty will be to do that act *for that purpose*, and the whole action will be chosen as your duty.

1.2.5

Let me introduce some terminology in order to express these ideas more clearly. Let's say that the basic form of a Kantian maxim is "I will do act-A in order to promote end-E." Call that entire formulation the description of an *action*. An *action*, then, involves both an *act* and an *end*, an act done for the sake of an end. In the examples we've looked at, making a false promise

---

[17] I defend the claim that this interpretation of the categorical imperative test, which I call the "practical contradiction" interpretation, is the best one in "Kant's Formula of Universal Law" (CKE essay 3).

and committing suicide are what I am calling "acts"; making a false promise in order to get some ready cash, committing suicide in order to avoid misery are what I am calling "actions." Now a slight complication arises from the fact that *acts* in my sense are also sometimes done for their own sakes, for no *further* end, from some non-instrumental motive like anger or sympathy or the sheer pleasure of the thing. In this case, doing the *act* is itself the end. To describe the whole *action*, in this kind of case, we have to put that fact into the maxim, and say that we are doing it for its own sake, for its inherent desirability, or however it might be. So for instance, if you choose to dance for the sheer joy of dancing, then *dancing* is the *act*, and *dancing for the sheer joy of dancing* is the *action*. We might contrast it to the different action of someone who dances in order to make money, or to dodge the bullets being shot at his feet. As I said before, it is the whole action that is strictly speaking the object of choice, which is why Aristotle says that our characters are revealed above all by our choices (NE 3.2 1111b5–6). And according to both Aristotle and Kant, it is the *action* which properly speaking is morally good or bad, noble or base.

1.2.6

The view that actions, acts-for-the-sake-of-ends, are both the objects of choice and the bearers of moral value sets Aristotle and Kant apart from many contemporary moral philosophers, less because of disagreement than because of unclarity about the issue. Contemporary philosophers tend to think of the reason for an action as something outside of or apart from the action itself, something that perhaps serves as its cause. This in turn leads to misinterpretation of our practices of asking and answering questions about people's reasons. We ask for *the reason* for an action, and as often as not, we give the answer by citing the agent's *purpose*. The purpose is separate from and behind the act, so if you think of a reason as separate from and behind an action, you will be led to confuse the act with the action. "Why did Jack go to Chicago?" we may ask. For Jack lives in Indianapolis, several hundred miles away. "To visit his mother who lives there" is the reply. Jack's purpose is offered in answer to the question about his reason. This makes it appear as if his purpose is the reason for his choice, and what he chose was the act. But this appearance is misleading.

To explicate this point I will first take a detour. One way to accommodate talk of reasons to the distinction between acts and actions would be to distinguish the reasons for acts from the reasons for actions. We could say that the act is performed for the sake of the purpose it serves, while the whole action is performed for its own sake—say because of its nobility or requiredness or rightness. Then we might think that confusion arises from thinking there is always "a reason" for what someone does, when in fact the phrase "the reason for what he does" is ambiguous between the reason for the act and the reason for the action. This proposal, although tempting, is not satisfactory. One problem springs from the fact that reasons are supposed to be normative. If a reason for an act is its purpose, and reasons are supposed to be normative, then it follows that the purpose itself is normative for the agent. This is certainly not what either Aristotle or Kant thinks. What is normative for the agent is for Aristotle the nobility, and for Kant the requiredness or rightness, of the action. The purpose, in most cases, is not a law to us, for in most cases the purpose may be abandoned if we find that there is no decent and reasonable and worthwhile way to pursue it. It is a different question whether there are *some* purposes it is wrong to give up; my point is that our purposes are not *in general* laws to us.[18] In Kant's theory, normativity arises from autonomy—we give laws to ourselves. But we do not first choose a purpose, enact it into law, and then scramble around for some way to fulfill it, now being under a requirement to do so. If it worked that way, we would be in violation of a self-legislated requirement every time we were unable to find a decent and reasonable way to achieve one of our purposes. What we will as laws are maxims, whole actions, and we normally adopt a purpose as a *part* of an action. Another problem with the proposal is that it suggests that in asking for "the reason" for what someone does, ordinary language is misleading, because there are always, so to speak, two reasons, one for the act and one for the action.

But that in turn suggests a different way of looking at the situation, which does not require us to say that the idea of a reason is ambiguous, but only that we tend to misinterpret what we are doing when we give a reason. If Aristotle and Kant are right about actions being done for their own sakes, then it may appear that every action is done for the same reason—because it is seen as a thing worth doing for its own sake. This obviously isn't what we are asking for when we ask for the reason why someone did something, because the answer is always the same: it seemed worthwhile to him. What may be worth asking for is an *explication* of the action, a complete description of it, which will show us *why* it seemed worth doing to him. Now normally we already know what the act was, so the missing piece of the description of the action is the purpose or end. "Going to Chicago to visit one's mother" is intelligible

---

[18] In Kant's theory there are some ends that are required of us, notably our own perfection and the happiness of others. See MM 6:385–394.

as a worthwhile thing to do, so once we have that missing piece in place, we understand what Jack did. That the purpose by itself couldn't really be the source of the reason shows up clearly in this fact: if the purpose supplied is one that fails to make the whole action seem worthwhile, even though the purpose is indeed successfully served by the act, we will not accept the answer. So if I tell you that Jack went to Chicago to buy a box of paperclips, you will not accept the answer, even though you can certainly buy a box of paperclips in Chicago. You will say "that can't be the reason," not because the purpose isn't served by the action, but because going several hundred miles from Indianapolis to Chicago to buy a box of paperclips is so obviously not worthwhile. So when we ask for the reason we are not just asking what purpose was served by the act—we are asking for a purpose that makes sense of the whole action. And as Aristotle saw, there will be cases where supplying the purpose will not be sufficient to make the action intelligible even where it is, so to speak, weighty enough to support the act. "Why did Jack go to Paris?" we ask. "He has always wanted to see it" is the reply. "No, but why just now?" urges the questioner, for Jack has taken off quite suddenly in the middle of the semester. And as Aristotle insists, in order to be worth doing the action must also be done at the right time and in the right way. So the practice of answering the motivational question "why" by citing the agent's purpose does not really suggest that actions have purposes outside themselves and are not performed for their own sakes. It is just that the purpose is often, though not always, the missing piece of the agent's maxim, the piece we need to have in place before we can see why the agent thought of this action as a thing worth doing for its own sake. On this view, importantly, the reason for an action is not something outside of or behind or separate from the action at all, for explicating the action, and explicating the reason, are the same thing. Rather, an action is an essentially intelligible object that *embodies* a reason, the way a sentence is an essentially intelligible object that embodies a thought.[19]

1.3 Aristotle and Kant

1.3.1

In attributing a common view about the nature of action and the locus of its value to Aristotle and Kant, I am flying in the face of received opinion, which holds that these two philosophers hold diametrically opposed views on the evaluation of action. According to the received story, Kant's categorical imperative test assesses the value of an action (or rather an act) by ascertaining

---

[19] For more on this point see "Acting for a Reason" (CA essay 7), pp. 225–9.

whether it is in accord with some general rule, while Aristotle insists that general rules cannot help us much in the evaluation of action. Instead he says, famously, that the decision about the goodness of action "rests with perception" (NE 2.9 1109b23), presumably the perception of the *phronemon*, or practically wise person. Actually, the decision that Aristotle says rests with perception in this imperfectly famous passage is how far one may deviate from the right before one becomes blameworthy, not whether the action is right, but I won't insist on that point here. When these views about the usefulness of general rules are combined with the assumption that the rules in question concern act-types, we arrive at the received story: Kant thinks that some act-types are identified by the categorical imperative as always wrong, while Aristotle thinks that act-types are at most generally wrong, and that only perception will identify the exceptions. One problem with this picture is that, as I have been arguing, neither of these philosophers thinks that moral characteristics attach to act-types. And Kant has no more use for general rules than Aristotle does. The categorical imperative test is directed to the quite particular action an agent proposes to perform, and it asks whether the maxim of *that* particular action, with all the relevant features of the action specified, has the *form* of a universal law.[20]

1.3.2

But what does that mean? As I've argued elsewhere, when Kant talks about the form of the maxim, he is using "form" in Aristotle's sense. In Aristotle's metaphysics, the form of a thing is that arrangement of its parts that enables it to do what it does, to serve its function. The parts of the action as described in a Kantian maxim are, primarily, the act and the end. (An Aristotelian *logos* has these parts but also others—notably the time, the place, and the manner—and that is a point I will come back to.) Kant's question is whether the act and the end are so arranged, or related to one another, that the maxim can serve as a law. I'll use the same example to illustrate this that I used in the *Sources of Normativity*, namely Plato's example of the three maxims (R 331c):

(1) I will keep my weapon, because I want it for myself.
(2) I will refuse to return your weapon, because I want it for myself.
(3) I will refuse to return your weapon, because you have run mad and may hurt someone.

Maxims 1 and 3 describe good actions; maxim 2 describes a bad one. What gives them these moral properties? Not just the acts, for maxims 2 and 3 involve the

---

[20] For more on this point see 4.4.2.

same types of acts; not just the purposes, for maxims 1 and 2 involve the same purposes. The goodness does not rest in the parts, but rather in the way the parts are combined and related; so the goodness does not rest in the matter, but rather in the form, of the maxim. If the action and the purpose are related to one another *so that* the maxim can be willed as a universal law, then the maxim is good.[21]

The maxim describes the action; the action is good if its maxim is fit to be a law in virtue of its form. That means that being fit to be a law is an *internal* property of the maxim, a property it has in virtue of the way the parts are related. It is not that there is some law existing outside of or independently of the action, with which the action happens to be in accord. It is not, say, as if God had laid it down in the commandments that promises are to be kept, the truth told, and weapons returned to their owners unless their owners have run mad, and that explains the lawfulness or its failure in these maxims.[22] Rather, the maxim itself, and therefore the action, has the property of lawfulness. What is the property of lawfulness? A law lays down what is to be done, so we might say it is *to-be-doneness*, that famous property that John Mackie claimed nothing in the world as we know it could possibly have.[23]

1.3.3

Actually, Mackie talks about *not-to-be-doneness*, and there is a good reason for this, for I am skirting over a complication here. For of course there are two kinds of rightness—permissibility and obligation—and accordingly there are two senses in which a maxim may be fit to be a law. A maxim is fit to be a law in one sense, the sense corresponding to permissibility, if it *could* function as a law. It is fit to be a law in a stronger sense, the sense corresponding to obligation, if it not only can but *must* be a law. The way we ascertain this is by showing that the maxim of doing the opposite is unfit to be law, and must be rejected. So, for instance, when we find that we cannot will the maxim of false promising just to get a little ready cash, we arrive at the duty of promising sincerely for purposes of this kind. Similarly, in Aristotle, an action may be noble, or merely not ignoble, or it may be demanded by the fact that its omission would be ignoble. So accordingly there are two kinds of to-be-doneness, one corresponding to the idea that an action is fit to be done (permissible, not dishonorable or ignoble), and the other corresponding to

---

[21] SN 3.3.5, p. 108.
[22] See "Kant's Analysis of Obligation: The Argument of *Groundwork I*" (CKE essay 2), pp. 61–6.
[23] John Mackie, *Ethics: Inventing Right and Wrong*, p. 40.

the idea that an action demands to be done: to omit it would be a violation of duty or ignoble.

1.3.4

So just as Kant thinks a good action embodies the property of lawfulness, which is found in the form of its maxim, Aristotle thinks a good action embodies a property of rightness or nobility, which is found in the *logos* that describes it. And I am prepared to claim that for Aristotle as for Kant it is in virtue of the *form* of the *logos* that the action has this property. For it is not the act, the aim, the time, the place, or manner that makes an action right, but rather that these should all be related to one another in just the right way. An action for Aristotle is like a work of art, with the parts working together to produce a beautiful and harmonious whole. It is *well formed*. A bad action by contrast is something misshapen and defective.

But for Aristotle is this form — the form of *to-be-doneness* — also the form of universality? Certainly, Aristotle does not say anything like that. I see no reason to doubt that Aristotle thinks that once the relevant features of the action are completely specified in its *logos*, it has the property of universality — that is, it would be the proper action for anyone in exactly the circumstances specified. Indeed, Aristotle repeatedly affirms that vice perverts and destroys the "first principle," which he identifies with "the universal," while virtue maintains and preserves it.[24] Actions are particulars, and objects of perception, but the business of perception for Aristotle is to grasp the universal that inhabits the particular: the perceptions of the vicious have been warped so that this is no longer possible.[25] But admittedly, even if Aristotle thinks that the action embodies a universal form of nobility or to-be-doneness, that is not quite the same thing as identifying the to-be-doneness with the universality or universalizability. So I do want not to understate the differences here.

And of course there are other, perhaps related differences. Just as Aristotle seems to think that moral judgment is more aesthetic and less ratiocinative in its workings than Kant does, so also he seems to think of its objects in a more aesthetic way. The Aristotelian idea of a good or noble action includes not only such things as sacrificing yourself for the sake of the *polis*, but also telling tasteful jokes for the delicate amusement of your audience and avoiding the error of dressing the chorus all in purple (NE 4.2 1123a19–24). It's hard to

---

[24] For the tendency of virtue to preserve and vice to destroy the first principle see for instance NE 6.5 1140b15–19; NE 6.12 1144a29–37; NE 7.8 1151a15; for the identification of practical first principles with "universals" see for instance NE 6.8 1141b26; NE 6.8 1142a12–21; NE 7.3 1147a1–5.

[25] For a defense of this interpretation see my "Aristotle on Function and Virtue" (CA essay 5).

imagine Kant caring much about things like that. On the other hand, Kant did manage to come up with some rather detailed recommendations about what to serve to drink at parties (MM 6:428), whether to express respect by bowing (MM 6:437), how to sign letters (MM 6:431), and things of that kind. But again, I won't insist on this point.

1.3.5

The important thing for my purposes here is the conception of action that Aristotle and Kant have in common, and that sets them apart from both the empiricist and the rationalist traditions. Both of them think that the objects of choice are actions, acts done for the sake of ends. Both of them think that actions in this sense are the bearers of moral value, and that moral value, that is, dutifulness or nobility, is a property internal to actions—a formal property embodied in the principles that describe them.[26] And both of them think that actions in this sense are chosen for their own sakes, because they embody this property.

1.4 Agency and Practical Identity

1.4.1

With that conception of action before us, I am ready to try to state my view. I believe that it is essential to the concept of action that an action is performed by an agent, rather in the same way that it is essential to a thought that it be thought by a thinker. One must be able to attach the "I do" to the action in the same way that, according to Kant, one must be able to attach the "I think" to a thought. As the invocation of Kant here suggests, this is not yet to say whether the agent or the thinker needs to be a separately existing entity—as I will explain later (7.1.3), I don't think that. But an action requires an agent, someone to whom we attribute the movement in question as its author. And I also believe it is essential to the concept of agency that an agent be unified. That is to say: to regard some movement of my mind or my body as *my action*, I must see it as an expression of my self as a whole, rather than as a product of some force that is at work *on* me or *in* me. Movements that result from forces working *on* me or *in* me constitute things that happen to me. To call a movement a twitch, or a slip, is at once to deny that it is an action and to assign it to some part of you that is less than the whole: the twitch to your eyebrow, or the slip, more problematically, to your tongue.

---

[26] If they are right about this, utilitarianism is not a moral theory, for utility is a property of acts, not of actions.

For a movement to be my action, for it to be expressive of *myself* in the way that an action must be, it must result from my entire nature working as an integrated whole.

1.4.2

Now this is where things get complicated. You might suppose that this requires that an action be the effect or result or expression of a *prior* unity in the agent, an integrity already achieved. You first achieve the sort of psychic unity or integrity that makes you the master of your own movements, that is, that makes some of your movements attributable to you as *yours*, and then the choices that lead to your actions express the unified selfhood you have already achieved. But I will argue that this cannot be how it works. This is where the problem of personal identity comes into the picture. I am going to argue that in the relevant sense there is no *you* prior to your choices and actions, because your identity is in a quite literal way *constituted* by your choices and actions.

1.4.3

The identity of a person, of an agent, is not the same as the identity of the human animal on whom the person normally supervenes. I believe that human beings differ from the other animals in an important way. We are self-conscious in a particular way: we are conscious of the grounds on which we act, and therefore are in control of them. When you are aware that you are tempted, say, to do a certain action because you are experiencing a certain desire, you can step back from that connection and reflect on it. You can ask whether you should do that action because of that desire, or because of the features that make it desirable.[27] And if you decide that you should not, then you can refrain.[28] This means that although there is a sense in which what a non-human animal does is up to her, the sense in which what you do is up to you is deeper.[29] When you deliberately decide what sorts of effects you will bring about in the world, you are also deliberately deciding what sort of a cause you will be. And that means you are deciding who you are. So we are each faced with the task of constructing a peculiar, individual kind

[27] Here I am leaving it open whether our reasons are desires or the features that make things desirable. For my views on this point see 6.3.1 and also my "Acting for a Reason" (CA essay 7).
[28] See SN 3.2.1–3.2.3, pp. 92–8; and the Introduction to *The Constitution of Agency*, pp. 3–5 and 10–12.
[29] For this contrast see my "Morality and the Distinctiveness of Human Action," in *Primates and Philosophers: How Morality Evolved*, especially pp. 107–12.

of identity—personal or practical identity—that the other animals lack. It is this sort of identity that makes sense of our practice of holding people responsible, and of the kinds of personal relationships that depend on that practice.

You will already see that I think those who claim that judgments of responsibility don't really make sense unless people create themselves are absolutely right—only unlike most people who believe this, I don't think it's a *problem*. It is as the possessor of personal or practical identity that you are the author of your actions, and responsible for them. And yet at the same time it is in choosing your actions that you create that identity. What this means is that you constitute yourself *as* the author of your actions in the very act of choosing them. I am fully aware that this sounds paradoxical. How can you constitute yourself, create yourself, unless you are already there? Call this the paradox of self-constitution. This is a problem to which I will return in the next chapter (2.4), after I have explained the metaphysical conception which will enable us to grasp the solution.

1.4.4

Before going on, I'd like to clarify the relationship of these claims about identity to things I have said about identity elsewhere. In *The Sources of Normativity*, I argued that the basis of choice is what I called a "conception of practical identity," a description under which you value yourself and find your life worth living and your actions to be worth undertaking.[30] Conceptions of practical identity include such things as roles and relationships, citizenship, memberships in ethnic or religious groups, causes, vocations, professions, and offices. It may be important to you that you are a human being, a woman or a man, a member of a certain profession, someone's lover or friend, a citizen or an officer of the court, a feminist or an environmentalist, or whatever. Our conceptions of our practical identity govern our choice of actions, for to value yourself in a certain role or under a certain description is at the same time to find it worthwhile to do certain acts for the sake of certain ends, and impossible, even unthinkable, to do others. If you are someone's friend, then you will find cooking a meal in order to share it with her or going shopping in order to buy her a gift to be actions worth doing, while committing adultery with her husband will be ruled out of court. If you are a parent, then you will see saving money for your child's education as a thing worth doing for its own sake, while you will see refusing to help him with his homework because

---

[30] SN 3.3.1, p. 101.

you want to watch a movie instead as an action that is ruled out. If you are a scientist, then carrying out arduous experiments to establish the truth of certain theories will seem a thing worth doing for its own sake, while you will reject as unprofessional and dishonorable an invitation to scramble your colleague's data so that you can beat him to the discovery that you are both trying to make.

One might think of a particular practical identity, if a little artificially, as a set of principles, the dos and don'ts of being a teacher or a citizen, say. But I think it is important, at least in some cases, to think of a form of identity in a more general way, as a role with a point. For there is room for argument about whether a particular way of acting is the best way or the only way to go about being, say, a teacher or a citizen—think of an argument about civil disobedience, for example—and it is with reference to the role or point of that form of identity that thought and argument about different interpretations of that form of identity can go on. There is room for creativity here, as well as argument: one might find a new way of being a friend.

Such identities are the sources of our reasons, but of course the idea is not just that we decide which ones we want and conform to them. We have many particular practical identities and so we also face the task of uniting them into a coherent whole.

1.4.5

In claiming that such identities are the sources of our reasons, I am not claiming that thoughts about your identity need to come into your reasoning in any explicit way. But just as I have rejected the Good Dog theory of virtue, so I reject the Good Dog theory of identity, and that means I want to grant that for beings like us, temptation to resist the claims of our practical identities is possible. And *then* you might have thoughts that explicitly invoke your identities: "I can't do that, she's my best friend!" "What do you take me for? I'm a scientist." Or they might even be offered by another: "You *are* his mother, you know. Who's going to help him if you don't?" The structure here is not that of means/end reasoning: it is not that your *purpose* is to be a friend or a parent or a scientist. Rather, these conceptions of our identity govern choice in the way that Kant and Aristotle think morality does. As I have already argued, when Kant and Aristotle talk about an action's being done "from duty" or "for the sake of the noble," they are not talking about alternative purposes for which we may perform certain acts, but rather about a kind of value that may be possessed by a whole action—an act done for the sake of an end. In the same way, practical identities confer a kind of value on certain whole actions. They define, as I might put it, contingent forms of duty and the noble.

1.4.6

It is an essential part of Kant and Aristotle's conception of moral motivation that considerations of duty and the noble must be the source of what Kant called "incentives." As I will explain at greater length later (5.6), Kant believes that every action involves two factors, an incentive and a principle. The incentive is the thing that presents the action to your mind as eligible; the principle is what determines whether it is in fact to be chosen or not. Now suppose that your principle is the categorical imperative: your principle is to act only on a maxim that you can will as a universal law. Suppose also that, with some ordinary desire serving as the incentive, you formulate a maxim that turns out to be incompatible with that principle. Wanting to spend the day at the beach, you are tempted to break your promise to help your neighbor paint his house on the first sunny day. You test your maxim, it is rejected, and you therefore do help your neighbor paint his house as you had promised. If rational action always involves both an incentive and a principle, what is your incentive for doing that? What presents "keeping your promise" to your mind as an eligible action? According to Kant, it is respect for law, the moral law's operation as its own incentive. In other words, the thought that you are required to keep a promise can itself serve as the incentive for keeping it. Of course we do not always have to perform this mental operation to find out what is required: the educated moral agent finds standing incentives to act from respect for law in his general knowledge of the sort of thing that is right.

I believe that our practical identities govern choice in exactly this way. They are standing sources of incentives, as well as principles in terms of which we accept and reject proposed actions. "I can't do that, it would be wrong" and "I can't do that, I'm his mother" are claims with the same structure. Since I argued in *The Sources of Normativity* that morality itself is grounded in an essential form of practical identity, our identity as rational or human beings, this should come as no surprise.[31]

1.4.7

It will be worth repeating here how the first step in that last mentioned argument—the commitment to our own human or rational identity as a form

---

[31] SN 3.4.1–3.4.9, pp. 113–25.

of practical identity—is supposed to work. Our practical identities are, for the most part, contingent. We acquire them in various ways. Some we are born into, like being someone's child or neighbor or being the citizen of a certain country. Some we adopt for reasons, like joining a profession that is worthwhile and suits your talents or devoting yourself to a cause in which you ardently believe. Many we adopt voluntarily, but without anything that is in more than a marginal sense a reason. Contrary to romantic notions, you don't marry a person who is made for you. You marry a person who is about your age, lives in your vicinity, and is feeling ready to marry at around the same time that you are. You may drift into a profession by way of a summer job, or champion a moral cause out of fellowship with a friend, or have undying loyalty to a nation because you happened to be born there.

However it goes, reasoned or arbitrary, chosen or merely the product of circumstance, the sorts of identities I am talking about remain contingent in this sense: whether you treat them as a source of reasons and obligations is up to you. If you continue to endorse the reasons the identity presents to you, and observe the obligations it imposes on you, then it's you. Leaving morality aside for the moment—because there may be moral reasons for not doing the things I am about to describe—you can walk out even on a factually grounded identity like being a certain person's child or a certain nation's citizen, dismissing the reasons and obligations that it gives rise to, because you just don't identify yourself with that role. Then it's not a form of *practical* identity anymore: not a description under which you value yourself. On the flip side, you can wholeheartedly endorse even the most arbitrary form of identification, treating its reasons and obligations as inviolable laws. Making the contingent necessary is one of the tasks of human life and the ability to do it is arguably a mark of a good human being. To do your job as if it were the most important thing in the world, love your spouse as if your marriage was made in heaven, treat your friends as if they were the most important people in the world—is to treat your contingent identities as the sources of absolute inviolable laws.

But why should we do that? I said a moment ago that these forms of identification are contingent, and we can walk away from them. Their hold on us depends on our own endorsement of the laws they give us. We ratify their laws whenever we act in accordance with them. For us even the reasons that spring from our animal nature are optional—for unlike the other animals, we can choose to turn our backs on our animal identity, and deliberately die. But there is a reason not to abandon all of our identities. The reason is given by the problem I started out from: the human plight. We must act, and we need reasons in order to act. And unless there are *some* principles with which we identify we will have no reasons to act. Every human being must make himself into someone in particular, in order to have reasons to act and to live. Carving out a personal identity for which we are responsible is one of the inescapable tasks of human life.

And that is the point on which the argument turns. Go back for a moment to the case of contingent practical identity. I said that a contingent practical identity was a description under which you value yourself and find your life to be worth living and your actions to be worth undertaking. What does it mean to say that you value yourself under a certain description? The actions or activities that constitute valuing something vary, depending on what sort of thing it is. Valuing doesn't always consist in producing or promoting or even preserving the thing that you value. Valuing beauty, for instance, consists in contemplating it with appreciation. Valuing people consists in respecting their reasons and choices and interests, not in having lots of babies.[32] Valuing yourself under a certain description consists in endorsing the reasons and obligations to which that way of identifying yourself gives rise. To say that a citizen of a certain nation values himself under that description is not to say that his purpose is to be a citizen of that nation. It is to say that he ratifies and endorses the reasons and obligations that go with being a citizen of that nation, because that's how he sees himself.

Suppose now that I conform to my obligations as an American citizen, treating the duties of citizenship as duties to which I must indeed conform. Someone might say to me: okay, sure, I see that you must do that insofar as you identify yourself as an American citizen, but why must you take that way of identifying yourself so seriously? It's only an accident that you were born in America. And here part of the answer is that I must take *some* ways of identifying myself seriously, or I won't have any reasons at all. Insofar as I take that fact—the fact that I need some way of identifying myself—to be a reason, I express the value I set upon myself as a human and rational being.

So in valuing ourselves as the bearers of contingent practical identities, knowing, as we do, that these identities are contingent, we are also valuing ourselves as rational beings. For by doing that we are endorsing a reason that arises from our rational nature—namely, our need to have reasons. And as I've just said, to endorse the reasons that arise from a certain practical identity just is to value yourself as the bearer of that form of identity. We owe it to ourselves, to our own humanity, to find some roles that we can fill with integrity and dedication. But in acknowledging that, we commit ourselves to

---

[32] See also T. M. Scanlon, *What We Owe to Each Other*, 103–7.

the value of our humanity just as such. That, roughly speaking, was what I had in mind in *The Sources of Normativity*.[33]

1.4.8

The argument from my earlier work that I just reviewed says that in order to be a person—that is, to have reasons—you must constitute yourself as a particular person, and that, in order to do that, you must commit yourself to your value as a person-in-general, that is, as a rational agent. In this book I will argue for the same conclusion, but with a more direct focus on agency—on what is necessary to constitute yourself as the author of your actions. So let me return now to the other part of my thesis: the part about the nature of action. I said that you constitute yourself as the author of your action in the very act of choosing it. I am proposing that this, not production as Mill thought, is what action is. Action is self-constitution. And accordingly I am going to argue that what makes actions good or bad is how well they constitute you.

The task of self-constitution involves finding some roles and fulfilling them with integrity and dedication. It also involves integrating those roles into a single identity, into a coherent life. People are more or less successful at constituting their identities as unified agents, and a good action is one that does this well. It is one that both achieves and springs from the integrity of the person who performs it. But since action requires agency, it follows that an action that is less successful at constituting its agent is to that extent less of an action. So on this conception, "action" is an idea that admits of degrees. An action chosen in a way that more successfully unifies and integrates its agent is more authentically, more fully, an action, than one that does not. And this in turn is where the principles of practical reason, the hypothetical and categorical imperatives, come in to the story. For I am going to argue that the principles of practical reason are principles by means of which we constitute ourselves as unified agents. And I will argue that that explains their normativity. The principles of practical reason bind us because, having to act, we must constitute ourselves as unified agents.

I know that at this point this is all very abstract, since I haven't yet said how an action can unify or constitute its agent. That has to wait for later. But here's the conclusion I am looking for. The necessity of conforming to the principles of practical reason comes down to the necessity of being a unified agent. And if it is correct that agency requires unity, then the necessity of being *a unified*

---

[33] In the passage above I have not tried to reproduce the part of the argument that links valuing one's identity as a rational being with morality. That part of the argument concerns the essential "publicity" of reason. For that see SN 4.2.1–4.2.12, pp. 132–45, and 9.4.5–9.7.6 below.

agent comes down to the necessity of being *an agent*. And if it is correct that action requires an agent, the necessity of being an agent comes down to the necessity of acting. And the necessity of acting, as we have seen, is our plight. The principles of practical reason are normative for us, then, simply because we must act.

1.4.9

It will be evident that in what I have said so far I am talking about *human* agency—that is to say, self-conscious agency. In fact some of the things I have said suggest that only human beings are agents, and if you aren't puzzled by that, you should be, because it isn't true. The nature of action more generally, and the differences between the actions of human and non-human animals, will be one of my subjects in this book. But one of those differences is immediately relevant here to the thoughts with which I began. Because human beings are self-conscious, we are conscious of threats to our psychic unity or integrity. Sometimes these threats spring from our own desires and impulses. The element of truth in the image of the Reformed Miserable Sinner who must repress his unruly desires in order to be good rests in the fact that we deliberate in the face of threats to our integrity, and as against them. What is false about the picture is the idea that we must repress these threats *in order to be good*. Rather, we must repress them in order to be one, to be unified, to be whole. We must repress them in order to maintain our personal or practical identity. And we must do that in order to maintain our agency itself. And the person who succeeds in that is good—not because he is striving to be good, but because he is striving to be unified, to be whole. On the picture I will be developing, being a person, having a personal identity, being a rational agent, is in itself a form of *work*. And the experience of *necessitation*, with its elements of effort and even of pain, is the experience of a form of *work*. A good person, it follows, is one who is good at this work. A good person is someone who is good at being a person.

That is what I will argue in the rest of this book.

2

The Metaphysics of Normativity

2.1 Constitutive Standards

2.1.1

In Chapter 1, I proposed that the principles of practical reason serve to unify and constitute us as agents, and that is why they are normative. Behind this thesis lies a more general account of normativity that I believe to be common to the philosophies of the three thinkers who are the heroes of this book: Plato, Aristotle, and Kant. According to this account, normative principles are in general principles of the unification of manifolds, multiplicities, or, in Aristotle's wonderful phrase, *mere heaps*, into objects of particular kinds (M 8.6 1045a10).

The view finds its clearest expression in the central books of Aristotle's *Metaphysics*, so that is the place to start.[1] According to Aristotle, what makes an object the kind of object that it is—what gives it its identity—is what it does, its *ergon*: its purpose, function, or characteristic activity. This is clearest in the case of artifacts, which are obviously functionally defined. An artifact has both a form and a matter. The matter is the material, the stuff or the parts, from which the artifact is made. The form of the artifact is its functional arrangement or teleological organization. That is, it is the arrangement of the matter or of the parts which enables the object to serve its function, to do whatever it does that makes it the kind of thing that it is. Say for instance that the function of a house is to serve as a habitable shelter, and that its parts are walls, roof, chimney, insulation, and so on. Then the form of the house is that arrangement of those parts that enables it to serve as a habitable shelter—or rather, to be more precise—it is the *way* the arrangement of those parts enables it to serve as a habitable shelter. The walls are joined at the corners, the insulation goes into the walls, the roof is placed on the top, and so on, so that the weather is kept out, and a comfortable environment is created within. That is the form of a house.

---

[1] The views that follow are primarily from *Metaphysics* 7–9.

On this view, to be an object, to be unified, and to be teleologically organized, are one and the same thing. Teleological organization is what unifies what would otherwise be a *mere heap* of matter into a particular object of a particular kind. Teleological organization, according to Aristotle, is also the object of knowledge. To know an object, that is, to *understand* it, is to see not only what it does and what it is made of, but also *how* the arrangement of the parts enables it to do whatever it does. After all, anybody knows that a house is a shelter, and anybody knows that its parts are walls and roofs and chimneys and things, and even roughly where they go. What distinguishes the architect is his knowledge of *how* the arrangement of those parts enables the house to serve the purpose of sheltering. And this means that according to Aristotle the form of a thing governs both theory and practice. To understand houses is to have their form in your mind, and to build one is to be guided by that form.

At the same time, it is the teleological organization or form of the object that supports normative judgments about it. A house with cracks in the walls is less good at keeping the weather out, less good at sheltering, and therefore is a less good house. The ancient metaphysical thesis of the identification of the real with the good follows immediately from this conception, for this kind of badness eventually shades off into *literal* disintegration. A house with enough cracks in the walls will crumble, and cease to be a house altogether: it will disintegrate back into a *mere heap* of boards and plaster and bricks.

2.1.2

It is essential here to observe the distinction between being a good or bad *house* in the strict sense and being a house that happens to be a good or bad *thing* for some external reason. The large mansion which blocks the whole neighborhood's view of the lake may be a *bad thing* for the neighborhood, but it is not therefore a *bad house*. The normative standards to which a thing's teleological organization gives rise are what I will call "constitutive standards," standards that apply to a thing simply in virtue of its being the kind of thing that it is.

An especially important instance of the constitutive standard is what I will call the constitutive *principle*, a constitutive standard applying to an activity. In these cases what we say is that if you are not guided by the principle, you are not performing the activity at all. In the case of essentially goal-directed activities, constitutive principles arise from the constitutive standards of the goals to which they are directed. A house-builder is, as such, trying to build an edifice that will keep the rain and weather out. But all activities—as opposed to mere sequences of events or processes—are, by their nature, directed, self-guided, by those who engage in them, even if they are not directed or guided with reference to external goals. And the principles that describe the way in which an agent engaged in an activity directs or guides himself are the constitutive principles for that activity. So it is a constitutive principle of walking that you put one foot in front of the other, and a constitutive principle of skipping that you do this with a hop or a bounce. Or, to use a controversial example, it is a constitutive principle of thinking that you *swerve* when you see a contradiction looming ahead in your path. And in all these cases, we can say that unless you are guided by the principle in question, you are not performing that activity at all.

2.1.3

The idea of a constitutive standard is an important one, for constitutive standards meet skeptical challenges to their authority with ease. Why shouldn't you build a house that blocks the whole neighborhood's view of the lake? Perhaps because it will displease the neighbors. Now *there* is a consideration that you may simply set aside, if you are selfish or tough enough to brave your neighbors' displeasure. But because it does not make sense to ask why a house should serve as a shelter, it also does not make sense to ask why the corners should be sealed and the roof should be waterproof and tight. I mean, of course you can ask these questions in a technical voice, you can ask how sealed corners and waterproofed roofs serve the function of sheltering. But once you've answered the technical questions, there is no further room for doubting that the constitutive standard has normative force. For if you fall too far short of the constitutive standard, what you produce will simply not be a house. In effect this means that even the most venal and shoddy builder must try to build a good house, for the simple reason that there is no other way to try to build a house. Building a good house and building a house are not different activities: for both are activities guided by the teleological norms implicit in the idea of a house. Obviously, it doesn't follow that every house is a good house, although there is a puzzle about why not. It does, however, follow that building bad houses is not a different activity from building good ones. *It is the same activity, badly done.*

2.1.4

Let's consider that puzzle. If building bad houses is the same activity as building good ones, why are there any bad houses? In the case at hand, we have an object, a house, characterized by certain constitutive standards. It is in terms of those standards that we understand the activity of producing a house. The producer of the house looks to the normative standards that are constitutive of houses—in Aristotle's terms, to its form—and tries to realize that form in appropriate matter—in building materials. Since building is a goal-directed activity, that is what the activity of building essentially is. The description of the form of a house could be read as a sort of recipe, or a set of instructions, for building a house: join the walls at the corners, put the insulation in the walls, put the roof on the top . . . So trying to produce a house is not a different activity from trying to produce a good house. One is trying to build a good house if one is building a house at all. How then is the shoddy builder even possible?

The problem is a general one, not limited to productive activities. Here are a couple more examples. In the *Groundwork*, Kant argues that hypothetical imperatives, the principles of instrumental reason, are analytic, because "whoever wills an end wills the means" is analytic (G 4:417). This seems to suggest that if you don't will the means, then it logically follows that you don't really will the end. But if that were true in the plainest sense, no one would ever be guilty of violating a hypothetical imperative. For if someone didn't will the means, then it would follow logically that he didn't will the end, and in that case, of course, he wouldn't have violated the hypothetical imperative, which only tells him what to do if he *does* will the end. This, however, leaves us unable to give sense to the claim that instrumental principles are imperatives—for how can they be imperatives, if they are impossible to violate?[2] Later I will argue that the hypothetical imperative is constitutive of action (4.3; 5.1.3), but it cannot follow that it is not normative for it as well. Here's another example that you might find more readily convincing. The presence of both a noun and a verb in an English sentence is *constitutive* of its being a sentence, that is, of its expressing a complete thought. Yet those of us whose work includes grading papers have all encountered the verbless string of words that wants to be a sentence and fails, and yet is not mere gibberish. There is such a thing as speaking English badly, and it is not quite the same as not speaking it at all, although—importantly—it tends in that direction. For if you ignore the rules of English altogether, what you speak will simply not be English.

---

[2] For a more complete version of this argument, see "The Normativity of Instrumental Reason" (CA essay 1).

2.1.5

So we are looking at a quite general problem about finding the conceptual space between performing an activity perfectly and not performing it at all, space into which we can fit the person who does it badly. Among the ancient Greek philosophers this seems to have been one of the standard puzzles about art or craft. At least it comes up in the first book of the *Republic* with respect to the art of ruling. Thrasymachus says that justice is the advantage of the stronger, for the rules of justice are imposed on the weak by the strong, and the strong rule for their own advantage. Socrates pretends to be puzzled by the question where justice lies when the strong make a law that is not *in fact* to their advantage (R 339c–e). Thrasymachus replies that the problem is the result of a loose way of talking. In the *precise sense*, he says, no craftsperson, expert, or ruler, is a craftsperson, expert, or ruler, at the very moment when he makes an error (R 340d–341a). In other words, Thrasymachus concludes you are not practicing an art at all if you practice it badly. Socrates proceeds to make mincemeat of Thrasymachus with this "precise sense" by showing that a ruler, in the *precise sense*, rules for the benefit of whatever he rules, and not for his own benefit (R 341c–343a).

In fact the "precise sense" or perfect version of an activity stands in a complex relation to the activity, because it is at once both normative and constitutive. Although it is not true that you are not performing an activity at all unless you do it precisely, it is true that you have to be *guided by* the precise version of the activity in order to be performing the activity at all. And at the same time the precise sense sets normative standards for the activity. It is tempting to say that the actual activity must *participate* in the perfect or precise one. In other words, Plato's Theory of Forms is true for activities.

The shoddy builder doesn't follow a different set of standards or norms. He may be doing one of two things. He may be guided by the norms, but carelessly, inattentively, choosing second-rate materials in a random way, sealing the corners imperfectly, adding insufficient insulation, and so on. But he may also, if he is dishonest, be doing this sort of thing quite consciously, say in order to save money. In that case, surely we can't say that he is trying to build a good house? No, but now I think we should follow Socrates's lead, and say that he is not trying to build a house at all, but rather a sort of plausible imitation of a house, one he can pass off as the real thing. What guides him is not the aim of producing a house, but the aim of producing something that will fetch the price of a house, sufficiently like a real house that he can't be sued for it afterwards. Socrates, in the passages from the *Republic* that I have already mentioned, makes rather a fuss about this point, insisting that a craftsman in the precise sense is not a money-maker, but simply a practitioner of his craft (R 341c–342a).

2.1.6

So on this conception, every object and activity is defined by certain standards that are both constitutive of it and normative for it. These standards are ones that the object or activity must at least try to meet, insofar as it is to be that object or activity at all. An object that fails to meet these standards is bad in a particular way. It will be useful to give this kind of badness, badness as judged by a constitutive standard, a special name, and in English we have a word that serves the purpose well: *defect*. So in the somewhat special sense that I will be using the term, a house that is so constructed as to be ill-adapted for sheltering is *defective*; while a house that blocks the neighborhood's view, though it may for that reason be a bad thing, is not *a defective house*. Since the function of action is self-constitution, I am eventually going to argue (Chapter 8) that bad actions, *defective* actions, are ones that fail to constitute their agents as the unified authors of their actions.

2.1.7

Constitutive standards are important, I claimed above, because they meet skeptical challenges with ease. But the importance of the idea is deeper than that, for I believe—and I know this is more controversial—that the *only* way to establish the authority of any purported normative principle is to establish that it is constitutive of something to which the person whom it governs is committed—something that she either is doing or has to do. And I think that Kant thought this too. The laws of logic govern our thoughts because if we don't follow them we just aren't thinking. Illogical thinking is not merely bad, it is *defective*, it is bad *as* thinking. The laws of the understanding govern our beliefs because if we don't follow them, we just aren't constructing a representation of an objective world (9.7.5). And as I will argue, the laws of practical reason govern our actions because if we don't follow them we just aren't acting, and acting is something that we must do. A constitutive principle for an inescapable activity is unconditionally binding.

How could it be otherwise? Constitutive standards have unquestionable authority, while external standards give rise to further questions, and leave space for skeptical doubt. How then can we ever give authority to an external standard, except by tracing its authority back to a constitutive one? Consider again that house that blocks the neighbors' view of the lake. Why shouldn't the house-builder build it? For I'm supposing that we all do agree that really, after all, he shouldn't do it, in spite of the fact that it wouldn't therefore be a *defective* house. Well, perhaps he identifies himself as a good neighbor, a citizenly type, and doesn't need to ask why he shouldn't build a house that is a blight on the neighborhood. Or perhaps he loves his neighbors, and wouldn't want to harm them. Or perhaps—to anticipate the success of the views we are working on here—it would be morally wrong to build a house that blocks the view of the neighbors, and so although it might be all very well as a bit of *house-building*, it would be *defective* as an *action*.

2.1.8

There is another reason why the idea of a constitutive standard is important—or rather, this is the same reason, described a different way, coming from a different direction. It is that we *need* the concept of the *defective*, in the sense described above. Say we have two objects, call them A and B, and they are in some respect different from each other. They have some different non-accidental properties. Now we need to distinguish two ways that A and B can be different from each other in this way: A can be a different *kind* of thing from B, or A can be a *defective instance* of the same kind of thing as B. Suppose A is a defective instance of the same kind of thing as B. Then say we have two objects Y and Z, which differ in regard to the same property, but which *are* of different kinds. Should we treat these two cases, the case of A and B and the case of Y and Z, any differently? Does it matter what *kinds of things* things are?[3] Why shouldn't all that matters be the properties themselves? If properties are all that matter, then we need not—and cannot—distinguish the different from the defective: different collections of properties will just be different, and that is all.

Well, consider again the case of instrumental reasoning. Kaspar says he resolves to begin a course of exercise tomorrow, in order to get in shape, but he does not do it. If he has changed his mind about the value of

---

[3] One place the question of difference and defect comes up in the philosophical literature is in discussions of the moral standing of animals. The so-called "marginal cases" argument holds that if we accord defective human beings a certain moral standing, then there is no reason not to accord that standing to animals who lack the property with respect to which the human being in question is defective. I believe that this argument is mistaken. I think that a better argument can be made for according moral standing to the other animals. I sketch such an argument in my "Fellow Creatures: Kantian Ethics and Our Duties to Animals" and in "Interacting with Animals: A Kantian Account," forthcoming in *The Oxford Handbook on Ethics and Animals*, ed. Thomas Beauchamp and R. G. Frey (Oxford, 2010).

getting in shape, or if he was lying when he announced his resolution, his volition is merely different from what we expected it to be. But if he does not exercise because he is suffering from weakness of the will, his volition is defective: he has performed an abortive act of will. It must be possible to distinguish these two cases. If his shifting volitions can only be different, and not defective, then he has not violated, and cannot violate, any principle or norm.[4]

Or to take once again a similar but more troublesome case, think of language. Someone violates the rules of English as you understand them. Is he speaking a dialect, or making a mistake? Perhaps he is speaking a dialect—we must certainly admit the possibility, to avoid intolerance—and then what he is doing is simply something different. These cases can be vexed—the adults may regard as merely erroneous what the children take to be a legitimate form of slang, for instance. But if everyone who speaks differently is allowed to counter criticism with the claim that he is simply using a different dialect, then there are no rules of English.

Another example: some physical differences, say hair color, are just that—differences. We regard others as defects, and those who suffer from them as unfortunate. Sometimes people try to deny this, often from laudable motives of respect and consideration. Being deaf, they claim, is not a defective condition, but is just a difference—the source of a different way of learning from and communicating with others. But we offer those who suffer from defective conditions special aid and compensation from society. If they were only different, why should we do that?

Distinguishing cases of difference from cases of defect can be difficult. As some of the examples I've given show, it can even be politically charged or delicate. It can also be largely pragmatic. Being short makes it harder to do certain things, just as being deaf does, but we do not regard this as a handicap. Perhaps this is because in a species like ours, not all of a single height, some people will necessarily be short. Some differences become defects only when they reach certain extremes. We should grant all these points about how hard it is to distinguish the different from the defective. Nevertheless, we need the concept of the defective for all sorts of purposes. And if we try to banish the concept of the defective from the world altogether, we will banish normativity along with it: nothing will violate any standard that necessarily applies to it; everything will just be different. And that is why we need constitutive standards.

---

[4] As I argue in "The Normativity of Instrumental Reason" (CA essay 1), especially pp. 48–50. But for some complications about that argument, see also the discussion below at 4.3.4.

2.2 The Constitution of Life

2.2.1

In 1.4.3, I mentioned what I called "the paradox of self-constitution." How can you constitute yourself, create yourself, unless you are already there? And how can you need to constitute yourself if you *are* already there? With Aristotle's view before us, we are now ready to start working our way towards the solution of this problem.

Aristotle extended his account of artifactual identity to living things with the aid of the view that a living thing is a thing with a special kind of form.[5] A living thing is a thing so designed as to maintain and reproduce *itself*: that is, to maintain and reproduce its own form. It has what we might call a self-maintaining form. So it is its own end; its *ergon* or function is just to be—and to continue being—what it is. And its organs, instincts, and natural activities are all arranged to that end. The function of a giraffe, for instance, is to be a giraffe, and to continue being a giraffe, and to produce other giraffes. We might therefore say that a giraffe is simply an entity organized to keep a particular instance, a spatio-temporally continuous stream, of giraffeness going—primarily through nutrition—and also to generate other instances of giraffeness, through reproduction. A healthy giraffe is one that is well-organized for keeping her giraffeness going, while an unhealthy giraffe suffers from conditions that tend to her disintegration. So health is not, strictly speaking, a *goal* for giraffes, but rather is our name for the inner condition which enables the giraffe to successfully perform her function—which is to go on being a giraffe. This parallels the way in which, as I said in 1.1.5, goodness is not a goal for people, but rather is our name for the inner condition which enables a person to successfully perform her function—which is to maintain her integrity as a unified person, to be who she is. This is why Plato and Aristotle always compared health to virtue.

It is important to notice the complex role that teleological organization plays with respect to the giraffe's activities and actions. The giraffe's actions are both dictated by, and preservative of, her giraffeness. A good giraffe action, such as nibbling the tender green leaves at the tops of the trees, keeps the giraffe going, for it provides the specific nutrients needed to constantly restore and refurbish her giraffeness through the nutritive processes. Yet the giraffe's action is one to which she is prompted by instincts resulting *from*

---

[5] To the aforementioned central books of Aristotle's *Metaphysics*, now add *On the Soul*, especially Book 2. *Physics* 2 is also helpful.

her giraffe nature. This is related to an apparent difference between living things and artifacts, which is that living things are made of parts that strictly speaking cannot exist independently of the living things themselves. You can't build a giraffe out of tender green leaves, but a giraffe's nutritive processes turn tender green leaves into the kinds of matter out of which a giraffe *is* built—giraffe tissues and giraffe organs and so on. Furthermore, the living tissues that make up organisms are comparatively fragile, and in need of constant renewal. It follows from all this that if a giraffe ceases her activities—if she stops nibbling the tender green leaves, or stops digesting them when she does—she will fall apart. And this means that, strictly speaking, being a giraffe is not a state, but rather an activity. Being a giraffe is *doing* something: a giraffe is, quite essentially, an entity that is always *making* herself into a giraffe. In fact, the *entity* that I just mentioned is derivative, arrived at only by an artificial freezing of the observer's mental frame, for nothing that stops working at being a giraffe, that stops making herself into a giraffe, will remain a giraffe for long. So to be a giraffe is simply to engage in the activity of constantly making yourself into a giraffe: this is what a giraffe's life consists in.

2.2.2

I said that living things are apparently different from artifacts because, strictly speaking, the parts of living things do not exist separately from the living things themselves. But actually, speaking *very* strictly, this is true of artifacts too—their parts cannot exist independently of the artifacts themselves. For example, large slabs of sheetrock or plaster can exist apart from houses, but *walls* cannot, for walls are functionally defined, and a slab of sheetrock or plaster that isn't part of a house cannot divide one room from another, or help to hold up a roof. But perhaps the only reason to bother making this point is to support the parallel with organisms.

But perhaps not. If we don't draw the parallel, and regard artifacts as having separately existing parts, then it seems as if artifacts are, or can be, static entities, not essentially activities, the way living things are. And I don't think they can. An artifact is defined in terms of its *essential* activity: it is the thing that can perform that activity. But in fact, most artifacts cannot perform their activities all by themselves. They need either a power source, or to be wielded by a human being, or both, before they can perform their functions. It isn't quite right, then, to say of the vacuum cleaner in your closet that it "can clean floors," since, actually, until you plug it in and wield it, it cannot. So strictly speaking, artifacts, when they are just sitting around doing nothing on our shelves or in our closets, are *incomplete objects* that will only start to perform their function when some last part is plugged in or inserted. In fact, the truth about this matter looks as if it may be depressing: there is no such artifact as a vacuum cleaner at all. Instead, what you call your vacuum cleaner is actually an entity that, when properly incorporated by you, makes *you* into a vacuum cleaner.

All sorts of strange conclusions follow from this line of thought: reality is essentially activity, for all static entities are in general only the result of freezing the observer's mental frame; all those objects in your attic and garage are not entities after all, but only half-constructed heaps waiting to be finished; and indeed there is no such thing as an artifact, although human beings and the other tool-using animals throw themselves into an enormous variety of artifactual modes . . . Okay, I'll stop.

2.2.3

To be a giraffe is simply to engage in the activity of constantly making yourself into a giraffe: this is what a giraffe's life consists in. And for the same reasons that we considered earlier there is no real difference between the activity of living a giraffe's life, and the activity of living a healthy giraffe's life, for in order to live a giraffe's life, you must follow the teleological principles implicit in the form of giraffeness, the constitutive principles of being a giraffe. And so leading the life of an unhealthy giraffe is not a different activity from leading the life of a healthy giraffe. *It is the same activity, badly done.*

2.3 In Defense of Teleology

2.3.1

We are almost ready to solve the paradox of self-constitution, but first I want to address another issue. The account of the normativity of practical reason that I am working on here grounds normative standards in a frankly teleological, Aristotelian, conception of objects and activities. Many philosophers are worried by teleological ways of conceiving the world. Hasn't Aristotle's idea that there are natural purposes, or that the world and the things in it were made for a purpose, long since been discredited by the Modern Scientific World View? My response to these worries will come in three parts: first, I will give an account of the target and scope of the teleological conception I propose to use; second, I will give an account of what justifies its use; and finally I say a few words about the resulting status of teleological claims.

First the target and scope of teleological thinking. The Aristotelian conception that I have just laid out identifies objects as having an internal teleological organization. This is clearest in the case of living things, where the claim is simply about how the living thing's organs and activities are conceived and explained as contributing to its life. A living thing is not assigned a purpose outside of itself—its "purpose," or more properly function, is to be what it is, to live its particular form of life.[6] Thus there are no such claims here as that horses are meant for riding into battle or that cows are meant for human beings to eat or that women are meant for housework or that oil is meant for lamps and automobiles. The teleological claims are made at the level of the individual object: they are claims about its internal organization. It is of course true that we can identify something as having an internal teleological organization only to the extent that we can identify it as *doing something*. Serving a human purpose is one recognizable way of *doing something*; but doing what we ourselves do—namely, living—is another. (Even in the case of an artifact its purpose need not be thought of as external to the object, since in the case of an artifact it is the whole nature of that object to serve the purpose in question.) In fact what I want to claim—although I will have to be a little vague here—is that this is how we pick out the object, how it emerges from what Kant called the sensible manifold as a unified thing. That is to say, we pick out an object as a region of the manifold that appears to be doing something, and we understand it as a single and unified object by understanding it as internally organized for doing whatever it does.[7]

This brings me to the second point—the justification of teleological thinking. That justification falls into two related parts. The first is the claim I have just made. Teleological thinking need not be grounded in a claim about the world. It may be grounded in a claim about how human beings conceptualize the world. The idea, of course a Kantian one, is that human beings are faced with the task of carving the sensible manifold into objects. The claim is that we pick out objects by identifying functional unities. *Very* roughly speaking, the idea is this: in dividing the world into objects, we need some reason for carving out more particular unities from the sensible manifold. And the kind of unity that grounds the identification of a particular object is a functional unity. To put it a bit fancifully, when a cluster of forces are all contributing to something that we, by our admittedly human standards, would call a *result*, then we bunch these forces together, and call them an object. When a cluster of natural forces works together to produce something I can sit down on, say

---

[6] For a more complete account of what I think Aristotle means by function, and a defense of his "function argument" in NE 1.7, see my "Aristotle's Function Argument" (CA essay 4).

[7] I think this is roughly what Kant means by "reflective judgment."

a flat rock, then I call it a *seat*. When I try to reproduce that cluster of forces, I call the result a *chair*. When a cluster of forces works together to maintain and continually reproduce that same cluster of forces, or a cluster of forces spatio-temporally continuous with itself, thus constantly making itself and copies of itself, then I call it a *living thing*.

And that has implications for the status of the resulting teleological claims. If we are to pick out self-maintaining regions of the manifold as living things, of course, there must be such things, so I do not mean to imply here that living things are merely human constructs, or anything of that sort. Not that that would necessarily be so bad. "Seats" are human constructs, since the concept of a seat is relative to the purposes of an erect-standing creature so constructed as to be able to sit down. "Chairs" like other artifacts are human constructs, but then, no one doubts *that*—the concept and its object are born together in the original craftsman's mind. For all that, however, there are chairs. Why do we pick self-maintainers out of the manifold as a kind of thing? As anyone who watches animals knows, animals or at least middle-sized multicellular animals in fact recognize one another as fellow animals without any fancy powers of conceptualization, so perhaps this question needs no answer. But our later recognition of living things as self-maintainers could have been inspired by the analogy with ourselves. Nothing I'm saying here is incompatible with a Darwinian account of how the world became populated with items fit to be thus conceptualized. And nothing I'm saying here is incompatible with all the ways in which the Darwinian account implies that teleological thinking can be wrong. We can wrongly assign a purpose to a useless vestigial organ, for example. We can conceive of something as relative to our purposes, when it has interests of its own that make a different understanding of its organization available. So there is no claim here that everything has one and only one purpose that is in fact its natural purpose. The claim is simpler—it is that the way we conceptualize the world, the way we organize it into a world of various objects, guarantees that it will appear to be teleologically organized at the level of those objects.

2.3.2

The idea that teleological thinking is inherent in our powers of conceptualization is a development of a point that is implicit in what I have already said. A teleological conception of the world is essential to our functioning as agents. We need the world to be organized into various objects in order to act. To recognize an object as *doing something* or as producing a *result* of some kind is to identify it with reference to our own purposes and powers of action. Since we must act, the world is for us, in the first instance, a world of tools and obstacles, and of the natural objects of desire and fear. An object is identified as a locus, a sort of force field, of particular causal powers, and the causal powers in question are identified as those we might either use or have to work against. And if we did not identify objects in this way, we could not act at all.

Let me put this point more specifically. As I will be arguing later on, Kant's hypothetical imperative is a normative principle essential to, constitutive of, action itself (4.3). To act is essentially to take the means to your end, in the most general sense of the word "means." And to take the means to your end is, as Kant himself pointed out, to determine yourself to cause the end—that is, to deploy the objects that will bring the end about. Thus action requires a world of objects conceived as the loci of causal powers. You intend to cut, for instance, so you look for a knife, conceiving the knife as the cause of cutting.

Now perhaps some people suppose that as long as you conceive the knife merely as *the cause of the cutting*, rather than as *for the purpose of cutting*, you are not conceiving of the world teleologically. The view that the knife is *the cause of the cutting* is mechanistic. But is it? In the purest form of the mechanistic view, the knife is not the cause of the cutting. It is rather—say—the knife wielded by the hand directed by the brain operating through the nervous system stimulated by certain forces determined in turn by certain events caused in certain ways. Assuming something like determinism is true at the level of middle-sized objects, the cause of the cutting is the state of the world a nanosecond ago determining the state of the world now. Why then do we say that *the knife*, rather than the state of the world a nanosecond ago, is the cause of the cutting? That is easy—because we can *use* the knife for cutting. From the purely mechanistic point of view, the identification of a particular object or even a particular event as *the cause* of another is artificial, a piece of shorthand, a sort of conception of thumb, if I may put it that way. The teleological view—the view of the world as a realm of tools and obstacles—stands behind the slightly artificial idea that particular objects are "causes." But the teleological conception of the world is essential to creatures who are inside of the world and must act in it.

2.3.3

The teleological view of the world as a realm of tools and obstacles, of objects of desire and fear, the conception of the world from which as agents we must start, is modified by rationality in two ways. One modification occurs within the teleological conception itself, and as I will argue is an inevitable development of it. It is the moral conception of the world. To act, I have already suggested, is to determine yourself to be the cause of a certain end. So to act *self-consciously* is to conceive of *yourself* teleologically—as the cause—that is, the *first* cause—of a certain end. It is to conceive yourself as an agent, as efficacious to achieve certain subjectively held ends. Thus in addition to tools and obstacles and objects of fear and desire, a rational, self-conscious agent comes to conceive the world as containing agents, with ends of their own. She comes to conceive the world, in Kant's language, as a Kingdom of Ends: a whole of all ends in themselves or first causes, with the ends that each sets before him or herself (G 4:433).

The other modification, which eventually emerges as an alternative conception, is the scientific or mechanistic conception of the world (6.1.6). It is a conception that results among other things from pressing the notion of cause, as I did above, until the idea of *a* cause within the world begins to look spurious. Or, to put the same point another way, it is the result of pressing our understanding of the world until the idea of an object, as a unified and independent being within the world, begins to look spurious. You think you're an object, indeed even an agent, but to a flea or a nit you are merely a rather nutritious and specific region of the environment, like a Pacific island. If the flea or nit could think, it would think itself an object, perhaps even an agent, but to the cells in its body it is merely a rather nutritious and specific environment . . . and so on. Even we self-identifying self-conscious and supposedly self-maintaining substances fail to see how thoroughly embedded we are in an environment that supports us from outside, how thoroughly our perceived internal unity and cohesion depends on what goes on around us. A chemical change, a rise in the temperature, a stray bullet, and the transient whirling vortex of forces that thought itself an immortal *thing* puffs away . . .

Are the teleological and moral conceptions of the world then related to the Scientific World View as illusions to fact? If that were so, whose illusions would they be?

2.4 The Paradox of Self-Constitution

2.4.1

Now we are ready to talk about the paradox of self-constitution. According to the Aristotelian picture of the nature of living things, a living thing is engaged in an endless activity of self-constitution. In fact to be a living thing is just to be self-constitutive in this way: a living thing is a thing that is constantly making itself into itself. But notice that the apparent paradox involved in the idea of self-constitution does not seem to arise here. No one is tempted to say: "how can the giraffe make itself into itself unless it is already there?" The picture here is not of a craftsman who is, mysteriously, his own product. The picture here is of the self-constitutive process that is the essence of life. The paradox of self-constitution, in this context, is no paradox at all.

And the same applies to personhood. Aristotle believed that there are three forms of life, corresponding to what he called three parts of the soul.[8] Each supervenes on the one below it. At the bottom is a vegetative life of nutrition and reproduction, common to all plants and animals. According to Aristotle, animals are distinguished from plants in being alive in a further sense, given by a functionally related set of powers that plants lack. Aristotle emphasizes perception and sensation, but notes that these are necessarily, or at least usually, accompanied by imagination, pleasure and pain, desire, and local movement (OS 2.2 413b22–24). What is distinctive of animals is that they carry out part of their self-constitutive activities through action.

The third form of life, distinctive of human beings, or as I will say, of persons, is the life of rational activity. Rational activity, as I have already suggested, is essentially a form of self-conscious activity, and it is this that leads to the construction of personal identity. Thus personhood is quite literally a form of life, and being a person, like being a living thing, is being engaged in an activity of self-constitution.

In other words, what it is to be a person, or a rational agent, is just to be engaged in the activity of constantly making yourself into a person—just as what it is to be a giraffe is to be engaged in the activity constantly making yourself into a giraffe.

2.4.2

One way to bring out the force of this point is in terms of the idea of practical identity. In 1.4, I proposed that we constitute our own identities in the course of action. In choosing in accordance with the principles of a form of practical identity, I claim, we make that identity our own.

It is sometimes said, in opposition to this sort of point, that it involves an overly voluntaristic conception of identity. I did not choose to be an American citizen, or my parents' daughter. Even many of my personal friendships, the older ones especially, are as much the outcome of circumstance as of choice. So I am these things—this country's citizen, these people's daughter, this

---

[8] These views are found especially in *On the Soul* 2–3. See also NE 1.7 1097b32–1098a5.

person's old friend—*perforce*, and not because I chose to be them. And yet these identities give rise to reasons and obligations, as much as the ones that I do more plainly choose, like a profession or an office or a friendship quite deliberately sought out. But I want to argue that while that is true in one way, in another way it is not. For whenever I act in accordance with these roles and identities, whenever I allow them to govern my will, I endorse them, I embrace them, I affirm once again that I am them. In choosing in accordance with these forms of identity, I make them my own.

The idea that to be a person is to be constantly engaged in making yourself into that person helps to explain what is going on in this debate. To see how this works, consider one of the standard dilemmas of contemporary moral philosophy. Some people have complained that the Kantian self is "empty."[9] If you conceive yourself simply as a pure rational agent, and are not committed to any more specific conception of your identity, you are, as it were, too distant from yourself to make choices. There are two problems here. The more formal problem is that it looks as if your empty self can have no reason to do one thing rather than another. But even if you can find some particular reasons, there is also a problem about wholeheartedness, about commitment. How can you be a true friend, a true citizen, a true Christian, say, if the relevant commitments are always up for question and open to choice? The self, it is argued, must be not empty but rather determinate and full: it must take certain identities and relationships as unquestionable law.

And then of course the other side replies that there are also two problems with the determinate self. In the first place, the determinate self is not free, for its conduct is governed by a principle or a law which is not reason's own. In the second place the determinate self must in the end be unjust. For tolerance requires exactly that distance from our roles and relationships that the defenders of the determinate self deplore. "Christianity is my religion, but just in the same way, Islam is his," says the tolerant person. Tolerance demands that you see your religion not as *you* but as *yours*, yourself not as essentially a Christian but as essentially a person who *has* a religion—and only one of many you might have had. So you cannot identify with your religion all out and still be a tolerant person. Or so says the defender of the empty self.

Now this is a false dilemma, arrived at by an artificial freezing of the observer's mental frame. It assumes that the endorsement of our identities, our self-constitution, is a state rather than an activity. If self-constitution were a state we would be stuck on the horns of this dilemma. Either we must

---

[9] See for instance Michael Sandel in *Liberalism and the Limits of Justice.*

already have constituted ourselves—in which case the self would be full and determinate. Or we must not have done so yet—in which case the self would be empty.

But we don't have to choose between these two options, because self-constitution is not a state that we achieve and from which action then issues. As I will try to show in the course of the next four chapters, it is action itself.

3

Formal and Substantive Principles of Reason

3.1 Formal versus Substantive

3.1.1

In Chapter 1, I explained the general thesis for which I am arguing in this book: that action is self-constitution. By this I mean that we human beings constitute our own personal or practical identities—and at the same time our own agency—through action itself. We *make* ourselves the authors of our actions, by the way that we act. As I said before, this apparently paradoxical thesis depends on the ideas that action requires agency, and agency requires unity. An action is a movement attributable to an agent considered as an integrated whole, not a movement attributable merely to a part of an agent, or to some force working in her or on her. Since some ways of acting unify their agents better than others, the extent to which a movement is an action is a matter of degree: some actions are more genuinely actions than others (1.4.8). The actions that are most genuinely actions, I will argue, are the ones that accord with the principles of practical reason. These principles are therefore constitutive principles of actions, principles that we must be at least trying to follow if we are to count as acting at all. And this is what explains their normativity, or the way that they bind us.

In Chapter 4, I will make a first stab at defending this thesis—or anyway, at making it less abstract—by showing how the principles of practical reason unify and so constitute the will. I will also contrast this account of the grounds of their normativity to some other familiar accounts of the way that practical principles motivate and bind us. Strictly speaking, I believe that the conclusion I reach in Chapter 4 is not short of the conclusion I hope to reach in the book in general, but I don't think that will be obvious. In the chapters that follow, I will be developing richer conceptions of action, agency, and identity that I hope will make it clearer what self-constitution involves.

But before any of that happens, I need to say a word about which principles I am talking about when I talk about the principles of practical reason, and to introduce a crucial distinction: the distinction between substantive and formal principles of reason. For it will be an important part of the argument of Chapter 4 that only formal principles can be directly normative: our substantive principles must be derivable from formal ones if they are to be binding on the will.

3.1.2

In the philosophical tradition, three kinds of practical principles have been proposed as rational principles. First, there is the principle of instrumental reason, the principle that instructs us to take the means to our ends. Kant identifies the instrumental principle as one kind of hypothetical imperative, as he calls it an imperative of skill (G 4:415). It says that if we will an end, we must also will the means to that end. Kant's derivation of this principle, which I will be discussing in 4.3.1, identifies the means to an end with the *causes* of the end. But nowadays the hypothetical imperative is widely taken to extend to ways of realizing ends that are not in any technical sense *causes* of those ends, for instance to what is sometimes called "constitutive" means. Say that my end is outdoor exercise; here is an opportunity to go hiking, which is outdoor exercise; therefore I have reason to take this opportunity, not exactly as a means to my end, but as a way of realizing it. When we take this line of thought to extremes, it appears that any case in which your action is guided by the application of a concept to an actual particular object or event in the world is governed by the hypothetical imperative. Compare, for example: I need a hammer; *this* is a hammer; therefore I shall take *this*, not exactly as a means to my end but as a way of realizing it. Some of Aristotle's examples of practical syllogisms are exactly like this. Consider for example this one from *On the Movement of Animals*: "I want to drink, says appetite; this is drink, says sense or imagination or thought: straightaway I drink" (MA 7 701a32–34). Or take the notorious "dry food" syllogism of *Nicomachean Ethics* 7, in which Aristotle toys with the idea that weakness of will occurs in a man who believes that "Dry food is good for every man" when he reasons that "I am a man" and "such and such food is dry" but then fails to exercise his knowledge that "this food is such and such" (NE 7.3 1147a1–7), and so fails to conclude that he should take *this food*. In this way the hypothetical imperative may be extended to cover *any* case of action in which the agent is self-consciously guided by a conception of the state of affairs he is trying to realize in the world.[1] In this guise, the hypothetical imperative appears to

---

[1] The preceding passages are partly lifted from a discussion in "The Normativity of Instrumental Reason" (CA essay 1), pp. 27–8 and p. 28 n. 2.

be the general normative principle of practical application, or as we might put it the general principle of practical *judgment*—the practical application of a universal thought about what must be done or would be good to do to a particular movement in the world. It is the hypothetical imperative in this most general form, as the principle of practical application or judgment, which I will be discussing in this book, and which I claim is constitutive of volition and action. For there is a sense in which an action *just is* a practical judgment of this kind.[2]

3.1.3

Moving to the other extreme, moral principles have often been identified as principles of practical reason. Here there are two important distinctions to make. The first is the distinction between views according to which moral conduct is in fact rational, as judged by some *other* principle of reason, and views according to which moral principles are themselves principles of reason. Neo-Hobbesian arguments purporting to show that morality is in our self-interest are examples of the first type of view. Morality is deemed rational judged by the standard of self-interest, which is supposedly a rational standard. That is not the sort of thing I am talking about here: I am talking about the view that moral principles themselves are direct dictates of reason.

The second distinction, within that area, is the distinction between substantive and formal moral principles. Roughly speaking—and I'm afraid all of the speaking will be a bit rough here—a substantive conception of morality identifies morality in terms of its content, while a formal conception of morality identifies it with a method of reasoning about practical issues. Most people, intuitively, think of morality in substantive terms. What does it mean to act morally? Well, it means to keep your promises, tell the truth, be helpful to others, respect people's rights, give to charity—stuff like that. In the philosophical tradition, intuitionistic philosophers and dogmatic rationalists have proposed that reason is the source of certain substantive principles directing the performance of act-types of these kinds.[3] Or more modestly, they may suppose that certain substantive characterizations of actions—for instance, that an action would be kind, or help someone in need—count

[2] See my "Acting for a Reason" (CA essay 7), especially pp. 228–9.

[3] For some examples see Samuel Clarke, *A Discourse Concerning the Unchangeable Obligations of Natural Religion, and the Truth and Certainty of the Christian Revelation* (the Boyle lectures, 1705); Richard Price, *A Review of the Principal Questions in Morals*, and W. D. Ross, *The Right and the Good*.

as reasons for those actions. Another version of this view is that of some consequentialists, such as Sidgwick, who are also rationalists, and who have proposed that a principle directing that we maximize the good, in some form, is a principle of reason.[4] I know that the categorization of the consequentialist principle as substantive may occasion some surprise, since consequentialism may seem more like a method of reasoning. Bentham and Sidgwick, in fact, both presented it that way.[5] But the principle of utility, like all maximizing principles, is in fact a substantive principle, as I will argue below.

The clearest example of a formal conception of morality, on the other hand, is Kant's. What does it mean to act morally? According to Kant, it means to act autonomously, that is, to always make sure that the maxim on which you act is one that you could will to be a universal law. Morality, on Kant's account, is not a certain set of considerations, identified by their content, but a *way* of deliberating: the categorical imperative, as I will argue later (4.2.4), is part of the structure or *logic* of practical reason. Of course Kant tries to show that the things that we usually regard as our substantive duties will be shown to be necessary by this way of reasoning, in order to make a plausible case for it. But what distinguishes the moral agent, on Kant's account, is not first and foremost *what* he thinks about when he decides, but rather *the way* he deliberates when he makes his decisions. This sense of "formal" is related to the sense of "formal" I introduced in Chapter 1, when I argued that universalizability or lawfulness is a formal property in the Aristotelian sense—a property of the functional relations among a maxim's parts (1.3.2). For the method of deliberation proposed is one of ascertaining whether the parts of the maxim are related in such a way that the maxim can serve as a law.[6]

A more contemporary example of a formal account of moral reason is found in Thomas Nagel's view in *The Possibility of Altruism*. Nagel does not quite give us a conception of morality, but he does present a formal characterization of altruism: in this formal sense, to act altruistically is just to be moved by someone else's reason.[7] We don't need to say anything about the content of that reason in order to identify the conduct as altruistic: in the formal sense, helping someone to slaughter his enemies is altruistic (however imperfectly so), if you do it simply because you are moved by this other person's reason.

---

[4] Henry Sidgwick, *The Methods of Ethics*. See especially Book 3, chapter 13.

[5] I have in mind Bentham's claim that anyone who reasons practically at all must reason in a utilitarian way (*The Principles of Morals and Legislation*, pp. 128–9) and Sidgwick's characterization of utilitarianism as a "method."

[6] In 5.1.3, I will link these senses of formal in turn to another closely related sense: these formal principles capture the essential form of an action, an autonomous and efficacious movement.

[7] Nagel, *The Possibility of Altruism*, pp. 15–16.

Nagel argues that altruism is made possible by a formal requirement on reasons: that they should be formulable in an objective or agent-neutral way, that is, in terms of reasons for certain states of affairs to obtain, rather than merely in terms of what I, or even anyone in my position, has reason to do.[8] On these views, the requirements of morality and altruism are not requirements that we should act on a special *kind* of reason, identified by its content. They are conditions on the adequacy of *any* practical reason.

3.2 Testing versus Weighing

3.2.1

The distinction between substantive and formal conceptions of morality has frequently been ignored in philosophy, and I believe that this has been a source of confusion. On a substantive conception of morality, it is natural to identify a special category of reasons that we call "moral reasons." They are the particular reasons that spring from substantive moral principles: the fact that an act is unjust or unkind is a moral reason against it, say. On a Kantian conception, we can also identify a special category of "moral reasons," if we want to, but it takes a little more work. As I have already explained in 1.4.6, when an action is disallowed by the categorical imperative—because its maxim cannot serve as a universal law—that thought and the associated feeling of respect provide us with an incentive (respect for law) to perform the action. It is natural to say that someone who acts on that incentive acts on a "moral reason." And because this reason is also in a sense the result of applying the moral principle to a case, it can look just like a "moral reason" in the substantive sense. But the sense is really very different. In Kant's sense, a "moral reason" is an unconditionally binding reason that emerges as such from the correct process of deliberation in general. In the substantive sense, a "moral reason" is simply one among many considerations, and its status as unconditional can therefore be called into question.

3.2.2

This is exactly what happens in Bernard Williams's argument in the opening chapter of *Ethics and the Limits of Philosophy*. Williams tells us that Socrates' question—"how should one live?"—should not be identified with the question "how morally ought one to live?" For, Williams claims, if we identify those two questions, then we cannot *argue* that we should live a moral life,

---

[8] Nagel, *The Possibility of Altruism*, chapter 10.

since we are effectively *presupposing* that we should live a moral life. Williams also rejects one possible response to the point he is making, which is that we should distinguish a moral and a non-moral meaning of "should."[9] Rather, Williams wants to take "should," in its unmodified form, to be the word we use when we ask the most general deliberative question, the question we ask when we are, so to speak, actually making a decision. But sometimes, Williams admits, in the course of deliberation, we ask what we *should* do from the point of view of some particular *type* of consideration. What should I do from a moral point of view? What should I do from a self-interested point of view? Or perhaps even what should I do from a family point of view? Williams refers to these as questions of "subdeliberation."[10] The picture seems to be that, on the way to making a decision, you marshal together the considerations of a certain common type before balancing them against considerations of another type.

There is an intuitive conception of practical reasoning that fits with this picture fairly well. I call this conception "the weighing model." Suppose you have to make a decision for or against some course of action. You take a piece of paper, draw a line down the middle of the page, and write "for" on one side and "against" on the other, and then you start listing the relevant considerations—as some philosophers would have it, the prima facie or pro tanto reasons. Then you add them all up somehow to see how strong the balance of reasons is "for" and how strong the balance of reasons is "against." When you imagine a decision that way, it is natural to think that there are different kinds of considerations and that they could result in what Williams calls "subdeliberation." On the "for" side you might write: "I would earn a lot of money" and "I would have more prestige." Those, you say to yourself, are self-interested considerations. But perhaps on the "for" side you also write: "It would give employment to the local population" and on the against side you write: "It would damage the environment." Those, you say to yourself, are moral considerations. Then you might do some subdeliberation on these various types of considerations, and then balance out the results against each other. When you make your final decision, you might say something like: "well, there are some moral reasons against it, but they are outweighed by the moral reasons in favor of it, so on the whole morality favors it. And self-interest favors it too. Therefore, all things considered, it is what I *should* do." And there is Williams's general deliberative *should*, the all things considered *should*, while moral considerations are just one type of consideration.

---

[9] Bernard Williams, *Ethics and the Limits of Philosophy*, p. 5.   [10] Ibid., p. 6.

If you think about deliberation this way, it is perfectly natural to talk about *moral reasons* and contrast them with other *types* of reasons. When you conceive practical reason substantively in this way—as Williams, by the way, generally does—it makes sense to insist that though we can ask what we morally ought to do, we should not take for granted that that is what we *should* do, all things considered. Or at least, it makes sense to insist that we cannot arrive at this conclusion—that what we ought to do morally is the same as what we should do all things considered—simply by equating the idea of "should" with the idea of "morally ought."

Here and elsewhere, Williams tends to write as if those who do equate "should" with "morally ought" are trying to show that we always should do what is morally right by a kind of verbal maneuver or trick. But on a formal conception of reason like Kant's, deliberation itself looks very different. Kant offers us what I think of as a "testing" rather than a "weighing" model of reasons. On his view, the way you are supposed to deliberate is to formulate a maxim, stating the complete package of considerations that together favor the performance of a certain action. Of course, some of the reasoning that I described above, the marshalling of relevant considerations, will still go on, but now it will be part of the work of formulating the maxim. You will still do some weighing and balancing, although now it will only be of considerations that plainly are generally commensurable—we need not assume a metric that makes any possible consideration commensurable with any other. Your maxim, once formulated, embodies your proposed reason. You then test it by the categorical imperative, that is, you ask whether you can will it to be a universal law, in order to see whether it really is a reason. Universalizability is a condition on the form of a reason, and if a consideration doesn't meet this condition, then it is not merely outweighed—rather, it is not a reason at all.[11] On this kind of formal account, it makes good sense to identify the general *should* of deliberation with the *moral ought*. This is not because we should do everything we do for what, in this kind of theory, counts as a "moral reason"—that is, it is not because the incentive of our action should always be respect for law—but precisely because the theory proposes

[11] Obviously, the workability of all this depends on the truth of Kant's claim that his formal principle can rule some considerations out as non-reasons, and require others as unconditional reasons. See my "Kant's Formula of Universal Law" (CKE essay 3), and Chapter 9, especially 9.4.5, below. In Nagel's account, objectifiability is the formal condition, but Nagel doesn't think this condition rules anything out—any reason can be given objective form, although certain claims of reason will appear very implausible when objectified (*The Possibility of Altruism*, p. 126). So in Nagel's theory the formal device does not serve as a test. Relatedly, the reasons that emerge from formalization in Nagel's theory still must be balanced, although Nagel does not favor a maximizing view (*The Possibility of Altruism*, pp. 135–8).

the moral law as a formal principle, and so as a way of deciding what we *should* do.[12]

Of course, describing these two models of itself doesn't settle the question whether the deliberative *should* is the same as the moral *ought*: it just means that before we can approach that question we have to ask whether a formal or a substantive conception of morality is correct. That is what I propose to do in Chapter 4. For it is the formal principle of morality, the categorical imperative, which I will argue is constitutive of action.

3.3 Maximizing and Prudence

3.3.1

Now let me mention, only to lay aside, the problem of what I will call the missing principle. Kant identified what he thought was a second sort of hypothetical imperative, a principle of prudence, which instructs us to take the means, in a broad sense of means, to our own happiness (G 4:415–16), which he thought of as something like a maximum or completeness of the satisfaction of desire. And many philosophers have agreed with Kant about this, believing that there is some sort of rational principle of prudence or self-interest, instructing us to promote or to maximize our own good, the satisfaction of our desires or whatever it might be. They have also agreed with Kant in categorizing this principle along with the instrumental principle as a hypothetical imperative. Often it is treated as a mere extension or application of the instrumental principle itself, as when philosophers or social scientists characterize self-interested reasoning as "instrumental."

I believe that this last way of thinking of the principle of prudence or self-interest, as an application or extension of the instrumental principle, is completely confused. The instrumental principle tells us only to take the means to any given end; it tells us nothing about what our ends should be. It therefore cannot possibly tell us that we ought to pursue a maximum of satisfaction, or any other form of overall good. In fact it does not even say that we ought to prefer the satisfaction of a conjunction of any two of our ends, even when there is no conflict, to the satisfaction of any one of them. No doubt there is some rational requirement of that sort—that's

---

[12] Kant himself gives the impression that there are two kinds of reasons in certain places in the *Groundwork* (see for instance G 4:419). According to a common interpretation, these are associated with the two kinds of imperatives—roughly speaking, self-interested reasons with the hypothetical imperative and moral ones with the categorical imperative. For additional discussion of why this should not be Kant's considered view see "Acting for a Reason" (CA essay 7), pp. 222–3.

why I call the principle "missing" rather than "non-existent"—but it is not the principle of instrumental reason. Nor of course does the instrumental principle say that we ought to prefer a maximum of satisfaction or pleasure or good to any particular satisfaction or pleasure or good when there *is* a case of conflict.

This is particularly obvious when the supposed maximum is composed of quite disparate objects. Suppose one can argue that it is irrational to prefer a penny to a dollar, on the grounds that a dollar is more of the same thing. It certainly wouldn't follow from *that* sort of argument that it is irrational to prefer a torrid though ultimately heartbreaking love affair to a lifetime of amicable matrimony, or a whole bottle of champagne to a hangover-free Sunday. For the argument that one must prefer the dollar to the penny will work only, or at most, on the assumption that one values both of them for the sake of their exchange value alone, while only the crudest hedonist thinks one values everything for the sake of some common experience or result.

But in fact the problem is much greater than that makes it seem, for there is a problem even for the crudest hedonist. Even the argument for preferring the dollar to the penny can't be made on the basis of instrumental reason alone. If I want to buy a piece of penny candy, the instrumental principle judges a penny and a dollar to be *equally good* means so far as *that* end is concerned. It is only on the assumption that I ought to pursue or stand ready to pursue more than one of my ends, and also of course that my other ends might cost money, that I am *required* to prefer the dollar to the penny. And as I have just pointed out, the instrumental principle does not require us to prefer the achievement of a conjunction of our ends to the achievement of any one of them. An argument in favor of pursuing one's greater good, and also of always preferring it to one's lesser good, can't follow from the instrumental principle, because it must be in place *before* the instrumental principle even tells us to prefer the greater means to the less.

And of course if we leave crude hedonism and its easy commensurabilities behind, any argument that is to show that one ought to prefer the hangover-free Sunday to the bottle of champagne or the years of happy matrimony to the torrid love affair on grounds of greater good will have to do that in terms of some substantive conception of the good. The maximization of satisfaction over time, as well as any other form of overall good, is a *substantive* end, not a formal one, and any principle directing us to promote and prefer it would be a substantive principle. It would not be a hypothetical imperative, since it dictates the adoption of a particular end, and it would certainly not be arrived at by an application of instrumental reason.

3.3.2

Why do people tend to think of maximizing as a formal requirement? I think they make a mistake like the one that John Stuart Mill makes in his proof of the principle of utility. Mill says that the only thing that "proves" that anything is desirable and therefore good is that it is desired. Each person desires his own happiness, so the sum of everyone's happiness is desirable and therefore good.[13] But, we may object, at least for all we know, no one desires the sum of everyone's happiness, so if only desire makes for desirability, what makes the sum desirable? Mill wants to mean that each *part* of it is desired, by the person whose happiness it is.[14] But of course a maximum does not include its parts in *that* way: maximizing happiness is not like adding one acre of ground to another that adjoins it. Conflicts are possible, and if the calculation turns out so, I may have to sacrifice my happiness in order to maximize the total, and then where is my part? In the same way, if my happiness consists in the maximum satisfaction of my desires, it is unlikely to include the satisfaction of each of my desires. And just as the individual person whose happiness is sacrificed for the sake of overall utility seems to have some right to protest, so also the individual desire whose satisfaction is sacrificed for the sake of overall happiness seems to have some right to protest. There are moments when the question "why should I be prudent?" is as much in need of an answer as its more famous cousin.[15]

3.3.3

Suppose that we say that a person's happiness is good for her (or just good, it does not matter for this argument), meaning that a maximum of the satisfaction of her desires is good for her. It seems natural to give one of two explanations of what makes happiness in this sense good. The first is that the satisfaction of each of her desires is a good thing for her, so that by maximizing her satisfactions she is maximizing good things. The second is that her happiness is good because she in fact desires it, and so good for her for the same reason that each of the objects of her particular desires is good for her. In whichever of these ways we establish the goodness of happiness,

---

[13] Mill, *Utilitarianism*, chapter 4, especially p. 34.

[14] Mill actually says this is what he meant in a letter to Henry Jones: 'As to the sentence you quote from my *Utilitarianism*; when I said that the general happiness is a good to the aggregate of all persons I did not mean that every human being's happiness is a good to every other human being; though I think, in a good state of society & education it would be so. I merely meant in this particular sentence to argue that since A's happiness is a good, B's a good, C's a good, &c., the sum of all these goods must be a good.' *The Later Letters of John Stuart Mill*, ed. Mineka and Lindley, 3. 1414. I owe the reference to Charlotte Brown and Jerome Schneewind.

[15] This section is lifted from "The Myth of Egoism" (CA essay 2), p. 72.

we get the result that each of the person's particular desires has exactly the same kind of normative claim on her that her happiness does. So if the aim of maximizing satisfaction comes into conflict with the aim of satisfying one of her desires, she now has a normative reason to do each of these things, and she needs some further reason to prefer the maximum satisfaction to the particular satisfaction. The problem of why she should be prudent, which before seemed to be a problem about *whether* there is a normative principle of prudence, has simply reappeared in the guise of a conflict among a plurality of normative principles. Why should she choose the maximum satisfaction of her desires, rather than the satisfaction of any one of them?

Now perhaps you will agree that this problem does arise for someone who claims that happiness is good because we desire it, and therefore places happiness exactly on a footing with the other objects of desire. But you may be tempted to think it does not arise for someone who claims that happiness is good because the satisfaction of each of her desires is a good thing, and therefore that happiness is a maximum of good things. For it is obvious that a maximum of good things is better than any one good thing, on the principle that more is better. But that argument only works on the assumption that satisfaction *itself* is the only thing you really want. And as Bishop Butler argued, that assumption is incoherent. For, as Butler argued, you cannot get any satisfaction from the fulfillment of your desire for an object, unless you want the desired object itself for its own sake.[16] But if we also want the particular objects of our desires, then it is not clear why we should be willing to sacrifice those particular objects for the sake of satisfaction, unless we—as it happens—in fact want satisfaction more than anything else. So the trouble with this argument is that it does not explain the authority of this version of the principle of prudence, but rather simply assumes that overall satisfaction is either the only thing a person wants, or what a person in fact wants most. But that is precisely what the person who questions the authority of the principle of prudence undertakes to deny. The imprudent person is not denying that he will get more satisfaction if he acts prudently—he is asking why he therefore has a reason to do so, given that he will have to give up something other than satisfaction—something else that he actually wants.

But there is one final move available to the defender of the principle of prudence. The last argument we looked at illicitly assumed either that a maximum of satisfaction is the only thing a person really wants, or, to meet Butler's point, that a maximum of satisfaction is what a person wants

---

[16] Joseph Butler, *Fifteen Sermons Preached at the Rolls Chapel*, Sermon 11. This is reprinted as Sermon 4 of *Joseph Butler: Five Sermons*, ed. Stephen Darwall. See especially pp. 47–51.

most. The defender of the principle of prudence can transform one of these psychological theses into a normative thesis instead. He can insist that only satisfaction, or only the set of desired objects that would yield a maximum of satisfaction, is really a *good* thing, and therefore that it cannot be *rational* to want anything but satisfaction, or those objects of desire that are consistent with your obtaining a maximum of satisfaction. But this defense of the principle of prudence wears its basis in a substantive theory of the good on its face. On this view, the good for a person *just is* either maximal satisfaction or the set of desired objects that will yield a maximum of satisfaction. And the goodness of happiness, in either of these senses, now cannot be grounded in the fact that it necessarily gets an agent what he *wants most*—for we have denied that assumption, which, as we have seen, begs the question against the challenger to prudence. Nor can it be grounded in the fact that it gets the agent *most of what he wants*—for we have denied that his wanting things in itself has any normative force, in order to avoid generating a plurality of normative claims that will conflict with the principle of prudence itself. On this view, the claim that it is irrational to pursue anything but maximum satisfaction, or those objects of desire that are consistent with your obtaining a maximum of satisfaction, is a pure dogmatic claim, based on nothing but a substantive conviction that maximal satisfaction, or the set of objects that would produce it, must be the good.[17]

3.3.4

Everything I've just said applies, *mutatis mutandis*, to the principle of utility. To see this, recall the comparison to Mill. The argument for the principle of utility depends on the idea that each person's happiness is a good. Therefore the utilitarian must grant that each person's happiness is the source of a normative claim. Again, what we get in the first instance is a plurality of normative principles, one telling us to promote each person's happiness, and one—assuming that adding in this case makes any sense at all[18]—telling us to promote the total. Someone who challenges the principle of utility when his own happiness is to be sacrificed is not denying that there will be more total happiness if we follow the principle of utility. He is asking why he therefore has a reason to give up his own happiness, which the utilitarian must agree is also a good. The utilitarian can try to block this challenge by insisting that a

---

[17] Later, I will also argue against the idea that this conception of the good could be a rational one (8.3.3). This section and that one are adapted from "The Myth of Egoism" (CA essay 2).

[18] I don't think it does make sense. The amalgamation of what is good for me with what is good for you isn't good for anybody, and everything that is good must be good for somebody.

maximum of happiness is obviously better, just as the defender of prudence can try to insist that a maximum of satisfaction is obviously better. But the utilitarian cannot base this claim on the idea that a maximum of happiness includes any given person's happiness and more, because it doesn't; someone's happiness may be left out. Just as the defender of prudence cannot insist that a maximum of satisfaction includes everything you want and more—because it doesn't; the satisfaction of some desire, and therefore of course its object, will surely be left out. So if the utilitarian insists that a maximum of satisfaction, or whatever will yield that maximum, is better, he is simply making a substantive, and apparently dogmatic, claim. The principle of utility, if it were a principle of reason, would be a substantive principle, not a formal one, based on the unsupported thesis that maximal happiness just is the good.

3.3.5

While I think the views I've mentioned about what I've tagged "the missing principle" are confused, there is a truth behind them. As I said before, it seems overwhelmingly plausible to believe that there is a rational requirement that we should prefer the achievement of a conjunction of our ends to the achievement of any one of them. And once that idea is on the table, we also do seem to need some method of balancing our various ends against one another when they cannot be practically combined. That is why we need the missing principle, something besides the instrumental principle and the categorical imperative, since neither of them will do this job. But there are many possible ways we could balance our various ends against one another in order to choose among them. Given this fact, it is perhaps unsurprising that there is more disagreement among philosophers about the correct formation of the missing principle than about any other part of the theory of practical reason. Some philosophers, as we have seen, think it requires us to maximize the sum total of our satisfactions or of our pleasures over the course of our whole lives; others, such as those who subscribe to what Derek Parfit calls "present-aim theory," require only that we try to satisfy our "present" desires, projects, and aims to as great an extent as possible.[19] But all of these principles must be based on dubious substantive theories of the good, which make it possible to assign our ends "weights" according to how well they promote that good.

I have suggested that maximizing principles and their closest cousins are substantive and not formal. Indeed this is why Kant's imperative of prudence

---

[19] Parfit, *Reasons and Persons*, especially chapter 6, section 45.

fits so badly with the rest of his theory, since his other principles are formal ones. I have no formulation to offer for a formal version of the missing principle. If we had it, it would be, like the instrumental principle, a principle for formulating maxims that would still have to be tested; it would not yield reasons by itself. But it seems clear to me that if we could formulate a version of the missing principle that is formal rather than substantive, then it should be easy for me to make my case about how its normativity is to be established. What I mean is that it seems rather *obvious* that a formal principle for balancing our various ends and reasons must be a principle for unifying our agency, since that is so exactly why we need it: so that we are not always tripping over ourselves when we pursue our various projects, so that our agency is not incoherent. Indeed, the argument in favor of crude hedonism is actually often *based on* this formal consideration. There must be some sort of common coin that makes our ends commensurable, says the hedonist, for how else could we ever choose among them? Here the need to balance precedes the theory of the good, instead of the possibility of balancing following from it. Perhaps in general a thought about the unity of our agency rests behind the conviction that there must *be* some single or unified human good that we can always see ourselves as striving for in our actions.

So I will leave the principle of prudence or balancing aside, and focus my attention on the instrumental and moral principles. In the next chapter I will defend two claims. First, normative principles of practical reason must be formal. In particular, I believe that they must be what I call the Kantian imperatives, the hypothetical imperative that tells you that if you will the end, you must will the means to that end, and the categorical imperative that tells you that you must will your maxim as a universal law. Second, I will argue that the way to establish these imperatives is by showing how they constitute a unified will.

4

Practical Reason and the Unity of the Will

4.1 The Empiricist Account of Normativity

4.1.1

In this chapter I will explain how the principles of practical reason serve to unify the will, and how that makes them normative. I will begin by arguing against two other accounts of the normativity of practical principles, grounded in the empiricist and rationalist traditions respectively. In each case, I will start by looking at their treatment of the hypothetical imperative.[1]

Empiricists have standardly assumed that hypothetical imperatives either are automatically normative or do not need to be normative because they are automatically motivating. This view has emerged not so much in direct arguments for the hypothetical imperative as in arguments against the normativity of supposedly more ambitious rational principles, such as the moral principle. Hume's famous argument to the effect that reason is the slave of the passions is the *locus classicus* for this sort of thing (T 2.3.3), and Bernard Williams's argument that internalism favors a view similar to Hume's is another example.[2] Indeed, I think we may see Williams's view as generalizing Hume's argument to fit the broader version of the hypothetical imperative that I mentioned earlier, the hypothetical imperative as the principle of practical application or practical judgment in general (3.1.2).

According to Hume, the role of reasoning is to ascertain the relations between things. The only relation he thinks could conceivably be directly relevant to action is the causal relation (T 2.3.3,413–414). Knowledge of that relation can motivate us, but only if we have a pre-existing desire to attain or avoid one of the two objects thus related. For as Hume seems to picture

---

[1] The arguments in this section are anticipated in "The Normativity of Instrumental Reason" (CA essay 1), and "The Myth of Egoism" (CA essay 2).

[2] See Bernard Williams, "Internal and External Reasons," in *Moral Luck*, pp. 101–13, and "Internal Reasons and the Obscurity of Blame," in *Making Sense of Humanity and Other Philosophical Papers*, pp. 35–45.

it, our knowledge of the causal relationship functions hydraulically, providing a conduit by which motivational force passes from the desire for the end to the idea of taking the means, thus making the idea of taking the means desirable.[3] It does not follow that there is any rational requirement to take the means, nor I think does Hume suppose that it does. On Hume's view we are reliably motivated in this way, and he says explicitly that it is only in cases of theoretical error, either about the nature of the object or about the means, that we ever do anything that might be called "irrational." That is, our desire for an object may be based on a mistake, as when we wrongly believe that something would be pleasant; or we may be wrong about what would constitute the means to achieving it. Even then, Hume says, it is strictly speaking the false belief, not the action or the desire that prompts the action, that is contrary to reason. Hume asserts quite explicitly that when mistakes of this kind are out of the case, we are *always* in fact motivated to take the means to our ends (T 2.3.3,416).

But if Hume is right about that, then we are never, really, instrumentally irrational. For there is a difference between making a theoretical error and being guilty of practical irrationality—that is, violating a principle of practical reason. When a person's action is based on a mistake, the person does the wrong thing, objectively speaking, but that does not show that the person is practically irrational. A person who adds a little dry vermouth and some olives to glass full of vinegar, believing it to be a glass full of gin, is not doing anything irrational, for by her own lights the action makes perfectly good sense. There is nothing amiss with her motivation, nothing wrong with her will: it is only her factual judgment that needs correcting. We would be violating the principle of instrumental reason only if, with the facts correctly in view, we failed to take the means to our ends. And this, according to Hume, never happens.

But Hume's apparently optimistic view of human rationality threatens to dissolve into tautology. The problem arises when we ask what makes something someone's end. Suppose someone claims to desire a certain object. We inform him that performing a certain act is the adequate and sufficient means to the achievement of that object, yet he fails to form the desire to perform that act. Then we are entitled to conclude that he does not desire the object, or does not desire it enough to inspire him to take those means. That being so, the object is not his *end*, and that being so, he has not failed to act on any instrumental reason that he has. If all we mean by your "end" is that which you in fact pursue, it is *conceptually* impossible for you to fail to take

---

[3] Or, of course, from our aversion to an effect to the idea of the cause of that effect, causing us to draw back from an action that would produce unwanted consequences.

the means to your end. If you fail to pursue something, then it isn't your end, and then you don't act irrationally in failing to pursue it.

But if people cannot ever be guilty of violating the instrumental principle by their own lights, then it is not a normative principle. For now in the case where you *do* perform an act that will achieve a desired end, the force of saying that you acted on an instrumental "reason" has become unclear. Your desire for the end plays a role in explaining why you did the act, but there is no rational requirement of taking the means to your end that has any normative force for you, and so no reason *on which* you act. What looks like the principle of instrumental reason turns out simply to be a *description* of the inevitable effect that a certain kind of judgment has on the human will: prove to a human being that a certain act will promote a sufficiently desired object, and that will cause her to desire to do that act.

4.1.2

Why couldn't rational principles turn out to be essentially descriptions of the effects that certain judgments or ideas have on the will? The answer is that this conception of what a rational principle is cannot support the normative use of "ought." Some philosophers—I think Williams may be among them—believe that the possibility of theoretical error or ignorance is sufficient to support the normative "ought." But I think that this is mistaken. For according to the empiricist view, if I say to you "you really ought to see a dentist about that tooth" all that I can mean—*all*—is that if you came to understand that a visit to the dentist is essential to the achievement of your end of avoiding a toothache, you would in fact be motivated to go to the dentist. And this is not a consideration *on which* you can act. For how would it work? I assert it as a truth that if you knew Fact-F, you would be motivated to do Act-A. You now know Fact-F, so can you act *on* the truth that I have asserted? All you can do is check, and if you are not motivated to do Act-A, you need not adjust your conduct, for if you are not motivated to do Act-A, then my assertion was false. So the "ought" judgment here is not really a recommendation, but rather a sort of hypothetical prediction. And it is *not* that I predict that you would be motivated to go to the dentist—if you understood that going to the dentist was a means to your end of avoiding a toothache—because you would then see that you have a *reason* to go. It is not *that*, for on the empiricist view, the claim that you have a reason to go *just amounts to* the claim that if you made the means-end judgment in question, you would then be motivated to go. So it turns out that what looks like the normative "ought" is really just a version of the "ought" of expectation. On the empiricist view, saying of someone on the brink of toothache that he *ought* to go to the dentist is exactly like saying of someone who is late that he *ought* to be home by now. Given human nature, we would have predicted that the person on the brink of toothache would be motivated to go to the dentist; just as given the distance, we would have predicted that the person who left the office an hour ago would be home by now. If these predictions turn out to be false, then we know that something has gone wrong. But *what* has gone wrong can no more properly be described as a failure of practical reason in the case of the person who doesn't go to the dentist than in the case of the person who isn't home by now. In both cases, what we would have predicted hasn't happened, and that is all.

The inadequacy of the view is clear from this fact: there may be many principles that accurately describe the way human beings are characteristically motivated, or the effects that certain judgments have on the will. And the empiricist conception of rationality leaves us with no way of distinguishing which ones are principles of reason and which ones are not. We *can* reliably predict that people will be motivated to take the means to their ends, mistakes and ignorance being out of the case. But we also can reliably predict that people will buy objects that come in packages with erotic pictures on them. And no doubt the transfer of libido from the package to the object occurs in the same way that, on Hume's account, desire is transferred from the end to the means. We are not therefore tempted to think that buying seductively packaged objects is rationally required of us.

4.1.3

What does make the difference between those two cases? As Nagel points out in *The Possibility of Altruism*, the specifically rational character of going to the dentist to avert an unwanted toothache depends on *how* the belief (that a trip to the dentist would avert a toothache) and the desire (to avert the toothache) are "combined."[4] It is certainly not enough to say that they jointly *cause* the action, or that their bare co-presence produces a motive, for a person might be conditioned to respond in totally crazy ways to the co-presence of certain beliefs and desires. In Nagel's own example, a person has been conditioned so that whenever he wants a drink and believes the object before him is a pencil sharpener, he wants to put a coin into the pencil sharpener. Here the co-presence of belief and desire reliably lead to a certain action, but the action is a mad one. (My example of the marketing technique is no different, except that nature has done the conditioning for us.) What

---

[4] Nagel, *The Possibility of Altruism*, pp. 33–5.

is the difference between this person and one who, rationally, wants to put a coin in a soda machine when she wants a drink? One may be tempted to say that putting a coin in a soda machine, unlike putting a coin in a pencil sharpener, is a means to a drink, so that the right kind of conceptual connection between the desire and the causal belief obtains. But so far that is only to note a fact about the relationship between the belief and the desire themselves, and that says nothing about the rationality of the *person* who is influenced by them. If the belief and desire still operate on that person merely by having a certain causal efficacy when co-present, the rational action is only accidentally or externally different from the mad one. After all, a person may be conditioned to do the correct thing as well as the incorrect thing; but the correctness of what she is conditioned to do does not make *her* any more rational. So neither the joint causal efficacy of the belief and the desire, nor the existence of an appropriate conceptual connection between them, nor the bare conjunction of these two facts, enables us to judge that a person acts rationally. For the person to act rationally, she must be motivated by her own *recognition* of the appropriate conceptual connection between the belief and the desire. We may say that she *herself* must combine the belief and the desire *in the right way*.[5] And that right way is the one described by the hypothetical imperative. And that means that, following Kant, we may say that a rational instrumental reasoner acts not merely *in accordance with*, but *from*, the hypothetical imperative. The normativity of the hypothetical imperative cannot be explained in terms of its effects on the will, because we must establish that normativity before we know that the effects on the will are of the right sort.

4.1.4

But why does the hypothetical imperative represent the right way to combine the means and the end? As I will be arguing later in this chapter, and again in the next, the reason why we are confident that taking the means to your end is rationally required, while buying seductively packaged objects is not, is that taking the means to your end is constitutive of volition and action, while buying seductively packaged objects is not. That difference is not adequately captured by the theory that rational principles essentially describe the effects of judgments or ideas on the will. Hume's view, in fact, ultimately depends on an inadequate conception of action. For Hume an action essentially is nothing

---

[5] The foregoing passages are lifted from "The Normativity of Instrumental Reason" (CA essay 1), pp. 32–3.

more than a movement caused by a judgment or idea that regularly has an effect on the will (T 2.3.1,403–404).[6] That, I will argue, is not what action is.

4.2 The Rationalist Account of Normativity

4.2.1

The rationalist view seems to take a step in the right direction, for on a rationalist view action is not merely *caused* by a judgment, but rather is *guided* by it. The traditional or dogmatic rationalist is a substantive realist about moral principles. The view is one of the most common and regularly recurring positions in the tradition of modern moral philosophy, and versions of it have been held by Samuel Clarke, John Balguy, and Richard Price in the eighteenth century, William Whewell in the nineteenth century, and W. D. Ross, H. A. Prichard, and more recently Derek Parfit in the twentieth and twenty-first. The combination of this rationalist view of normativity with a formal principle of reason is unusual, but as I have argued elsewhere, there is evidence that Kant himself somewhat confusedly held such a view in his earlier writings.[7] I won't rehearse those arguments here. In any case, it is certainly not uncommon for people to interpret Kant as holding this sort of view. Sidgwick, I think, reads Kant in this way.[8]

Hume famously accused this sort of view of what we nowadays call externalism. That is, he argued that it is impossible to explain how rational principles of the type in question are supposed to motivate us (T 3.1.1,457–462). His own contemporaries, philosophers such as Clarke and Price, saw no difficulty here: they simply claimed that the perception of rightness necessarily motivates.[9] That dispute, I think, may be a standoff. But if we think about normativity, rather than motivation, then we will find that there is something in Hume's complaint.

The realist supposes that there are eternal normative verities of some sort—facts about which act-types or actions are right, or facts about what counts as a reason for what. How do we act on these verities? Apparently, by applying them in particular instances. We apply our knowledge that an action is right by choosing it. That sounds natural enough. But notice that this

---

   [6] Those who believe that Hume is responsible for the "belief/desire" model may be startled by this claim. But Hume doesn't insist that we are always moved by a passion: he makes it clear that he thinks we can be moved by a judgment about a probable passion. See T 1.3.10, "Of the Influence of Belief."

   [7] See "The Normativity of Instrumental Reason" (CA essay 1), pp. 51–2.

   [8] Sidgwick, *The Methods of Ethics.* See for instance pp. 385–6.

   [9] See Clarke, *A Discourse Concerning the Unchangeable Obligations of Natural Religion* (the Boyle lectures, 1705), in the selections in Raphael's *British Moralists*, vol. 1, pp. 199–200. For Price, see *A Review of the Principal Questions in Morals*, in the selections in *British Moralists*, vol. 2, p. 194.

sort of account could not possibly explain the normativity of the hypothetical imperative. We can see this by thinking about how it would have to work. The agent would have to recognize, as some sort of eternal normative verity, that it is good, or that it is required, or that there is a reason, to take the means to his ends. Let's say, just to make a choice, that it is rationally required. How does he act on this recognition? How does he apply it to the case at hand? The problem is that the extended version of the hypothetical imperative is itself, as I mentioned earlier (3.1.2), the principle of practical application. But we cannot explain how we are motivated to act on the hypothetical imperative, much less how we are bound by it, by appealing to the hypothetical imperative *itself*. We would have to say that an agent's end is to do what is rationally required, and that he sees that actions conforming to the hypothetical imperative are rationally required. Taking the means to his ends is therefore *itself* a means to his end of performing rationally required actions, and he chooses to conform to the hypothetical imperative under the influence of—the hypothetical imperative itself. The point is that the hypothetical imperative cannot be a normative truth that we *apply* in practice, because it is the principle *in accordance with which* we are acting when we apply truths in practice.

4.2.2

Even if this were not an incoherent way of thinking about what happens when we act on the hypothetical imperative, it would be an incoherent way of thinking about its normativity. For on the picture I have just sketched, the hypothetical imperative can bind us only by way of a prior commitment to doing what is rationally required. So the very phenomenon we are trying to explain—rational requiredness—must be, so to speak, front-loaded into the picture. And for this reason, the realist picture in fact works no better for moral principles than it does for the hypothetical imperative. For even if we know what makes an action morally required, so long as that is just a piece of knowledge, that knowledge has to be applied in action by way of the hypothetical imperative. But the hypothetical imperative cannot itself bind us to do what is morally required. There would have to be some further obligation to take the performance of morally required actions as our end. And this further obligation could not just be another piece of knowledge, for the same problem would then arise once again. What obligates us to apply it?

The problem here rests in thinking of the principles that define the obligatory and the forbidden as standards we *apply* when we are deliberating about what to do. Normative standards for things other than action do work in this way.

Having decided, say, that you are going to buy a car, you then ask yourself what makes for a good one, or perhaps what makes for a good one for you. These standards exert their normativity, if they do so at all, through action itself—we allow them to guide our choices. But the normative standards for actions themselves cannot work the same way. To see the problem, consider the fact that, in the case of things other than action, you don't absolutely *have to* apply the normative standards. Usually you have the same reason for choosing a good X (or a good X for you) that you have for choosing an X. But it is at least imaginable that you might just *pick* an X without reference to its goodness, like someone picking a number from one to ten or randomly picking a cookie from a passing tray. So if you are *obligated* to pick the best X or a good X, we need some further argument for that. But no further argument could be given why we are *obligated* to choose obligatory actions.

So long as we think of the principles of rational action as something that we *apply*—and therefore as something that we may or may not apply—when we deliberate about what to do, then we cannot really be obligated to perform morally required actions. For either we are obligated to apply the standard for morally required action or we are not. If we say we are not, morality is not normative, whereas if we say that we are, because the standard is known to hold, the whole argument starts all over again—why must we apply this piece of knowledge? This is the truth in Hume's complaint about the rationalists. Mere knowledge is external to the will, and external standards cannot obligate the will.[10]

4.2.3

Of course, if my arguments succeed, and if you believe them for the right reasons, you will then have knowledge that the hypothetical and categorical imperatives are normative, and perhaps this will move you to conform to them. So won't I then have to say that you have applied your knowledge of the normativity of these principles after all? No. Since Philosophy leads to a conceptual grasp of the issues that it deals with, there is a standing tendency to think that what Philosophy wants is always some piece of knowledge, which will then be applied. Knowledge of the normativity of practical principles doesn't transform them into premises which are then applied, any more than knowledge of the normativity of logical principles, like modus ponens, transforms those into premises which are then applied. What Philosophy leads to when it formulates such principles and reveals the sources

---

[10] This discussion is adapted from "Realism and Constructivism in 20th Century Moral Philosophy" (CA essay 10), pp. 315–17.

of their normativity is not knowledge which is then to be applied, but rather self-knowledge. That is to say, it leads to a self-conscious appreciation of what you are and of how you work, which will make you better at being what you are and at working in that way.

That, by the way, is how I intend the arguments in this book to work—if of course they work at all.

4.2.4

As I have just hinted, the argument I gave in 4.2.2 is essentially the same as a now-familiar argument to the effect that the standards of logic cannot enter into reasoning as premises.[11] Suppose George does not reason in accordance with modus ponens. He does not see how you get from "If A then B" and "A" to the conclusion that "B." As is often pointed out, it does not help to add modus ponens as a premise, that is to say, to add "if A and B, and also A, then B." For you still need to reason in accordance with modus ponens in order to get any conclusion from these premises, and this is what George does not do. The argument I've just given against the rationalist account of normativity amounts to an argument that the principles of practical reason cannot obligate us to act if they enter into practical deliberation as premises. Adding practical principles as premises cannot bind us to act, just as adding logical principles as premises cannot bind us to draw the conclusion. And this fact is related to the case I am trying to make here in another important way. For it is important to notice that if George lacks logic, his mind will be a disunified jumble of unrelated atomistic beliefs, unable to function as a mind at all. It will be a *mere heap* of premises. And that is where the normativity comes in. What obligates George to believe B in these circumstances is not merely his belief that "if A then B" and also that "A," but rather modus ponens itself. And it is not his *belief* in modus ponens that obligates him to believe B, for that, as the argument we have just looked at shows, is irrelevant. What obligates him to believe B is that, if he does not reason in accordance with modus ponens, he will not have a mind at all.

The principles of practical reason, if they are to be normative, must be principles of the *logic* of practical deliberation. They must be formal principles. For without such principles the will, like George's mind, will be a *mere heap*, not of ideas now, but of impulses to act. And this brings us at last to Kant.

---

[11] I show what kind of trouble it makes if we try to use the principle of instrumental reason as a premise in "The Normativity of Instrumental Reason" (CA essay 1), pp. 50–1.

4.3 Kant on the Hypothetical Imperative

4.3.1

Kant's derivation of the hypothetical imperative is simple. The hypothetical imperative says that if you will an end, you must will the means to that end. And as Kant says:

> Whoever wills the end also wills (insofar as reason has decisive influence on his actions) the indispensably necessary means to it that are within his power. This proposition is, as regards the volition, analytic; for in the volition of an object as my effect, my causality as an acting cause, that is, the use of means, is already thought . . . (G 4:417)

Taking the means to an end, and determining yourself to cause the end, are so closely linked that Kant characterizes the relationship as "analytic." While obviously apt in one way, the term is unfortunate in another, for it suggests that if someone fails to take the means to a certain object, we are logically entitled to conclude that that object is not after all his end. If this were right, Kant's view, like Hume's, would degenerate into tautology: your end would be whatever you in fact pursue. What the argument establishes is rather that the hypothetical imperative is a constitutive principle of willing. What makes willing different from merely desiring or wishing or thinking-it-would-be-nice-if is that the person who wills an end determines himself to bring the end about, that is, to cause it. And to determine yourself to be the cause of an end is to determine yourself to set off a chain of causes that will lead to the achievement of the end. Thus the person who wills an end *constitutes himself* as the cause of that end.

4.3.2

This account goes back to Kant's original definition of rationality. A rational being, according to Kant, is distinguished from everything else in nature by the fact that it acts not merely in accordance with laws, but in accordance with its own representation or conception of a law (G 4:412). If I toss my pen into the air, it will act in accordance with the law of gravity: it will eventually fall back down to the earth. But it doesn't say to itself when it reaches its acme, "I guess I'd better go back down now." But this is the sort of thing we do when we act. We don't choose to obey the law of gravity, of course. But in certain circumstances, we might choose to go back down. For instance, maybe I am climbing a mountain, and if I don't go back down now I won't make it home before sunset. So I say to myself: "I guess I'd better go back down now, in order to make it home before sunset." That thought—I will go back down now, in order to make it home before sunset—is my maxim and it is also my conception of a law. And it is because my maxim determines what I do that my movements count as willed—that is to say—as an action. In other words, it is because I determine myself to go back down that my movement is attributable to me. Rationality is a power of self-determination.

This is a general point, not just a point about practical reason. Consider again the case of logic. Perhaps you don't arrive at all your beliefs through reasoning, but when you do, it's an act of self-determination, in the sense that the activity of your own mind is part of what produces the belief in you. Suppose you believe two premises, and a certain conclusion follows. You won't automatically believe that conclusion, because you might not notice the connection between them. But if you do notice the connection, and put the premises together in the way suggested by the connection, then you *do* something: you *draw* the conclusion. In drawing the conclusion—or, as we say, in making up your mind, in *constituting* your mind—you determine yourself to believe it. The principle of modus ponens describes what you do when you draw the conclusion, but it is also a normative principle. In the same way, the hypothetical imperative describes what you do when you will an action: you determine yourself to be a cause, the cause of some end. But it is also a normative principle. It is a constitutive principle for the will.

4.3.3

So how does the hypothetical imperative unify and constitute the will? Suppose I decide to get some work done on my book today. At this moment, now, I decide, I *will*, to work; at the next moment, at any moment (importantly, maybe even at *this* moment), I will certainly *want* to stop. If I am to work I must *will* it—and that means I must determine myself to stay on its track. Timidity, idleness, and depression will exert their claims in turn, will attempt to control or overrule my will, to divert me from my work. Am I to let these forces determine my movements? At each moment I must say to them: "I am not you; my will is this work." Desire and temptation will also take their turns. "I am not a shameful thing like timidity," desire will say, "follow me and your life will be sweet." But if I give in to each claim as it appears *I* will do nothing and I will not have a life. For to will an end is not just to cause it, not even if the cause is one of own my desires and impulses, but to consciously pick up the reins, and *make myself* the cause of the end (5.5.2). The reason that I must conform to the hypothetical imperative is that if I don't conform to it, if I *always* allow myself to be derailed by timidity, idleness, or depression, then I never really *will* an end. The *desire* to pursue the end and the desires that draw me away from it each hold sway in their turn, but *my will* is never active. The distinction between my will and the operation of the desires and impulses in me does not exist, and that means that I, considered as an agent, do not exist. Conformity to the hypothetical imperative is thus constitutive of having a will. It is, in fact, an essential part of what *gives* you a will.[12]

4.3.4

Now for a slight complication. In 1.2, I argued that, according to both Aristotle and Kant, the object of choice is what I there called an *action*—an-act-for-the-sake-of-an-end—not a mere *act*. And if this is so, then there is a sense in which *there is no hypothetical imperative*. What I mean by that is that we never make a choice that is governed only by the hypothetical imperative; every choice we make is governed by the categorical imperative. As I said in 1.2.6, we do not first will some end as a law, and then scramble around for some way to fulfill it, now being under a requirement to do so. And that, strictly speaking, is how choice would have to work if we were ever to find ourselves directly governed by the hypothetical imperative. The hypothetical imperative is not really a separate principle at all; rather, it captures an *aspect* of the categorical imperative: the fact that the laws of our will must be *practical* laws.[13]

This has one important ramification. In "The Normativity of Instrumental Reason," I argued that the existence of a normative principle of instrumental reason depends on the possibility of instrumental irrationality. And the idea that there is such a thing as instrumental irrationality, in turn, depends on our being able to distinguish different kinds of failure.[14] Suppose Kaspar says that he wills to lose weight, and acknowledges that exercise is, as Kant puts

---

[12] I have lifted this passage with a few modifications from my paper "The Normativity of Instrumental Reason," pp. 59–60. As I mention in the Afterword to that paper, it was when writing it that I first noticed the connection between Kant's and Plato's accounts of the normativity of practical principles that led to this book.

[13] In recent years, there has been a flurry of papers worrying about the question how merely having or adopting a certain end can give you a reason to take the means to it. For one thing, your end may be awful—are we to say that the assassin has *reason* to aim carefully? How could we ever forgive ourselves if we said *that*? And for another, the fact that you can give yourself a reason to take the means just by adopting an end seems to make an objectionable form of bootstrapping possible—for every action is, in a sense, a means to itself. Despite these worries, the writers agree that there does seem to be something rationally amiss about someone who is indifferent to the means to his own ends, and a great deal of work has been done to characterize this without generating the worrisome consequences. See, to name just a few examples, Jay Wallace, "Normativity, Commitment, and Instrumental Reason" in *Normativity and the Will*; John Broome, "Normative Requirements" and "Practical Reasoning"; and Joseph Raz, "The Myth of Instrumental Rationality." I think some of the worries are misguided, but in any case if what I say in the text is correct, no such problem ever arises. We do not ever come under the independent dominion, so to speak, of the hypothetical imperative.

[14] "The Normativity of Instrumental Reason" (CA essay 1), pp. 48–50.

it, indispensably necessary. But Kaspar does not exercise. What are we to conclude? It may be that when Kaspar announces his resolve he is either insincere, or self-deceived, and so that he has no real intention of losing any weight. In this case there is something to criticize in his conduct, but he cannot be held guilty of instrumental irrationality (I argued then), since if weight loss isn't really his end, there is no irrationality in his failure to will the means. If there is to be such a thing as instrumental irrationality, there must be a third possibility, which is that he does will the end, but cannot bring himself to take the means. And, as I also argued then, it does seem to us that there are such cases. For if someone shrinks from an agonizing medical procedure needed to save his life, it seems more plausible to say that he can't face the means than that he doesn't really will the end of continuing to live.

A number of people pointed out to me that there is a difficulty here, however, for it seems unclear how we could tell what the fact of the matter is about which of the three conditions Kaspar is in.[15] And that merely empirical problem is rooted in a much more serious metaphysical one, for there is a deep unclarity about how there could *be* a fact of the matter about which of the three conditions Kaspar is in. But if we reject the view that the hypothetical imperative is an independent principle, and accept the view that the objects of choice are actions, then this problem goes away. The agent decides that performing a certain act for the sake of a certain end is a thing worth doing. In a case of weakness, his grip on his decision is wavering and unsteady. We can still distinguish cases in which the source of the weakness is more likely some reluctance or fearfulness about taking the means from cases in which the source of the weakness is more likely a failure, say, to sufficiently imagine the importance or the delights of the end. But there may also be cases in which elements of both are contributing to his difficulty. Since the hypothetical imperative is not a separate imperative, this does not matter after all.

I am inclined to think that the right thing to say about this parallels what I take to be the right thing to say about Aristotle's theory of the unity of the virtues (NE 6.13 1144b30–35). There is really only one virtue, but there are many different vices, different ways to fall away from virtue, and when we assign someone a particular virtue, what we really mean is that she does not have the corresponding vice. In a similar way, there is only one principle of practical reason, the categorical imperative viewed as the law of autonomy, but there are different ways to fall away from autonomy, and the different

---

[15] I would especially like to thank Joseph Raz, Sidney Morgenbesser, and Michael Thompson for pressing this objection.

principles of practical reason really instruct us not to fall away from our autonomy in these different ways.

Nevertheless, I am going to continue to talk about the hypothetical imperative as if it were a separate principle, for it captures a distinctive feature of action, one that is somewhat different from the feature captured by the categorical imperative.[16] To act is to constitute yourself as the cause of an end. The hypothetical imperative picks out the *cause* part of that formulation: by following the hypothetical imperative, you make yourself the *cause*. As we are about to see, the categorical imperative picks out another part of that formulation—that the cause is *yourself*. By following the categorical imperative, you make *yourself* the cause.

4.4 Against Particularistic Willing

4.4.1

I have argued that action is a form of self-determination, and that we can derive the hypothetical imperative from the fact that acting is determining yourself to be a cause. The hypothetical imperative is a constitutive principle of action, for you are not acting unless you are determining yourself to be a cause. But as I've just indicated, Kant thought that the fact that action is self-determination has a further implication. It also implies that the categorical imperative is a constitutive principle of action. For determining yourself to be a cause is not the same as being moved by something within you, say some desire or impulse—or to use Kant's own language now, some *incentive*—operating as a cause. When you deliberate, when you determine your own causality, it is as if there is something over and above all of your incentives, something which is *you*, and which chooses which incentive to act on. So when you determine your own causality you must operate as a whole, as something over and above your parts, when you do so.[17] And in order to do this, Kant believes, you must will your maxims as universal laws.

To see why, we need only consider what happens if we try to deny it. The argument that follows is what I call "the argument against particularistic willing."[18] If our reasons did not have to be universal, then they could be completely particular—it would be possible to have a reason that applies only

---

[16] For the relationship between these two features see 5.2.

[17] I will say more about how you can understand yourself as something over and above your parts in 7.1.3.

[18] Previous versions of this argument appear in the first section of the Reply in *The Sources of Normativity* (pp. 225–33) and in "Self-Constitution in the Ethics of Plato and Kant" (CA essay 3), pp. 120–4.

to the case before you, and has no implications for any other case. Willing to act on a reason of this kind would be what I will call "particularistic willing." If particularistic willing is impossible, as I will argue, then it follows that willing must be universal—that is, a maxim, in order to be willed at all, must be willed as a universal law.

4.4.2

I need to preface this argument with a couple of caveats in order to avert confusion. First of all, the question before us—the question whether particularistic willing is possible—is not the question whether we can will a new maxim for each new occasion. We may very well do that, for every occasion may be different in relevant ways from the ones we have previously encountered. In Kant's theory, any difference in the situation that is actually relevant to the decision properly belongs in our maxim, and this means that our maxim may be quite specific to the situation at hand. The argument here is not supposed to show that reasons are general. It is supposed to show us that reasons are universal, and universality is quite compatible with—indeed it requires—a high degree of specificity.

The second caveat is that it will be enough for the argument if the principle that is willed be, as I will put it, provisionally universal. Let me define my terms so you will see what I mean by these caveats. There are three different ways in which we can take our principles to range over a variety of cases, and it is important to keep them distinct. We treat a principle as *general* when we think it applies to a wide range of similar cases. We treat a principle as universal, or, as I will sometimes say, *absolutely universal*, when we think it applies to absolutely every case of a certain sort, but all the cases must be exactly of that sort. We treat a principle as *provisionally universal* when we think it applies to every case of a certain sort, unless there is some good reason why not. The difference between regarding a principle as universal and regarding it as provisionally universal is marginal. Treating a principle as only provisionally universal amounts to making a mental acknowledgment, to the effect that you might not have thought of everything needed to make the principle universal, and therefore might not have specified it completely. Treating principles as general, and treating them as provisionally universal, seem superficially similar, because in both cases we admit that there might be exceptions. But in fact they are deeply and essentially different, and this shows up in what happens when we encounter the exceptions. If we think of a principle as merely general, and we encounter an exception, nothing happens. The principle was only general, and we expected there to be some exceptions. But if a principle is provisionally universal, and we encounter an exceptional case, we must now go back and revise it, bringing it a little closer to the absolute universality to which provisional universality essentially aspires.

The rough causal principles with which we operate in everyday life (I am not talking about quantum physics now) are provisionally universal, and we signal this sometimes by using the phrase "everything else equal." The principle that striking a match causes a flame holds everything else equal, where the things that have to be equal are that there is no gust of wind or splash of water or oddity in the chemical composition of the atmosphere that would interfere with the usual connection. There are background conditions for the operation of these laws, and without listing and possibly without knowing them all, we mention that they must be in place when we say "everything else equal." Although there are certainly exceptions, these kinds of natural laws are not merely general, for whenever an exception occurs, we look for an explanation. Something must have made this case different: one of its background conditions was not met.

To see how it works in the practical case, consider a standard puzzle case for Kant's universalizability criterion. It may seem as if wanting to be a doctor is an adequate reason for becoming a doctor, for there's nothing wrong with being a doctor because you want to—in fact, really, it's rather admirable—and if you ask yourself if it could be a law that everyone who wants to be doctor should become one, it seems, superficially, fine. But then the objector comes along and says, "But look, suppose *everyone* actually wanted to be a doctor and nobody wanted to be anything else. The whole economic system would go to pieces, and then you couldn't be a doctor, so your universalized maxim would have contradicted itself!" So does this show that it is wrong to be a doctor simply because you want to?

What it shows is that the mere desire to enter a certain profession is only a provisionally universal reason for doing so. There's a background condition for the rightness of being a doctor because you want to, which is that society has some need for people to enter this profession. In effect the case *does* show that it's wrong to be a doctor merely because you want to—the maxim needs revision, for it is not absolutely universal unless it mentions as part of your reason for becoming a doctor that there is a social need. Someone who decides to become a doctor in the full light of reflection also takes that into account.

That case is easy, but there's no general reason to suppose we can think of everything in advance. When we adopt a maxim as a universal law, we know that there might be cases, cases we haven't thought of, which would show us that it is not universal after all. In that sense we can allow for exceptions. But so long as the commitment to revise in the face of exceptions is in place, the maxim is not merely general. It is provisionally universal.

So particularistic willing is neither a matter of willing a new maxim for each occasion, nor is it a matter of willing a maxim that you might have to change on another occasion. Both of those are compatible with regarding reasons as universal. Instead, particularistic willing would be a matter of willing a maxim for exactly this occasion without taking it to have any other implications of any kind for any other occasion. You will a maxim thinking that you can use it just this once and then so to speak discard it; you don't even need a reason to change your mind.

4.4.3

I'm going to argue that that sort of willing is impossible. The first step is this: I said before that when you deliberate, when you determine your own causality, it is as if there is something over and above all of your incentives, something which is *you*, and which chooses which incentive to act on. This means that when you determine yourself to be the cause of the movements which constitute your action, you must identify yourself with the principle of choice on which you act. For instance, suppose you experience a conflict of desire: you have a desire to do both A and B, and they are incompatible. You have some principle that favors A over B, so you exercise this principle, and you choose to do A. In this kind of case, you do not regard yourself as a mere passive spectator to the battle between A and B. You regard the choice as yours, as the product of your own activity, because you regard the principle of choice as expressive, or representative, of yourself—of your own causality. You must do so, for the only alternative to identifying with the principle of choice is regarding the principle of choice as some third thing in you, another force on a par with the incentive to do A and the incentive to do B, which happened to throw in its weight in favor of A, in a battle at which you were, after all, a mere passive spectator. But then you cannot regard yourself as the cause of the movements which constitute your action. Self-determination, then, requires identification with the principle of choice on which you act.

The second step is to see that particularistic willing makes it impossible for you to distinguish yourself, your principle of choice, from the various incentives on which you act. Kant thinks that every action involves some incentive or other, for there must always be something that prompted you to consider the action. And in order to will particularistically, you must in each case wholly identify with the incentive of your action. That incentive would be, for the moment, your law, the law that defines your agency or your will.

It's important to see that if you had a particularistic will, you would not identify with the incentive as representative of any sort of type, since if you took it as a representative of a type you would be taking it as universal. For instance, you couldn't say that you decided to act on the inclination of the moment, *because you were so inclined.* Someone who takes "I shall do the things I am inclined to do, simply because I am inclined to do them" as his maxim has adopted a universal principle, not a particular one: he has the principle of treating his inclinations *as such* as reasons.[19] That is the law that defines his causality. A truly particularistic will must embrace the incentive in its full particularity: it, in no way that is further describable, is the law of such a will.[20]

But this means that particularistic willing eradicates the distinction between a person and the incentives on which he acts. And then there is nothing left here that is the *person*, the agent, that is his self-determined will as distinct from the play of incentives within him. If you have a particularistic will, you are not one person, but a series, a *mere heap*, of unrelated impulses. There is no difference between someone who has a particularistic will and someone who has no will at all. Particularistic willing lacks a subject, a person who is the cause of his actions. So particularistic willing isn't willing at all.

4.4.4

If a particularistic will is impossible, then when you will a maxim you must take it to be universal. If you do not, you are not determining yourself to perform an action, and then you are not willing. To put the point in familiar Kantian terms, we can only attach the "I will" to our choices if we will our maxims as universal laws. The categorical imperative is a constitutive principle of acting, according to Kant, because conformity to it is constitutive of an exercise of the *will*, of the determination of a person *by himself* as opposed to his determination by something within him.

4.5 Deciding and Predicting

4.5.1

Let me make what is really the same argument (I am *always* making the same argument) in a much simpler way. Let us say that on Monday I decide to go to

---

[19] We will meet this person again, in 8.3.4.

[20] Why can't the particularistic willer keep himself separate from his incentives by saying of each of them in turn, "I am the one who acts on *that* incentive," as it were, mentally pointing, since he cannot regard the incentive as a type and therefore cannot give it a name? That mental pointing is the problem. For what can he mean by "that incentive"? Simply "the one I am acting on now." So his thought would be "I am the one who is acting on the incentive I am acting on now." Obviously, the thought lacks content.

the dentist on Tuesday, in order to get a cavity filled. Consider the following fact: there is a difference between deciding to do something and predicting that I will do it. After all, if I know that a band of well-meaning kidnappers plans to seize me and drag me to the dentist on Tuesday, or to order me to go there at gunpoint, then I can predict that I will go there, but this does not mean that I have decided to go there.[21] And by the same token, if I predict (admittedly somewhat surprisingly) that I will *want* to go to the dentist on Tuesday and therefore that I will go then, I have not thereby decided to do so. After all, I can predict that I will *want* to drink a martini in half an hour, and therefore that I will do so, and that is unfortunately compatible with my deciding now *not* to drink one. So deciding is different from predicting. Deciding is *committing* yourself to doing the thing. That is another way of saying acting is determining yourself to be a cause. In this case, I am determining myself to be the cause of my appearing at the dentist's office in order to get my cavity filled on Tuesday.

4.5.2

Now ordinarily when we decide to do something in the future, we are aware that certain unexpected circumstances could arise, circumstances that would give us *good* reason not to do it. So my commitment implicitly takes this form:

> On Tuesday I will go to the dentist, in order to get a cavity filled, unless there is some good reason why not.

One way there might be a good reason why not is internal to the maxim at hand—my reason for going to the dentist might be cancelled. My tooth might fall out, or the cavity might magically fill in overnight of its own accord—one can always hope—so that I no longer can benefit from a trip to the dentist. But not all good reasons for canceling are like that. Some of them are external to the commitment itself. Perhaps on Tuesday morning I hear that a loved one is dying, and I catch a plane to go and tell her that I love her one last time.

---

[21] I realize one might worry that this example equivocates on a passive and an active sense of "go"; that is, that the sense in which I predict that I will "go" to the dentist if I am brought (by the well-meaning kidnappers) is different from the sense in which I predict that I will "go" if I betake myself. To obviate that problem, I have added the case of coercion (being ordered at gunpoint) as an example using a more active sense of "go." But now you might worry that the prediction that you will go if ordered at gunpoint is after all based on a decision, say a general policy that, if ordered at gunpoint, it is always wise to concede. To obviate this worry, notice that you might predict that you will do something if ordered at gunpoint even if you think you shouldn't do it. For example, making a canny assessment of your own courage, you might predict of yourself that if ordered at gunpoint to do so, you would shoot a complete stranger, even though you think you shouldn't do that. That shows that there is a difference between predicting one will do something, even in the active sense of "do," and deciding to do it.

Perhaps on Tuesday morning I find I must cash in a winning lottery ticket for three million dollars before the deadline, or I am unexpectedly summoned to a job interview with the company I want to work for most in the world. Since examples can be controversial, I stipulate that these are good reasons for canceling my appointment. If you don't like them, find others. And so you don't think I'm trading on the ease with which dental appointments may be rescheduled, let me also stipulate that I would cancel the appointment for these reasons even if I were sure it would cost me the loss of the tooth.

So if I wake up on Tuesday and one of these things happens, and I therefore don't go to the dentist, I have not violated my commitment, because I was committed to going only if there were no good reason not to go, and it turns out that I have such a reason. But now suppose instead that I wake up on Tuesday morning, and the thought of the drill fills me with terror. Although all examples are controversial, I stipulate that this is a *bad* reason to cancel the appointment. So if I cancel the appointment for *this* reason, then I have violated my commitment.

4.5.3

So the picture is this. Right now I am subject to a certain set of potentially motivating factors, incentives. I take one of these incentives to provide me with a reason to go to the dentist on Tuesday. When I commit myself (on Monday) to going to the dentist on Tuesday, I know that on Tuesday I will be subject to a different set of potentially motivating factors, or incentives, though I don't know exactly which ones they will be. What I have just said is that some of those incentives would count as good reasons for canceling the appointment, while others would not. And that means that my commitment has universal normative force: it holds over a range of possible different cases, namely all of the cases in which I am subject to different potentially motivating factors, and yet there is no good reason to cancel the appointment.

And to see this, once again, suppose that we deny it. Suppose I take it that *any* possible motivating factor to which I might be subject provides me with a good reason to cancel the appointment. That means that when Tuesday comes, unless it happens that I want to go to the dentist more than anything in the world, I won't go to the dentist. Or to put the point more properly—it means that when Tuesday comes, I won't go to the dentist, unless I decide to go to the dentist on Tuesday. But if all that I am doing on Monday when I commit myself to going to the dentist on Tuesday is committing myself to doing whatever I will decide to do on Tuesday regardless of my decision on Monday, then obviously I am not doing anything at all. The law that I give myself must have *universal* normative force, or I have not committed myself to anything at all.

And the truth is that, although I have used the case of a future-oriented decision in order to make the point perspicuous, the argument applies just as well to a decision in the present. For just as a decision you make to do something in the future is different from a prediction, so a decision you make to do something in the present is different from an *observation*. When I decide to do something now, I know that there is a range of hypothetical differences in my motivational state, some of which would constitute good reasons for not doing it, and some of which wouldn't. And if *any* possible change in my motivational state would count as a good reason to do something other than what I am doing, then I am not making a decision, but merely observing the workings of the motivational forces within me. So even a decision I make for the here and now must have universal normative force.

4.5.4

Come back to logic for a moment. Another argument with this structure is the famous argument in Aristotle's *Metaphysics* (M 4.4 1006a12–15), in which Aristotle claims that a person is committed to the principle of non-contradiction just by virtue of making an assertion—any assertion whatever—and meaning something in particular by it. The argument I have just presented is the analogue of this—it is that you are committed to universalizability just by virtue of willing something in particular—you are committed, so to speak, by willing a maxim and meaning something in particular by it.

4.5.5

To act is to constitute myself as the cause of some end. I have been arguing that this requires that I make a law for myself with universal normative force, a law that applies to my conduct over a range of cases. I have attributed this argument to Kant, because I believe that an argument along these lines must have been on his mind when he asserted, in the third section of the *Groundwork*, that because the will is a kind of causality, it must operate according to a law (G 4:446). From there Kant moved to the conclusion that "a free will and a will under moral laws are one and the same" (G 4:447). For if the argument is correct a free will, as a causality, must act in accordance with a universal law; yet because it is a free will, it cannot be a law that is imposed upon it from outside. Kant concluded that it must be its own law, the categorical imperative, the law of imposing laws on itself.

But I believe that the argument proves both more than and less than (or at least not obviously as much as) Kant thought it did—and both for the same reason. In *The Sources of Normativity*, I distinguished what I called "the categorical imperative" from what I called "the moral law."[22] The categorical imperative is the law of acting only on maxims that you can will to be universal laws. The moral law, as I characterized it there, is the law of acting only on maxims that all rational beings could act on together in a workable cooperative system. The arguments I've given above don't—or rather don't obviously—get us all the way to a commitment to the moral law in that more specific sense. To get from the categorical imperative to the moral law, two more things are necessary. First of all, we must establish that the domain over which the universal law ranges must be rational beings as such: that is to say, when you will your maxim as a universal law, you must will it as a law *for every rational being*. And second, we must establish that the reasons embodied in universal maxims must be understood as public, or shareable reasons: reasons that have normative force for all rational beings. These are issues to which we will return in Chapter 9. Kant either didn't see that these points still need to be established, or he didn't see that he needed to make it clear that they already have been established, and that is why Kant thought that his argument proved more than it does—or than it obviously does.

But it also proves more than he thought. For if I have interpreted it correctly, Kant's conclusion should not just be about what we must do insofar as we have free wills. The argument identifies the categorical imperative as a constitutive principle of volition, so it is about what we must do insofar as we act at all. In the next chapter I will provide an account of what action is that will make it explicit why this is so.

---

[22] SN 3.2.4, pp. 98–100.

5

Autonomy and Efficacy

5.1 The Function of Action

5.1.1

In Chapter 4, I argued that the hypothetical and categorical imperatives are constitutive principles of volition and action. Unless we are guided by these principles—unless we are at least trying to conform to them—we are not willing or acting at all. The conception of action that yields this conclusion is Kant's conception: that action is determining yourself to be the cause of some end. The hypothetical imperative binds you because *what* you are determining yourself *to be* when you act is the *cause* of some end. The categorical imperative binds you because *what* you are determining to be *the cause of* some end is *yourself*. In fact, the two things are so closely bound together that they seem to be inseparable, for nothing counts as trying to realize some end that is not also trying to determine *yourself* to realize that end, and nothing counts as determining yourself to realize the end that is not also trying to determine your own *causality*. In fact, as we saw (4.3.4), the two ideas are so closely linked that there is something artificial in the idea that there are *two* imperatives. There is really just one imperative here: act in accordance with a maxim you can will as a universal law. The hypothetical imperative merely specifies the kind of law we are looking for—a causal law, a practical law. And that thought is already contained in the idea that what we are looking for is a law that governs *action*. It appears that there is only one law of practical reason, and it is the categorical imperative.

5.1.2

As I noted in 4.5.5, this seems to be a stronger conclusion than Kant thought he had reached, for at least in the *Groundwork*, Kant appears to claim that there is such a thing as "heteronomous" action (G 4:441–4), action that is determined by "alien causes" (446) rather than being autonomously willed.[1] He also seems

---

[1] See also 3.1.3, n. 9. I say "at least in the *Groundwork*" because by the time he writes the *Critique of Practical Reason*, Kant characterizes the evil will as governed by "evil and unchangeable principles

to suggest that action of this kind is governed by hypothetical imperatives but not by categorical ones (G 4:441), and furthermore that the categorical imperative, unlike the hypothetical imperative, is "synthetic" rather than "analytic" (G 4:417–19). But there is something amiss here, at least if I am right in supposing—as I argued in 1.2.4—that on Kant's view the objects of our choices are "actions" rather than mere "acts." For if the object of your choice is always a whole action—that is, an act undertaken for the sake of a certain end—then it seems clear that your choice could not be governed by a hypothetical imperative alone. For the hypothetical imperative concerns only the relationship between the act and the end, and has nothing whatever to say about whether the whole package, the act for the sake of the end, is a thing worth doing for its own sake. If that is what we choose, then choice must be governed by a categorical imperative, for only a categorical imperative governs the choice of actions and not mere acts.

5.1.3

So how are we to sort this out? Is the categorical imperative constitutive of all action or not, or is there such a thing as heteronomous action, ungoverned by the categorical imperative? In 2.1, I argued that in order to establish what the constitutive standards of anything are, we must look to its form in the Aristotelian sense—to the teleological organization that makes it the kind of thing that it is. So in order to establish that my claims are true, I need to show you what the function or *telos* of an action is. My view is that action is self-constitution, so of course I am going to argue that the function of an action is to constitute an agent. More specifically, I will argue that the essential characteristics of an agent are *efficacy* and *autonomy*.

These terms mean pretty much what you think they mean. Speaking roughly, and putting the point in a way best suited to human agents, an agent is *efficacious* when she succeeds in bringing about whatever state of affairs she intended to bring about through her action. A reminder is important here. I do not mean in saying this to imply an *act* is never done for its own sake; that is, I am not suggesting that an agent must always be trying to accomplish some purpose beyond the act itself. You might, for example, dance for the sheer joy of dancing (1.2.5). But even someone who dances for the sheer joy of dancing is subject to a standard of efficacy, because he can fail. He can, for instance, fall flat on his face. And if his steps are not in any way guided by this standard of efficacy—if he makes *no* effort not to fall flat on his face—then he is not

freely adopted" (C2 5:100) rather than by "alien causes." We will come back to the question how to understand evil action in Chapter 8.

dancing, but merely flailing about. This much normativity—that the agent is guided by some norm of efficacy—is inherent in the very idea of action. And to that extent the very idea of action is a normative idea.

An agent is *autonomous* when her movements are in some clear sense self-determined or her own. These two properties, efficacy and autonomy, correspond to Kant's two imperatives, hypothetical and categorical. The hypothetical imperative commands us to be efficacious, and the categorical imperative commands us to be autonomous. That, as I noted before, is why I am still talking about the hypothetical imperative, even though I've denied it an independent existence: because it captures something quite fundamental about the nature of agency (4.3.4). Since the function of an action is to render you efficacious and autonomous, your action must, in order to be a good one—one that serves its function—conform to these imperatives.[2] If you fail to follow the Kantian imperatives you will not be efficacious and autonomous, and then you will not be an agent. Your action constitutes you as an agent by being chosen in a way that renders you, the agent, efficacious and autonomous.

5.1.4

Be patient with me. I know that it sounds backwards. How can the agent perform an action, you will ask, unless she is already autonomous and efficacious? This question, I believe, is based on a false picture of the way agents are related to their actions. It is based on the idea that actions are produced or caused by their agents, and that is not correct. We may indeed say that when an agent acts, her *movements* are produced or caused by her. But we can say that only after we have already identified the case as one of action. My question is about how we do that: in particular, what entitles us to attribute a movement to an agent as her own. For that—the authoredness of it—is the essence of an action.

To break the spell that makes you think the way I am talking is backwards, try it this way. If your action is unsuccessful and you do not bring about the state of affairs that you intended, it is not (or not just) the action that is ineffective. It is *you* that is ineffective. It is not as if you were effective in producing the action, but then the action, once out there on its own, failed, like a defective machine you have invented and then let loose on the world. The action is not your product: it was *you* that failed. An unsuccessful action

---

² As I mentioned earlier (n. 6 to 3.1.3), this gives us another sense in which these two imperatives can be said to be "formal." Their normative force is grounded in the fact that they reflect the *form* of an action, an autonomous and efficacious movement.

renders you ineffective. Therefore a successful action is one that renders you effective. A similar point holds for autonomy, as I will be trying to make clear in the rest of this book. In fact it almost has to, given what I have just said. For no question of your efficacy can arise unless the movements through which you are supposed to have been efficacious are *yours*, in the relevant sense of *yours*. If I shove Tom at Bernard, hoping that Bernard will topple over, and he does not, it isn't *Tom* who has been ineffective, it is *me*. It makes sense to evaluate movements as effective or ineffective only if they are self-determined movements, so it is my movements, not Tom's, that are subject to the hypothetical imperative in this case. Therefore it makes sense to evaluate movements as effective or ineffective, that is, as governed by the hypothetical imperative, only if they are also self-determined, that is, governed by the categorical imperative. As I said before, the hypothetical imperative is not really an independent principle. Therefore a successful action, an action that is good as an action, is one that renders its agent both efficacious and autonomous.

5.2 The Possibility of Agency

5.2.1

Before I go on, I want to talk about a problem. An agent, I just claimed, is autonomous and efficacious. Is it possible to be an agent? There's a problem about this, only one side of which, the side concerned with autonomy, is usually recognized. I want to discuss the other side of the problem, not because I know how to solve it, but because it reveals a way in which the two aspects of agency, autonomy and efficacy, are really just two sides of the same coin.

5.2.2

It's an old story that if you focus on the fact of the causes behind you, the ones in the past, it can threaten your sense of your agency. To be an agent, according to Kant, is to be a self-conscious causality: to think to yourself that you will bring about a certain end, and somehow, through that thought, to bring it about. When you think of yourself as an agent, you think that your effects are your own, and had you not taken thought to realize them, they would not, other things being equal, have happened at all. So you are their cause, and these effects are yours, and the world is different, because you've made it so. There's a touch of the divine in being an agent, and as Aristotle says, we love the effects of our actions, as poets do their poems, and parents their children, because we see them as our handiwork, and we see ourselves realized and completed in them (NE 9.7 1168a1–9).

But then you look back, over your shoulder, so to speak, and there they are: the prior causes. It's true, you *did* say to yourself that you would do this thing, and somehow that caused the thing to come to be. But your saying it to yourself in turn had a cause; some combination of the immediate stimulus of the decision, and of course of the causes of that stimulus, and of the forces at work within you—the forces we sometimes call your character—that determine how you respond to such a stimulus. And those forces in turn have *their* causes—your education, your training, your psychic formations—that eventually lead, taken backwards far enough, behind you and outside of you, into the past before you were born. And suddenly you do not seem to be *the* cause of this event, and it is in no special way *yours*, for in fact it was inevitable, and you, well, you are just one of the links—and there are millions of them—in a causal chain that has rolled inexorably along a preset path that can be traced back to the very beginning of time.

5.2.3

What I have just described is the problem of freedom and determinism, of the threat to our agency that arises from causes that are lurking behind us, and as I have said, it is perfectly familiar. But it took the genius of Kant to notice the threat to our agency that comes from the causes that loom up in front of us. And it is just as real a threat. For I say to myself that I will bring about this end, but what happens next? Earlier, I said that your thinking you would bring about an end brings it about "somehow"; I am now unpacking the question that is wrapped in that "somehow." Does my body obey the command of my will, and if it does, is *that* my doing? Suppose that I am paralyzed or partially anesthetized or simply tied up or bound down? Then my willing the end has no tendency to bring about the end that I will. And even if I do move, in just the way that I will to move, what happens then? Normally, I cannot bring about the effect that I intend directly, but rather move to set off some causal chain, which, if all goes well, will lead to the effect that I will. But that "if all goes well" contains a world of assumptions about the causes that loom up in front us.

As with the problem of freedom and determinism, the problem of the causes behind us, there are cases that make this parallel problem, the problem of the causes in front of us, seem especially vivid. Cases of rescue make good examples, for let's face it—the world you have saved for another is a very fine thing to see as your handiwork.[3] So you shoot off your gun to stop the attacker, only you mow down the escaping victim instead. Or you try to throw a gun to the victim, and the attacker, hitherto unarmed, catches it instead and turns it on the victim. Or you open the window to let out the smoke, and a gust of wind fans the flames yet higher. Or you open the window to let out the smoke, and the arsonist pitches a second grenade through the opening that you have now made for him.[4]

And as in the case of freedom and determinism, the vivid examples really serve only to bring out a problem that is always there. In the vivid cases, you set out to do something, set off a causal chain that ought to bring about a certain end, but the forces of nature and the actions of other people so to speak step in, divert the course of the chain, and make the result the opposite of what you intended. Your own incompetence, unexpected events, interfering agents, can all derail the train whose engine you have started, or worse: set it off on a course of destruction. But this only serves to bring out a standing fact, there in every case, which is that it is always true, in *every* case, that the effects of your actions depend not just on your will, but on the forces of nature, and the actions of other people. To act—that is, *if* such a thing is possible at all—is to insert yourself—your first-personal, deliberating self—into the causal network. But that inevitably means it is to become hostage to the causal network, to the forces of nature, and the actions of others.

5.2.4

How does this threaten our sense of our agency? Put in general terms, we might say that the problem is that the relation between the content of our wills, and the effects of our willings, seems completely contingent. To get a sense of why that's a problem, imagine that the relation between the content of your speech, and its effects on the minds of your audience, becomes (as perhaps it is already) completely contingent, or worse. "Let me help you" you say, and the person you say it to backs off in terror, or cowers as if expecting a blow. "You're wonderful" you say, and find you have given the gravest offense. "Kiss me" you say, and get punched in the stomach. Somehow your words are always taken up in some different sense than you meant them, do not relate you to others as you thought that they would, and things do not turn out, as

---

[3] In fact, "benefactors" are the agents Aristotle is most directly discussing in the passage cited in 5.2.2 (NE 9.7 1168a1–9), although his point is general.

[4] Or, to take Kant's own example, you lie to the watchman at the front door to save your employer from disturbance, and your employer slips out the back way and commits a great crime—which will now be imputed to you by your own conscience, according to Kant (MM 6:431).

you had set yourself to make them turn out, when you opened your mouth up to speak. Could you still see yourself as a speaker? Of course, it does *not* always happen that way—and yet sometimes it does. And acting, according to Kant, is like this, for the meanings of our actions are determined, not just by what *we* mean by them, but by the way the world takes them up.[5] And so our actions are like children in a different way, a more unsettling way, than the way that Aristotle had in mind, namely, that there seems to be no telling what might happen to them out there in the dangerous world, and so how they will turn out.

We cannot regard ourselves as agents, that is, as the causes of certain effects through our wills, if in fact our wills have no power at all to make our effects be the ones that we will. And yet we must regard ourselves as agents, that being our situation, and not negotiable, for to be human is to have no choice but to choose (1.1.1). And so, just as she who must speak must cross her fingers and hope that her listener will take up her words in the sense in which she means them, so we who must act must cross our fingers and hope that the world, starting with our own bodies, will take up our willings in the sense in which we mean them. And this means that, just as the speaker is forced to take up an attitude of trust towards her hearer, so the agent is forced to take up an attitude of trust towards the world itself.

5.2.5

I say that last thing, about taking up an attitude of trust towards the world, because these thoughts about efficacy are the essential starting point for Kant's philosophy of religion. That's why I credit Kant with spotting this problem. Kant focused on the problem of the efficacy of *moral* action, but as I will explain shortly, I believe that the general problem is the same. A commitment to morality, according to Kant, essentially involves a commitment to the realization of a certain end, the highest good, which he describes as the state of things in which human beings achieve virtue and *necessarily* achieve happiness in proportion to their virtue (C2 5:113). If this end is impossible to achieve, and nothing we can do even counts as promoting it, then we cannot intelligibly be committed to its realization; and if a commitment to morality involves a commitment to its realization, then we cannot intelligibly be committed to morality either. Yet because of the very factors we've just been discussing—the forces of nature, and the actions of others—it seems impossible to see how anything we can do can bring about a necessary connection between virtue

---

[5] I am indebted to many useful conversations about these issues with Tamar Schapiro.

and happiness, and so promote the realization of the highest good. But since we must be committed to morality—for that, of course, isn't optional—it follows that we must suppose that the highest good is possible, and that we can, through our moral efforts, contribute to its realization. And this rational necessity or non-optionality licenses us to have faith—*Glaube*, a word also used for "trust"—that the conditions under which the highest good would be possible are indeed realized, even though we cannot know for sure that they are. According to the argument of the second *Critique*, these conditions are that the soul is immortal, so that we may progress unendingly towards moral perfection or virtue; and that a God exists, that is, an Author of the laws of nature, who will so adjust those laws that our good moral intentions will, ultimately, bring us happiness, and so have the effect of promoting the highest good.[6]

You might think that Kant's argument for religious faith isn't a response to the general problem of efficacy, for it matters to his argument that the end that he thinks we are supposed to promote is one commanded by morality, and so one that we cannot possibly give up. But I'm inclined to think the force of his argument is not limited in this way, since the essential point is that the need for faith arises only if you think that it actually *matters* that you achieve the end you are trying to achieve. This, however, is built right into the structure of agency, since to act without thinking that it matters how your action turns out is just to flail, and to flail is not to act. But precisely because of this, the religious solution, on reflection, seems to be much too strong.

5.2.6

For consider what it actually implies. The problem, Kant says in the second *Critique*, is that:

the acting rational being in the world is, however, not also the cause of the world and of nature itself . . . for that reason [he] . . . cannot by his own powers make it harmonize thoroughly with his practical principles. (C2 5:124–125)

So the trouble is that we are not the cause of nature. And the solution is that:

the existence of a cause of all nature, distinct from nature, which contains the ground . . . of the exact correspondence of happiness with morality, is . . . *postulated*. (C2 5:125)

---

[6] Famously, Kant claimed to deny knowledge in order to make room for practical faith (C1 Bxxx). He discusses practical faith in many places in his work, but the main discussions are in "The Canon of Pure Reason" in the *Critique of Pure Reason*, the "Dialectic" of the *Critique of Practical Reason*, and in sections 83–91 of the *Critique of Judgment*. The description I have given in the text corresponds most closely to the way Kant describes it in the *Critique of Practical Reason*.

This postulated cause of nature must have the traditional attributes of God, Kant says, because:

He must be *omniscient* in order to cognize my conduct even to my inmost disposition in all possible cases and throughout the future, *omnipotent* in order to bestow results appropriate to it, and so too *omnipresent, eternal*, and so forth. (C2 5:140)[7]

This suggests that what God is going to do is look into our hearts, know our moral character, and so arrange the laws of nature that each of us is made happy in proportion to the goodness of her own moral character.

But if this is supposed to be a solution to the problem of efficacy, then it seems as if something has gone terribly wrong. For if this is the world I live in, how is it that my effects are ever really *mine*? Think back to the examples I mentioned earlier, of cases of rescue, and rescue gone awry. Can I ever rescue you, or fail to? God has designed the laws of nature so that your fate will be determined by your moral character. If you are good, I cannot—in the long run, of course, and with many qualifications—harm you. And if I help you, I am only the instrument of God, doing something that would have been done another way if I had not taken thought to do it. Where then is my dream of agency, of efficacy, of effects that are my own, and that would not have taken place at all, had I not taken thought to produce them? How can I do anything to make this all too perfect world a better place—or for that matter, a worse one?

5.2.7

Anyway, my point in bringing all this up is not to make a brief for Kant's philosophy of religion, or for the need for agency to be supported by faith. For in fact, the issue here is really just the same as one we've already looked at in 2.3.2, where I argued that the notion of a particular cause, within the world, is essentially a teleological notion, one that we deploy when we conceptualize the world in a way that makes it possible for us to act in it. Why do we say that *the knife*, rather than the state of the world a nanosecond ago, is the cause of the cutting? Because we can *use* the knife for cutting. The conception of a particular cause within the world makes the world a scene for action. And why do I say that *I* was the cause of the cutting, or that *you* were? For the same reason: so that we can act and interact. My point here is rather to show how closely the ideas of efficacy and autonomy are actually linked, and how ambitious the ideal of agency is. The ideal of agency is the ideal of inserting yourself into the causal order, in such a way as to make a genuine difference in the world. Autonomy, in Kant's sense of not being determined by an alien

---

[7] Yes, that bored-sounding "and so forth" really is Kant's own.

cause, and efficacy, in the sense of making a difference in the world that is genuinely your own, are just the two faces of that ideal, one looking behind, and the other looking forward. That is why Kant's two imperatives together are the laws of agency.

5.3 Non-Rational Action

5.3.1

There's a problem with what I have been saying, which I flagged earlier (5.1.3) when I mentioned that my remarks were most appropriate to the case of human agents and human action. It is a problem that emerges very starkly in Kant's own account of the foundation of the categorical imperative, in section three of the *Groundwork*. Kant's account begins with the claim that volition *is* "a kind of causality of living beings insofar as they are rational" (G 4:446). The remark harks back to Kant's initial definition of rationality in section two, in a passage that I discussed in 4.3.2. Kant says:

Everything in nature works in accordance with laws. Only a rational being has the capacity to act *in accordance with the representation* of laws, that is, in accordance with principles, or has a *will*. Since *reason* is required for the derivation of actions from laws, the will is nothing other than practical reason. (G 4:412)

But in other works Kant apparently disavows this strong connection between rationality and volition. In several places he mentions the idea of *arbitrium brutum*, an animal choice or will (C1 A802/B830; MM 6:213). And in *The Metaphysics of Morals*, he identifies the capacity for action quite broadly—in fact a little too broadly—with "life." He says:

The *faculty of desire* is the faculty to be by means of one's representations the cause of the objects of these representations. The faculty of a being to act in accordance with its representations is called *life*. (MM 6:211)

The reason is obvious enough. Human beings are, after all, not the only creatures who act. The distinction between actions and events also applies to the other animals. A non-human action, no less than a human one, is in some way ascribed to the acting animal herself. The movements are her own. When a cat chases a mouse, that is not something that happens to the cat, but something that she does. To this extent, we regard the other animals as being the authors of their actions, and as having something like volition.

But Kant never tells us what difference this acknowledgement might make to his deduction of the moral law, which uses the claim that volition is the "causality of living beings insofar as they are rational" as a premise. And more generally his account as it stands leaves it obscure what non-free, non-rational volition could be. For the stark contrast between being self-determining, or autonomous, and being what Kant calls "heteronomous" or determined by natural laws seems to leave no place for the actions of non-human animals. If the movements of the other animals are directed from outside, by alien causes, then it is not clear how those movements are different from the movements of objects to which we do not ascribe actions, or from those movements of animals which we do not ascribe to the animals themselves. The antelope perceives the approaching lion, and runs away. The antelope is tackled by the lion, and falls over. Running away is something an antelope does while falling over is something that happens to him. But if both are equally cases of the antelope's movements being determined by alien causes, where does the difference lie?

This brings us back to the issue I began with, Kant's apparent conviction that some actions, heteronomous actions, are governed only by hypothetical imperatives. For the problem we are considering now is intimately related to the more notorious problem how on a Kantian conception we are supposed to conceive of bad action. The *Groundwork* portrays bad action as heteronomous action. Commentators often complain that if that is supposed to mean action that is caused by external forces, it is impossible to see how people are ever responsible for bad action. But of course the problem is much deeper than that, for if a person's movements are caused by external forces, it is not clear why we should call them actions at all. And the same would be true of the actions of non-human animals.

5.3.2

A little surprisingly, there is a version of this problem even in Aristotle's apparently more naturalistic account of action. Aristotle distinguishes three kinds of action: the involuntary, the voluntary, and the chosen (NE 3.1–2). The chosen is a division of the voluntary, for all chosen action is also voluntary. Small children and non-human animals generally act voluntarily, while only adult human beings act from choice (NE 3.2 1111b7–10). For the voluntary, Aristotle tells us, it is sufficient that "the moving principle is in the agent himself, he being aware of the particular circumstances of the action" (NE 3.1 1111a23–24).

There are well-known problems about interpreting this criterion of the moving principle being "in" the agent. The moving principles of respiration, circulation, and digestion seem in some sense to be "in" us, but these things are not voluntary. Aristotle opposes the voluntary to the compulsory, defined as that "of which the moving principle is outside, being a principle in which nothing is contributed by the person who acts or is acted upon" (NE 3.1 1110a1–3). So the "internal" character of the moving principle must have something to do with the agent's contribution. The difficulty arises when Aristotle tries to explain the compulsory in more detail. He gives us three examples of the compulsory, which seem intended to be increasingly close to being voluntary (NE 3.1 1110a3–11). The first concerns a man carried somewhere by the wind, or by other men who have him in their power. This does not appear to be an example of compulsory action, for someone carried somewhere by a wind or by others doesn't do anything at all. We might do better to imagine that the man in the power of others is, say, tied to the back of a wagon, so that he is forced to walk.[8] The second example concerns coercion: a tyrant who has your loved ones in his power orders you to do something, threatening to harm them if you do not. The third example is one of unfortunate circumstances: it concerns some sailors who must throw their cargo overboard during a storm in order to save their own lives. These last two cases are actually mixed, Aristotle tells us, because "they are worthy of choice at the time when they are done" (NE 3.1 1110a12). We could also say this about the man who walks behind the wagon, for if he does not move his feet, he will be dragged, and it will be worse for him. Yet unless he chooses to walk, he performs no action, not even a compulsory one. And therein lies the problem. Action requires some contribution from the agent, and in all these cases, the agent's contribution appears to be that, given the circumstances, he chose to do the action. But if the agent's contribution rests in his choice, however constrained that choice might be, what becomes of the category of the merely voluntary? And if we lose the category of the merely voluntary, what becomes of the actions of non-human animals, who can never contribute their choice?

5.3.3

Obviously I inherit this problem. I have claimed that we cannot recognize someone as acting unless he is at least in some degree governed by the hypothetical and categorical imperatives. An agent must at least be trying to render himself efficacious and autonomous if we are to recognize what he is doing as acting at all. So how can the other animals possibly act? I surely do not want to claim they try to obey the Kantian imperatives. I seem to be faced with a choice—either give up the idea that the Kantian

---

[8] See 4.5.1, n. 21.

imperatives are constitutive standards of action, or give up the idea that the other animals act.[9]

But I don't intend to do either of those things. In what follows I will explain what I think action is. On the basis of that explanation, I will also explain how autonomy and efficacy can be constitutive standards for actions, even though the other animals do not try to conform to them. Apart from saving the phenomena—for I think it is clear that the other animals do act—the account will throw light on what is distinctive about human action, and why it is that human actions alone are governed by imperatives, and can be morally good or bad.

5.4 Action

5.4.1

Recall from 2.2.1 that according to Aristotle, a living thing is a thing with a special kind of form, a self-maintaining form. It is designed so as to maintain and reproduce itself, that is to say, to maintain and reproduce its own form. So it is its own end; its *telos* or function is just to be—and to continue being—what it is. And its organs, instincts, and natural activities are all arranged to that end. That much applies as much to plants as to animals: a plant also has a self-maintaining form.

But Aristotle tells us that animals are distinguished from plants in being alive in a further sense, given by a functionally related set of powers that plants lack. Aristotle emphasizes perception and sensation, but notes that these are accompanied by imagination, pleasure and pain, desire (*orexis*), and usually, local movement (OS 2.2 413b1–23). What is distinctive of animals, in other words, is that they carry out a part of their self-maintaining activities through action.[10] They are alive in a further sense than plants, for they spend their lives *doing* things. This brings us to our question: what is action, in the general sense that applies to them too?

---

[9] The idea of animal action has been neglected in philosophy, just as, at least until recently, the idea of animal cognition has. And it's a serious problem, because many philosophical theories do not seem to leave any *conceptual* space for animals to exist in—space, that is, for something that is neither a mere mechanism nor a rational person. There are also philosophers who deny that animals are agents, but that seems plainly false. Aristotle himself says that the other animals "have no share in action" (NE 6.2 1139a20). But what *he* means is that the other animals do not act in a sense associated with the view of action I laid out in 1.2: they don't choose whole actions, seeing them as things worth doing for their own sakes. The account of animal agency that I sketch in the rest of this chapter will vindicate that conclusion.

[10] Nowadays, an "animal" is defined as a complex multicellular eukaryotic organism that feeds on other life forms. This is not precisely coincident with Aristotle's definition, but for my purposes here this won't matter.

5.4.2

First, an action is an intelligent movement, in a simple descriptive sense: the animal's movement is responsive to a representation or conception that he forms of the world, or of his environment. That is why Aristotle associates action essentially with perception. When I say that action is intelligent, of course, I'm not using "intelligent" in a laudatory sense. In the sense I am using the term, a spider crawling towards the moth caught in her web or a cockroach running underneath the toaster as you try to swat him with a newspaper, exhibit intelligence, for they respond to representations or conceptions of their environment. A perception of something as *dinner* or *danger*—that is *to-be-eaten* or *to-be-avoided*—determines the course of the animal's movements. Kant, in a passage I quoted earlier, puts it this way:

The *faculty of desire* is the faculty to be by means of one's representations the cause of the objects of these representations. (MM 6:211)

The spider, for example, represents the moth to herself as dinner, and that is the cause of the moth's being dinner.

In the cases I have mentioned, an object desired or feared is represented as actually existing in the environment, but of course action may also begin from a conception of something that could be there, as when an animal goes looking for food or a mate. Even in that case, however, his movements are guided by a representation of his environment, for the shape or course of his movement—where he looks, how he goes about looking—is determined by his conception of the world he is moving through.

5.4.3

Before I go on I should clarify something about the way I am using "movement." When talking about spiders and cockroaches, it is natural enough to identify actions with physical movements, or at least to suppose that actions are a type of, or perhaps supervene on, physical movements. But we do not want to write this thought into our conception of action, for a variety of reasons. For one thing, not every action is physical: making a promise to someone, for instance, is not, nor are performatives generally. Of course one may insist that making a promise must have some physical manifestation, at least an utterance. But what about making a promise to yourself? Perhaps some physicalists will insist that even *that* must have some sort of physical manifestation or leave some sort of trace in the brain, but I do not think this thesis in the philosophy of mind should be made part of our conception of action. Not all agents are physical entities either: corporations and governments are not. Again, it might be argued that they and their actions must supervene on some sort of physical events, if only the recording of their decisions on paper. And what about God? Isn't the idea of divine action coherent?

In fact this question helps us to get at the relevant conception of movement. To act is to render a change in the world (or in the limiting case, to prevent or forestall one). When an agent acts, something must happen as a result of the action. Now we may be tempted at first to think that there is this difference between the actions of God and finite creatures. When a finite creature acts, or produces a change in the world, there has to be *a way* the creature does it, in the sense of a method, or even a means. Whereas when God acts, He needs no method: His very thought of what He would effect effects it. But I think we should resist this idea. Although many things we do involve a means or a method, not all of them do. For instance, suppose I decide to raise my arm. There is no way I do that, no method, no means—I just do it. To be sure there is a way it *happens*—nerve signals run down from my brain to my arm, or whatever—and because there is a way it happens I am constrained in a way that God could not be. If my nervous system isn't working properly, I may not be able to raise my arm. But that "way it happens" isn't a "way I do it" for I do not send nerve signals off to my arms, like a mother sending her children off to school.[11] So when I say that action necessarily involves a movement, the movement I am talking about is the effecting of a change in the world itself, not a *method* of effecting the change in the world.

Nevertheless, the example I just used to illustrate action without a method brings out something else important about the relevant notion of movement. Ordinarily, the way animals change the world is most immediately by moving their limbs. One of the few things that we can do that we don't do *by way of* moving our limbs is *move our limbs*. This gives rise to a certain tendency to confuse action with bodily movement, so that what we call an "action film" for instance, is one in which the protagonists jump around a lot. And there is a deep reason for this confusion, for it is not accidental that the only thing I can do without a method or a means is effect a change in myself. It does not have to be in my body, but it does have to be in myself. Even when we imagine cases in which someone produces an effect magically, we imagine the agent *disposing* himself somehow: chanting, or concentrating, or staring. For that matter, even when we imagine God creating the world, we imagine God most immediately effecting a change in himself: thinking a thought, or perhaps even uttering one, like "let there be light." So although the movement I am talking about is the effecting of a change in the world, it is essential to the idea of action that the agent produces the change in the world by producing a

---

[11] In the action theory literature, this sort of thing is called a "basic action."

change in himself. The reason all this matters is that it is another way of saying that action essentially involves self-determination. The cases where there is no method are limited to the cases where *all* that the agent is doing is producing a change in himself. So when an animal acts, she effects a certain change in the world by effecting a change in herself, in a way that is responsive to her conception of her environment. That is the sort of intelligent movement that is in question.

5.4.4

Now this sense of intelligent movement already implies that an action has intentional content. We say that spider is "crawling to the center of her web to eat the moth that is trapped there" or that the cockroach is "running under the toaster to avoid being swatted." Those phrases specify purposes, but for the kind of intentional content that characterizes action, we do not need to specify further or ulterior purposes. The important thing about action is only that it is done, as we say, "on purpose." To assign intentional content to a movement in this sense is to make it subject to a normative standard of efficacy, to a standard of success and failure. And being subject to such a standard, as I mentioned before, is essential to the idea of action. Suppose all we say about the cockroach is that "he is running under the toaster." This is still different from saying of a rock that it is rolling down the hill. If the rock runs into an obstacle and stops rolling before it gets to the bottom of the hill, it has not failed. But if the cockroach does not make it under the toaster, he *has* failed. What licenses us to talk in this way? Obviously, we do not want to say that the cockroach has formed the intention of getting under the toaster. This is really just the problem we started out from. Since the cockroach himself is not guided by any hypothetical imperative, why do we think of his movements as subject to the norms of efficacy that make those movements count as actions?

5.4.5

According to Aristotle, to assign intentional content to an object's movement we do not need to suppose that there is some thought process that accompanies the movement. What licenses intentional description is not the presence of accompanying thought, but rather appeal to the object's form and function. Intentional descriptions apply even to the movements of artifacts. A clock, for example, is an object functionally constructed so as to tell the time. And that is why when we say things like "This clock chimes out the hour" or "The alarm clock will wake me up at eight," we imply the existence of criteria of success and failure. If the clock chimes eleven times when both hands point to twelve, or if the alarm does not go off when eight comes round, then the clock has failed. It is because a clock is organized so as to tell the time that we can assign intentional content to its movements. And in the same way, it is because an animal has a self-maintaining form that we can assign intentional content to her movements. It is because an animal's function is the maintenance of her form that we describe even a very primitive animal as "looking for something to eat" or "trying to escape the danger," in a way that implies criteria of success and failure.

But of course a clock's chiming is not an action. We ascribe intentional movements to plants and machines, but they are not actions. The clock chimes out the hour, or it wakes you up. The plant turns towards the sun, or its roots grow down through the dry soil to where there is more water. As this last example suggests, these movements may even be reactions to events or conditions in the environment. But these reactions to the environment are not intelligent movements, in the sense I described earlier. They are not the result of the plant or machine forming a *conception* or *representation* of the environment. So to get at the idea of action, we must put these two elements—a movement with intentional content, and responsiveness to a conception of the environment—together. An action is an intentional movement of an animal that is *guided* by a representation or conception that the animal forms of his environment.

5.4.6

As I've just suggested, there are intentional movements that are not actions, and yet are reactions to environmental cues. Consider for example, the phototropic response of a plant, almost irresistibly describable in action-language as the plant *turning towards* the sun. Why isn't it an action? According to the account I just gave, only because it is not governed by perception, by a representation of the environment: if the plant saw the sun or felt it then it would be an action. Does the concept of an action then require us to make a hard and fast distinction between mere causal reactions to environmental cues on the one hand and perception or representation on the other? Only if we think that the concept of action itself should be hard and fast, but there is no reason to think that. There will not be a hard and fast line in nature between action and other forms of intentionally describable responses because there is not a hard and fast line in nature between mere reaction and perceptual representation. But this does not threaten what I am saying about action. It only suggests that there is not a hard and fast line in nature between what is action and what is not. And we knew that anyway. There are lots of things that linger on the vague conceptual fringes of action, for lots of different reasons: drumming your fingers (which is somewhere between mere expressiveness and action), breathing (for after all, you can hold your breath), omission in cases where it matters morally versus omission in cases where it does not (the first is a bad action and the second is nothing at all). There are many cases in which we need a hard and fast concept for the purposes of philosophical understanding and indeed for ethical and political life, even where there is not a hard and fast line in nature.[12] This is hardly surprising, since there are few hard and fast lines in nature.

5.4.7

The concept of action requires both an intentional movement and a representation or conception of the world. These together are what allow the agent to guide himself through the world. It is because both of these elements are needed for the idea of action, I believe, that philosophers fall too readily into an overly intellectualized conception of action. We tend to think that in order for something to be an agent, it must be guided by a conception of what it is doing, or even that it must actively entertain a purpose and a method of achieving that purpose—that it must, as philosophers say, "form an intention." This is an absurd thing to say about a cockroach running under a toaster. The animal must indeed be guided by a conception, and his movements must have a purpose, but he need not have a conception of his purpose. Action that is self-conscious in the particular way that, as I will soon argue, human action is, certainly does require that the agent has a conception of what she is doing and why. That much is true by definition. But action in the wider sense does not.

In fact I think it makes most sense to see the kind of intentionality that characterizes human action as being at the extreme end of a continuum. At the bottom of the continuum is simple intentional movement, of the sort that, as I have been saying, we ascribe to plants, organs, and machines. At the next level are the movements of simple animals whose movements are guided by perception. Here we begin to be tempted to use the language of action, and it is clear enough why: when an animal's movements are guided by her perceptions, they are under the control of her mind, and when they are under control of her mind, we are tempted to say that they are under the animal's own control.[13] At the next level, perhaps, would be the

---

[12] On this see my "Two Arguments Against Lying" (CKE essay 12).

[13] This is a bit mysterious, actually. Think of a mosquito. Why should a movement under the control of his "mind"—his representational capacities—be any more attributable to *him* than a

movements of animals that have some idea of what they are doing or trying to do. And finally—I'm getting ahead of myself here—there would be the movements of those animals who are aware of the principles upon which they act (6.1.7). Intentionality *itself* is not then something that makes human action radically different from every other movement in the world. But the form it takes in us does, as I will argue in Chapter 6, make the world radically different for us.

5.4.8

One more point about the phototropic responses of plants. The sun hits the plant, and the plant turns towards the sun. If the plant saw the sun, I said in 5.4.6, then that would be a case of action. There will be resistance to that idea. Some of you will be thinking that *that* cannot possibly be the difference that makes action action. For the case to be one of action, it must involve self-determination: the plant must move its own leaves. So the plant's turning its leaves toward the sun would only be action if the plant had a *will*, and when it saw the sun, it formed a volition that caused its leaves to turn towards the sun. The plant's will must issue its leaves a sort of order to turn towards the sun, just like all those orders we are always issuing to our arms and legs, and that must be what causes its movement. Right?

Wrong. That is a sort of homunculus or pineal gland theory of the will. We've got a philosophical problem here, so we invent or point to an organ or faculty and say "There! That is the faculty that solves the problem!" How is the will posited as a faculty supposed to solve the problem of making volition possible? Essentially, by being capable of volition.

You can't solve a philosophical problem by giving it a name. The will is not a faculty that makes self-determination possible; the will is the capacity for self-determination. That is what we need to understand in order to understand animal agency: why we attribute something like a capacity for self-determination to the other animals.

movement attributable to one of his other organs? We are certainly not more tempted to hold him responsible for it. We regard ourselves as autonomous because our actions are under the direction of our minds: the necessity of action is, so to speak, encountered in our minds. Therefore we take lower animals to be the authors of their actions when their movements are under the direction of their minds. Of course it helps that mind-directed movements exhibit the kind of flexibility of response that we take to differentiate action from mechanical motion. In 2.1.5, I said that the concept of an activity is a Platonic one: other movements count as activities to the extent that they participate in the ideal version. That's what's going on here: the concept of action gets its contours from the ideal case, which is the idealized versions of our own case: the case of someone reflectively in control of his own movements.

5.5 Attribution

5.5.1

But this way of putting it makes it clear that the account of action that I have given so far does not yet get to the heart of the matter. When an animal acts, she is supposed to determine herself to movement; the movement is supposed to be her own. On what grounds do we attribute the movement *to* the animal? This brings us to the third and most important feature of action (the first two are that action is an intentional movement and that it is guided by perception). So far I have not focused on the causes of an animal's movements, only on the causation the animal exercises *through* her movements, on her efficacy in achieving her ends. But to many philosophers it seems to be the most essential thing about actions that they are caused in some particular way. And in the case of human actions, this point has been associated with a moral issue, namely the fact that we hold people responsible for their actions. We could not do this, it is sometimes said, unless people were the causes of their actions.

Now this cannot be quite right, for to say that an agent is the cause of an action suggests that an action could be caused by something other than an agent. But I take it to be essential to the notion of action that it is attributable to an agent. So the question is not why we attribute an action to an agent, but rather why we attribute certain movements to an agent as her own, thus interpreting them as an action. One traditional response to this problem has been to identify action with movement produced by a particular sort of causal route through the person, say, a route through the person's psychology. The thought seems to be that a person is more essentially identified with her psychology than with her body, say. So a causal route through her psychology seems well suited to making the movement her own.[14]

But I believe this gets the story almost exactly backwards. The intimate connection between person and action does not rest in the fact that action is caused by the most essential part of the person, but rather in the fact that the most essential part of the person is *constituted* by her actions.

5.5.2

Let me try to explain my objection a little more clearly. Empiricists sometimes seem to believe that action is movement caused by a passion or desire, movement that inherits its intentionality from the passion or desire that causes it. For instance if a desire for the apple somehow causes your arm to

---

[14] See for instance Hume at T 2.3.2,410–12.

move towards it, we call this "reaching for the apple," where the intentionality of the movement springs from the content of the desire that caused it. But this cannot be right. For passions and desires cause movements and other physical alterations which are not, or not quite, actions. Blushing when you have been caught out in folly or sin, flinching as the needle draws near to your arm, giggling when you are amused, weeping when you are hurt, and dropping your books when you are nervous are not, or not quite, actions. Yet these movements do inherit something like intentionality from the emotions they express. The explanations we give of these movements not only explain how they came about, but also make them intelligible. We can say that he blushed because he was ashamed, just as we can say that he reached for the apple because he wanted to eat it.

In fact emotionally expressive movements may even inherit a certain subjection to normative standards from their causes—weeping, for example, may be deemed bad if the sadness that causes it is bad. "So you didn't get what you wanted. That's nothing to cry about," we say sternly. Weeping may even be deemed *morally* bad, say if you weep from a morally bad motive. Suppose, for example, that you weep when you learn that your rival was not after all killed in the accident; then we will find your weeping morally offensive.

Hume thinks that an action inherits its capacity to be morally right or wrong from the moral quality of its "motive" in *exactly* that way (T 3.1.1). According to this virtue-ethical account, we could just as well say that weeping from a despicable motive is not only morally bad, it is *wrong*, in exactly the same sense that, say, injuring someone is wrong. There is no difference, for according to Hume injuring someone inherits its wrongness from the viciousness of the cruelty that causes it, just as the despicable weeping inherits its moral badness from the badness of the sorrow that caused it. Moral rightness or wrongness, on this sort of account, is really just moral goodness or badness, and has no special connection to action. And in my own view this means that this account of action cannot be correct, because it is an *essential* feature of (human) actions as such that they can be right or wrong. Emotional responses may be subject to evaluation in terms of moral standards, but they cannot, in the same sense as actions, be right or wrong.

Now at this juncture someone may be tempted to say that we judge actions, unlike expressive responses, to be right or wrong because actions are voluntary while emotionally expressive responses are not. According to one familiar account, the concepts of right and wrong apply when we may follow or violate a rule, and this only happens in the domain of the voluntary. As it stands, this is just the pineal gland view of the will again (5.4.8). For absent some further analysis, "voluntary" is just another name for the problem we are working on: namely what makes actions different from emotionally expressive movements. Yet the response is pointing to the right place, for it is relevant here that emotionally expressive movements are not intentional in the exactly same sense as actions. For although emotional responses are subject to normative standards, they are not subject to standards of success and failure. When you say that someone is weeping, you do not invoke the possibility of failure that you do when you say that the cockroach is running under the toaster. What would count as failing? Of course you can *try* to weep, and fail, but if you try to weep and succeed, weeping to that extent is an action.

5.5.3

Now let me deal with a problem. I was asking in virtue of what we attribute a movement to an agent. I claimed that it was not enough that the movement had a psychological cause, because that is just as true of emotionally expressive responses as it is of actions. But actions—so I said—can be right or wrong, and emotionally expressive responses cannot. Now it may seem unclear what bearing this point has on the question of why we attribute certain movements to agents in the distinct way we do in cases of action, for that is a question about agency in general, whereas only human actions can be morally right or wrong.

But there is something analogous to being right or wrong in non-human action. For on my view, an action is wrong if it fails to constitute you as an agent, as the agent who you are. The parallel would be an animal action that fails to constitute the animal as the animal who he is—not simply because it happens to be ineffective, which can always happen, but because it is the wrong sort of thing altogether. This can happen, because an animal's instincts are relative to his environment, and when his environment changes in radical ways, they can lose their self-maintaining function. Think for instance of migrating birds who are thrown off course by human light pollution, or predators who attack livestock, perhaps seeing them as easy pickings, and get themselves shot.[15]

Of course the animals are not responsible for these failings, for they are not responsible for their principles in the way that we are. And our principles,

---

[15] Even though human beings no longer act on instinct, as I will explain in 6.1.7, our desires and incentives are still tied to our instincts, and we can see these effects in ourselves. Human beings are attracted to fatty foods, for instance, as a result of instincts telling us to store fat while we can, to survive the famines ahead. And when the famines are no longer forthcoming, then human beings become obese and can die as a result. Another case that parallels the situation of non-human animals whose instincts have become wrong is the case of trying to meet standards of etiquette in a foreign culture: your standards, once removed from your own cultural environment, can lead you to do exactly the wrong thing.

moral principles, are supposed to hold us together in any environment, any circumstance, come what may. They are supposed to be universalizable, and it is up to us to choose them that way.

5.5.4

My solution to the problem of attribution is implicit in what I just said. Earlier I mentioned Aristotle's view that an intentional movement's vulnerability to standards of success and failure, its intentionality in the sense we want here, derives from the fact that the moving object has a certain form or functional organization (5.4.5). To see a movement as an action, as subject to standards of success and failure, we must see it as a movement attributable to the animal's form. Since the animal's form is what unifies her into an individual object, her form is not merely something within the animal. So when the animal's movement can be attributed to her form, it is the animal herself, the animal *as a whole*, who moves. And when I say that the movement is attributable to the animal's form, I don't mean merely that the animal's form contributes importantly to the cause of the movement. I mean rather that the animal is formed—we view the animal as formed—*so as* to produce a movement of that kind.

Of course, an animal's form is also responsible for his emotionally expressive movements. So you may think my account is no better off than that of the empiricist, who wants to say what distinguishes action is that the causal chain runs through the agent's psychology, and who, I claimed, could not distinguish between emotionally expressive movements and actions. To reply to this objection, I need only remind you that we can distinguish between an object's form contributing importantly to the causation of a certain effect, and an object's being formed *so as* to cause a certain effect. An alarm clock's form may contribute importantly to its making a ticking noise, but that is not its function. When digital clocks were invented, we did not deem them to be failures on the grounds that they do not make ticking noises.

To avert confusion, not to mention howls of protest, let me remind you that I am not claiming that *experiencing an emotion* is just a sort of incidental byproduct of an animal's form, like making a ticking noise. I am claiming that emotionally expressive *movements* are more like by-products of that kind. But here again we run up against the lack of sharp lines in nature. In the animal world, many emotionally expressive movements serve a biological function: when terror makes your fur rise, it also makes you look big and scary to your enemy. So in this sort of animal, is raising the fur an action, subject to standards of success and failure? Is it something that the animal does? The line between emotionally expressive movement and action is not hard and fast, and it is even less hard and fast in the case of animal action than it is in our own. This is a point we will be coming back to (6.1.3). With that acknowledged, we can say that what makes a movement an action is that the animal is formed so as to produce a movement of that kind, in response to his conception of his environment.

5.5.5

So here is the view I have been arguing for. When an animal is guided by his perceptions through his environment, his movements are subject to a standard of efficacy, a standard of success and failure. He is subject to a standard of success and failure, because there is something he is trying to do—he is trying to be himself and continue being himself, and to reproduce others like himself. He is trying to do this not in the sense that he forms the intention of doing it, but in the sense that that is his nature: he has a self-maintaining form. The principles that govern an animal's movements as he guides himself through his environment—the principles that govern his reactions to his perceptions—are what we may call his instincts.[16] An animal's movements are self-determined when they are governed by his instincts, for when they are governed by his instincts, they spring from his own nature. An animal's instincts then are his will, the laws of his own causality. They determine what he does in response to what, what he does for the sake of what. When he acts from his instincts, then, the animal's movements are his own. He acts according to his own laws, and therefore autonomously.

It is even tempting to say that the animal's instincts are imperative for him. When you see an animal acting under the influence of a powerful instinct, it does have that look. But of course I am not saying non-human animals are therefore subject to imperatives, as human beings are. So what makes the difference? To answer this question we must look at action from the inside, at the psychology of action. And for this part of the argument I turn once again to Kant.

5.6 The Psychology of Action

5.6.1

In Kantian moral psychology, the starting point for action is what Kant calls an incentive (*Triebfeder*). An incentive is a motivationally loaded representation

---

[16] See 6.1.3–6.1.5 for a clarification of this notion.

of an object. I am using the term "object" broadly here to include not only substances but also states of affairs and activities. The object may be actually perceived, or conceived as a possible item in the environment, a way that things might be. You are subject to an incentive when you are aware of the features of some object that make the object attractive or appealing to you. Perhaps the object satisfies one of your needs; or perhaps because of the nature of your species or your own particular nature, the object is one you are capable of enjoying. It interests you, it arouses the exercise of your faculties, it excites your natural curiosity, or it provides some sort of emotional comfort or satisfaction. It doesn't matter what—something about you makes you conceive this object as appealing or welcome in a particular way. The object answers to something in you or to the condition you are in. Incentives can also be negative. You may represent an object to yourself as painful or threatening or disgusting, or in some other way unwelcome.

Incentives operate on animals causally, but they do not directly cause the animal's movements. If an incentive directly caused the animal's movement, it would be something within the animal, not the animal as a whole, that determined the movement, and then as we have seen it would not be a case of action. A desire for food, after all, can cause you to salivate. If it also could cause you to go to the refrigerator, then salivating and going to the refrigerator would equally be actions. If we are to count a movement as an action, the movement must be caused by the animal himself, not by his representations or perceptions. According to Kant, incentives work in conjunction with principles, which determine (or perhaps I should say describe) the agent's responses to those incentives, responses which are guided by the agent's conception of the world. The principle represents what Aristotle calls the agent's "contribution" to the action, the thing needed to make it voluntary. Every action must involve both an incentive and a principle: that is, something is presented to the animal's consciousness, *on* which he then acts.

In the human case, in the case of a person, it is easy to say what makes action different from mere response, for human beings act on reasons. A person's principles determine what the person counts as a reason. To the extent that the person *determines himself* to intentional movement, he *takes* his desire for food to provide him with a reason for going to the refrigerator; and that is not the same as its directly causing him to go to the refrigerator. We may represent this fact—his own causality or self-determination—by saying that it is his *principle* to get something to eat when he feels hungry, at least absent some reason why not.

5.6.2

According to the view I have just laid out, the agent's principle describes what Aristotle calls her "contribution" to the action: it tells us what she *does* in the face of the incentives that are presented to her, rather than merely describing the effect which those incentives have on her mind. This is not merely a view about the principles of practical reason, but a view about principles in general. We invoke principles whenever what we are dealing with is a case of self-determination. The principles of logic and the canons of evidence, for instance, describe what a thinker *does* with the incoming evidence: arriving at a belief through reasoning is an active process, a process by which the mind *determines itself* to a conclusion. In fact rational principles, the principles that govern *self-conscious* self-determination, may be seen as *instructions* in the most literal way (2.1.4). What makes your belief logical is that you follow the instruction: you *put* the two premises together in the way required by modus ponens, and so *cause yourself* to believe it (4.3.2). And if you do draw the conclusion, then we can ascribe modus ponens to you as your principle: it describes what you do when faced with these premises. In the same way, the principles of practical reason describe what you do with certain items, say incentives, or beliefs and desires, that are given to you. When you act instrumentally, for instance, you *put* the belief that these are the means and your determination to realize the end together in the way required by the hypothetical imperative, and so *cause yourself* to act. The point is that principles are not just rules and regulations that one might write down on paper: they describe something essential to the mental economy of an active or self-determining being. That—and not because of some fetishistic or puritanical love of rules and regulations—is why action *must* involve principles.

5.6.3

In a non-rational animal, the principles in question are the animal's instincts. The role of both instincts and rational principles in the model is to capture the element of self-determination that is essential to action. As I said before, the animal's instincts are the laws of her causality, definitive of her will. They determine the sort of thing the animal does when faced with a certain stimulus. An animal's instincts determine her to hunt when she is hungry, flee when she is afraid, fight when she is threatened, and so on. Instinctive action is autonomous in the sense that the animal's movements are not directed by alien causes, but rather by the laws of her own nature.

You can see from this description that incentives and principles exist in natural pairs. The fact that an animal has certain instincts explains why he is subject to the associated incentives. In this sense the animal's instincts play a double role in the account of his actions. They both explain why the animal is subject to certain incentives in the first place, and what he does in response to those incentives once they are present. A motive, one might say, is an incentive operating under a certain principle or instinct, or viewed from the standpoint provided by that principle or instinct. For example, for a person whose principle is to help those in need, the fact that another is suffering appears as an incentive to help, an occasion for action. For an animal with the instincts of a cat, a small scurrying rodent is an occasion to give chase. By putting it this way, I mean to convey the fact that it is in a certain way artificial to separate the work of incentive and the work of principle, or at least, to separate them in the non-human animal's experience. In the human case it will vary. The experience of acting from instinct is obviously not, phenomenologically, like the experience of applying a rational principle to a case. But for that matter, acting on a rational principle need not involve any step-by-step process of reasoning, for when a principle is deeply internalized we may simply *recognize* the case as one falling under the principle, where that is a single experience. Principles and instincts play a role in structuring our perceived environment. Yet the two aspects must be separated in our analysis of action in order to capture the difference between being *motivated*, which requires self-determination, and merely being *caused*, which does not.

5.6.4

When an animal acts, he is determined by his form, by his instincts, to produce a change in the world, guided by his conception or representation of the world. But an animal's form is what gives him his identity, what makes him the animal he is. So to say that an animal's form determines him to cause a certain effect is to say that the animal determines himself to be the cause of that effect. Action is self-determination, and, to that extent, it is autonomous. And as I have said before, it is only because action is autonomous that the question of its efficacy can come up. If one thing causes another, there is no room for success or failure. But if an animal determines herself to be the cause of something, and yet does not bring that thing about, then *she* has failed. Autonomy and efficacy are the properties of agents—all agents, not just human agents.

5.6.5

But we are subject to imperatives and non-human animals are not. So then what makes the difference? I think by now it should be clear. In one sense an animal constitutes his own will. He constitutes himself as the kind of animal that he is, and his will *is* essentially himself as the kind of animal that he is. He makes himself the kind of agent that does what he does by doing what he does. But an animal does not choose the principles of his own causality—he does not choose the content of his instincts. We human beings on the other hand do choose the principles of our own causality—we choose our own maxims, the content of our principles. And the categorical and hypothetical imperatives are rules for doing this—rules for the construction of maxims. It is because we, unlike the other animals, must choose the laws of our own causality that we are subject to imperatives.

What this shows is that there are actually two senses of autonomy or self-determination. In one sense, to be autonomous or self-determined is to be governed by the principles of your own causality, principles that are definitive of your will. In another, deeper, sense to be autonomous or self-determined is to *choose* the principles that are definitive of your will. This is the kind of self-determination that Kant called "spontaneity." Every agent, even an animal agent, is autonomous and self-determined in the first sense, or it would make no sense to attribute her movements to her. Only responsible agents, human agents, are autonomous in the second and deeper sense.

That is *where* the difference lies, but I have not said yet *why* it exists. That will be my task in the next chapter.

6

Expulsion from the Garden: The Transition to Humanity

6.1 Instinct, Emotion, Intelligence, and Reason

6.1.1

When an agent acts, even a non-human agent, the agent may succeed or fail. To that extent the very idea of action is a normative one: it is subject to a standard of efficacy. In the last chapter, I argued that actions are subject to a standard of efficacy only because they also exhibit at least a primitive kind of autonomy (5.1.4, 5.5.5). Mere causality is not subject to a standard of success and failure, but if an agent determines himself to cause something, and yet does not, then the agent has failed. So only movements that can be seen as the products of self-determination are subject to a standard of efficacy. Actions are movements that are determined by the acting animal himself in the sense that they are determined by the animal's form. When an animal's form determines his movements, his movements are determined or directed by his own nature, and in that sense the animal is autonomous. In general, then, efficacy and autonomy are the essential properties of agents. Since the Kantian imperatives, the hypothetical and categorical imperatives, tell us to be efficacious and autonomous, the Kantian imperatives in effect tell us to be agents, and so represent constitutive standards for actions.

Obviously, however, that does not mean that non-human animals are subject to imperatives. In 5.6, I explained where the difference lies. Both animal actions and human actions involve the interaction of two factors, an incentive and a principle. The incentive is a motivationally loaded representation of an object. It presents the object as desirable or aversive in some specific way—as a thing to be eaten, mated with, avoided, fled, investigated, defeated or what have you. The principle determines, or we may say describes, what the animal does, or tries to do, in the face of the incentive: catch it, eat it, seduce it, get downwind of it, or whatever it might be. Incentives and principles exist in natural pairs, for her principles determine which incentives a creature is subject to as well as what she does about them. If you are a human being whose principle is to help those in need, then the neediness of another is an incentive to help. If you are a cat whose principle is to chase small scurrying creatures, then the movements of a mouse or a bug are an incentive to give chase.

As that last example is intended to suggest, a non-human animal's principles are her instincts. Her instincts are her own laws in the sense that they arise from her form, and they are the laws of her causality in the sense that they determine what she does for the sake of what. She goes downwind to escape the notice of the lion, pounces to capture the scurrying rodent, digs a burrow to build her nest in, or whatever it might be. Since her instincts are the laws of her own causality, they are in effect the animal's will, and the movements that are determined by them are her actions.

But human beings are agents in a further, deeper sense. For we do not merely determine ourselves in the sense that we act *from* the principles of our own causality—we determine ourselves in the deeper sense that we *choose* the principles of our own causality. It is up to us to decide what we will do for the sake of what. How this difference between us and the other animals emerges, and what further ramifications it has for human life, is my subject in this chapter.

6.1.2

We attribute instincts only to conscious beings, for their role is to *structure* an animal's consciousness, his conception of the world, in ways that will enable him to survive and reproduce. A non-human animal lives in a world that is in a deep way his own world, a world that is *for* that animal. I don't mean by saying this that the animal's world is favorable to his interests; often it is not. But the world as perceived by the animal is organized around his interests: it consists of the animal's food, his enemies, his potential mates, and, if he is social, of his fellows, his family, flock, tribe, or what have you. To say that the animal is subject to incentives is just to say that his perceptions come already loaded with the practical significance of various objects for him. He confronts a world of things that are perceived directly, without calculation or conscious interpretation, as things *to-be-avoided*, things *to-be-chased*, things *to-be-investigated*, things *to-be-eaten*, things *to-be-fled*, things *to-be-cared-for*, and things *to-be-mated-with* if at all possible. If you think of it, you will see that it has to be this way. Consciousness first evolved in unintelligent animals, and would have been useless if all it did was flood their tiny minds with neutral information that needs to be processed by intelligence or reason before it is of any use. So the world comes to an animal already practically interpreted as a world of tools and obstacles, friends and enemies, of the to-be-avoided and the to-be-sought. The natural way of perceiving the world, in other words, is *teleologically*.

6.1.3

But this is not to say that non-human animals never use intelligence to find their way around in the world. Here it is important for me to clarify something about the way I am using the term "instinct." I am using the term in one way more narrowly and in another more broadly than it is generally used. First, I am using it to refer to an established connection between a representation (the incentive) and a certain primitively normative response, an automatic sense of the response as *appropriate* to or perhaps better *called for* by the representation. Sometimes people use the term "instinctive" for reactions and movements that are not experienced as called for but rather are wholly automatic and simply caused, like salivating. The smell of food to a hungry animal is an incentive for eating, not an incentive for salivating—it is only a cause of salivating. Still, it must be admitted that the line between such reactions and actions in nature is indistinct, and this is one of the ways in which the concept of action, especially when applied to the lower animals, is indeterminate (5.5.4). We can form a continuum going from, say, salivating at the smell of food, to blinking when an object comes close to your eye, to ducking when something is hurled in your direction, to running when you see a predator. As we move along this continuum we move from the wholly automatic to a case where there is room in consciousness to experience the response as called for or appropriate. It is more this latter kind of case that I have in mind when I talk about instinctive action. In that sense, my use of the term is narrower than usual.

6.1.4

Before I turn to the way in which my use of the term "instinct" is broader than usual, I want to address an objection to what I just said. I characterized an animal's instinctive response to an incentive as "primitively normative," and claimed that the animal experiences the response as "called for" by the occasion.

Some people balk at the idea that a non-human animal can experience things in this way. But nobody (well, almost nobody) balks at the idea that the higher animals, at least, experience emotions, and emotions do, at least in many cases, present certain responses as appropriate to us. In *The Sources of Normativity* I argued that pain and pleasure are the perceptions of reasons, and it is a natural corollary of that view that that is what the emotions are too: perceptions of reasons.[1] For, as Aristotle says, "every passion . . . is accompanied by pleasure and pain" (NE 2.3 1104b14). Now because it comes naturally to us to say things like "there is no reason to be afraid" or "there is no reason to be so angry," and to talk about "irrational" or "rational" feelings, many philosophers are prepared to say that emotions are things for which there can be reasons. But the sense in which we "have reasons" for our emotions isn't the same as the sense in which we "have reasons" for our actions: we do not undertake to have our emotions or decide to have them on the basis of our reasons; emotions are responses, and actions are something more (5.5.2–3). But to say that they are responses is not to say that they are mere caused reactions. In 5.5.2 I argued that emotions can sometimes be judged morally good or bad, and this is in turn because an emotion is subject to standards of appropriateness and intelligibility, while a mere reaction—a rash, say—is not. So what I am proposing is that we don't actually have reasons for our emotions, despite the natural way of talking, but rather that our emotions, or our affective experiences more generally, are perceptions of practical reasons, reasons for action. Fear is the perception of a reason to flee, pity is the perception of a reason to relieve another's pain, and so on. And in making this proposal, I want to emphasize a feature of perception that philosophers do not always attend to: namely, that it is not just a way of knowing, not just an epistemic state, but a way of being in the presence of its object. For I think that is why we place a high value on the emotions, even the negative emotions, and feel that we aren't really alive unless we feel them. To have an emotion is to stand *in the presence* of a normative fact: to feel fear is to stand in the presence of the dangerousness of danger; to feel grief is to stand in the presence of the infinite loss of death. And that is what the other animals do, through their instincts, through the normatively loaded way in which they perceive the world: they perceive their reasons, and they act accordingly.

Some readers may suppose that this doctrine requires normative realism of a kind that I would reject.[2] Don't reasons have to be "out there" in order to be perceived? No, that's the whole point. I am not claiming that reasons for an animal to survive and reproduce exist independently of the

---

[1] SN 4.3.4–6, pp. 147–50.
[2] Among other places see SN 1.4.1–1.4.9, pp. 28–47, "Realism and Constructivism in Twentieth-Century Moral Philosophy" (CA essay 10); and 6.3 below.

animal herself, and that the animal survives because she perceives them.[3] Rather, to have a set of instinctive and affective responses that organize the perceived world around your own needs and interests is in effect to conceptualize the world in your own image, as a place *for* you in the sense I described above. Though the animal perceives the reasons, they are there because of the animal's own nature. Although the animal's instinctive response is "normative" in this primitive sense, the animal knows nothing of the normative; she doesn't need to, because it is built right into the way she perceives the world.

6.1.5

Now let me return to instinct. I am using the term more narrowly than it is sometimes used, because I am using it only to describe a non-human animal's principles of *action*. But in another way I am using the term "instinct" more broadly than some people do. Some people contrast the idea of "instinctive response" with a "learned response." The term "instinct" as I am using it involves no such contrast. And this is what brings me to the issue of intelligence.

An intelligent animal is characterized by his ability to learn from his experiences. He is able to extend his repertoire of practically significant representations (or even just cues, for a machine may be intelligent) beyond those with which instinct (or the inventor) originally supplied him. So intelligence is a capacity to forge new connections, to increase your stock of automatically appropriate responses. Intelligence so understood is not something contrary to instinct, but rather something that increases its range and ramifies the view of the world that it presents. After the puppy's encounter with the porcupine and the beehive, the porcupine and the beehive get added to the category of things-to-be-avoided and are now perceived that way automatically. The human being you live with becomes a pack member and yowling in the kitchen becomes a way of getting food. Not the way you would have done it in nature but you can learn that it works. Hume's description of the process by which human beings and the other animals automatically come to make new causal inferences is a pretty good description of the workings of intelligence (T 1.3.6). Hume was right to deny that reason needs to come into the story at that level, though he was wrong to deny that it needs to do so later on.

---

[3] Indeed, although this is too long a story to tell here, I think it is only because the other animals fall within the scope of human moral legislation that they can be said to have reasons at all. See my "Fellow Creatures: Kantian Ethics and Our Duties to Animals."

Instrumental thinking of the kind found in the higher animals is a further stretch of intelligence. By instrumental thinking, I mean figuring out that something could work as a tool or an obstacle not by accidental experience but by noticing its properties. The intelligent animal learns about the practical significance of objects—although it wasn't always obvious, this object is a food, or a predator, or a source of pain. The animal capable of *instrumental* intelligence discovers the practical significance of the *properties* of objects: the heavy object can be used to smash coconuts or the sharp one to pierce the shell. For the intelligent animal, the world of tools and obstacles presented by instinct is elaborated and changed in ways that contribute to the animal's flexibility in dealing with changes in her environment and her success in getting around. But the world she perceives is still a world teleologically structured around her own interests by her instinctive responses.

6.1.6

And this is true for us as well. Our *natural* way of perceiving and conceiving the world is teleologically. Perceptual salience in everyday life is determined by our interests and commitments, even once those begin to change in the ways that are characteristic of the human. And this remains true even when we become *very* intelligent. Recall here the discussion from 2.3.2: as basic a fact as that we divide the world into objects, each associated with a cluster of causal powers, is a way in which our perceived world is a world that is for-us. Why do we say that the stone broke the window, rather than that the state of the world at Time T_1 produced the state of the world at Time T_2, which includes a broken window? Because we can *use* a stone to break a window. Our world is a world of means and ends because it is a world for intelligent action, a world for us. The scientific conception of the world, the view of the world as a system of neutral laws and forces whose impact on our own fates and interests is largely accidental, requires the *detachment* of perception from the rich normative significance that naturally inhabits it.

Some philosophers seem to suppose that we start from some crude but still purely theoretical conception of the world, and work out the practical significances of things, using intelligence and reason. This is backwards: the truth is that detachment of perception from practical significance, the detachment that makes the scientific conception of the world possible, is an extraordinary conceptual achievement (2.3.3). It is an achievement made possible, and also necessary, not by intelligence but by the interaction of intelligence with another power, namely reason, the thing that makes us us.

6.1.7

What is reason, anyway? It is sometimes said that human beings are the only animals who are self-conscious. Animals are aware of the world but not of themselves. I believe that the issue is much more complicated than that, for self-consciousness, like other attributes, comes in degrees and takes many different forms. A tiger who stands downwind of her intended prey is not merely aware of her prey—she is also locating herself with respect to her prey in physical space, and that is a rudimentary form of self-consciousness. A social animal who makes gestures of submission when a more dominant animal enters the scene is locating himself in social space, and that too is a form of self-consciousness. Parallel to these abilities would be a capacity to locate yourself in mental space, to locate yourself with respect to your own thoughts and emotions, and in particular, to know them as your own. This is what we more commonly think of as self-consciousness, a reflective awareness of our mental states as such. Do any of the other animals have this ability to locate themselves in subjective, mental space? Some of the language-trained animals can express the idea "I want"—Koko the gorilla and Alex the African gray parrot, two famous language-trained animals, can both do this—so perhaps they have the ability to think about their own mental states.[4] And some scientists have also pointed to cases of deception to suggest that some animals are aware of the thoughts of others, and therefore, presumably, of their own. The evidence on these questions is, I think, inconclusive.

But however it may be with the other animals, there is no question that we human beings are self-conscious in a very particular way. We are aware, not only *that* we desire or fear certain things, but also that we are inclined to act in certain ways on the *basis* of these desires or fears. We are conscious of the potential grounds of our actions, the principles on which our actions are based, *as potential grounds*. And this, as I have argued elsewhere, sets us a problem that the other animals do not have.[5] For once we are aware that we are inclined to act in a certain way on the ground of a certain incentive, we find ourselves faced with a decision, namely, whether we should do that. We can say to ourselves: "I am inclined to do act-A for the sake of end-E. But should I?" The same applies in the theoretical realm. An intelligent but non-rational animal may be moved to believe or expect one thing when he perceives another, having learned to make a certain causal connection or

---

[4] See *The Alex Studies*, pp. 197–208, for Irene Pepperberg's account of teaching Alex the parrot to use "wants" and her own very careful conclusions about what exactly he learned when he learned it.

[5] SN 3.2.1–3.2.2, pp. 92–7.

association between the two things in the past. But he does not think about that principle of association itself, and ask himself whether he should allow it to govern his thinking. But as rational animals we are aware that we are inclined to take one thing as evidence for another, and therefore we can ask whether we should. Our awareness of the workings of the grounds of our beliefs and actions gives us control over the influence of those grounds themselves.

The first result of the development of this form of self-consciousness is liberation from the control of instinct. Instincts still operate within us, in the sense that they are the sources of many of our incentives—in fact, arguably, though by various routes, of all of them. But instincts no longer *determine* how we respond to those incentives, what we do in the face of them. They *propose* responses, but we may or may not act in the way they propose. Self-consciousness opens up a space between the incentive and the response, a space of what I call reflective distance. It is within the space of reflective distance that the question whether our incentives give us reasons arises. In order to answer that question, we need principles, which determine what we are to count as reasons. Our rational principles then replace our instincts—they will tell us what is an appropriate response to what, what makes what worth doing, what the situation calls for. And so it is in the space of reflective distance, in the internal world created by self-consciousness, that reason is born.

6.1.8

Reason, therefore, is not the same thing as intelligence. Intelligence, as I said before, is a power of forging new connections, through thought and learning. It elaborates an animal's representation of the world in practically useful ways, making the animal more flexible and adaptive to change. Instrumental intelligence may enable an animal to make choices of a sort, as between two different hiding places or tools. And the forethought that comes with intelligence may enable a non-human animal to choose between quite different courses of action, based on her expectations of the results. But what makes either of the two options worth choosing, in these kinds of cases, is still determined by instinct: instinct settles it that the predator is *to be avoided* or the nut *to be cracked*. Intelligence still looks outward, at the world. It is only when we become self-conscious, when we look inward, that we are faced with normative problems, and must decide what is worth doing for the sake of what. It is reason, not mere intelligence, which puts us in the realm of the normative.

6.2 The Parts of the Soul

6.2.1

In his essay, "Conjectures on the Beginning of Human History," Kant explains one of the first results of the development of reason, namely the enormous proliferation in the possible objects of desire that is characteristic of the human. Intelligence can find new means, but when we enter the realm of reason, we begin to find new ends.

In this essay, Kant uses Genesis as the basis for a fanciful account of the historical development of the power of free choice. The first object of free choice in history is the apple in the story of Adam and Eve, and Kant explains how this choice came about. Initially, Kant explains, the primordial human animal must have been guided by instinct to her natural food, just as the other animals are. We need not suppose, Kant says, that there was some special instinct that has now been lost. Rather, the sense of smell carried with it an ability, "still in evidence today," as Kant says, to pick out our natural food (CBHH 8:111). But then reason, operating through a power that Kant calls comparison, begins to change things. Kant explains:

> *reason* soon made its presence felt and sought to extend [the human being's] knowledge of foodstuffs beyond the bounds of instinct; it did so by comparing her usual diet with anything which a sense other than that to which her instinct was tied . . . represented as similar in character (III.6). . . . The initial incentive to abandon natural impulses may have been quite trivial. . . . Thus, it may have been only a fruit which, because it looked similar to other agreeable fruits which she had previously tasted, encouraged her to make the experiment. There may also have been the example of an animal to which such food was naturally congenial. . . . this was enough to give reason the initial inducement to quibble with the voice of nature (III.1), and despite the latter's objections, to make the first experiment in free choice . . . (CBHH 8:111–12)

I'm taking some liberties with the translation of the pronouns here, for in Kant's story it is obviously *Eve* who makes the *first* free rational choice. How does it happen? Eve is naturally drawn by the sense of smell, say, to pears. They smell like food to her, and when she is hungry her instinct directs her to eat them. But then she becomes self-conscious and so she notices the working of this incentive within her. One day when she is hungry she finds herself thinking of pears. "I have an inclination to eat some pears," she says to herself. (Later in this chapter I'll explain exactly how that step happens, how she comes to think "I have an inclination to eat some pears.") There before her is the tree, dripping with juicy green apples. "Those apples look like pears," she says to herself, making the first comparison. And there is her playmate, the serpent, munching away on an apple. "He's like me, in some ways, and he eats apples," she says to herself, making the second comparison. And then it happens. "You know, I could eat one of those apples to satisfy my hunger," she says to herself.[6] That's the first maxim, of the first free action, and there our story, the human story, begins. Kant comments:

No matter how trivial the harm it did may have been, it was nevertheless enough to open her eyes (III.7). She discovered in herself an ability to choose her own way of life without being tied to any single one like the other animals. But the momentary gratification which this realization . . . afforded . . . was inevitably followed . . . by anxiety and fear as to how she should employ her newly discovered ability, given that she did not yet know the hidden properties or remote effects of anything. She stood, as it were, on the edge of an abyss. For whereas instinct had hitherto directed her towards individual objects of her desire, an infinite range of objects now opened up, and she did not yet know how to choose between them. Yet now that she had tasted this state of freedom, it was impossible for her to return to a state of servitude under the rule of instinct. (CBHH 8:112)

In the essay, Kant goes on to trace further steps by which the powers of reason are developed. Reason not only directs the human being to new objects of desire among the things she finds around her, but leads to the development of altogether *new kinds* of objects of desire. Kant anticipates Freud, for example, in suggesting that the senses of beauty and romantic love are the products of the suppression of our sexual instincts (CBHH 8:112–13), a suppression made possible by reason's power to say "no" to an incentive. In this way distinctively human desires and interests come about.

6.2.2

But our liberation from the government of instinct is also our expulsion from the Garden, our banishment from a world that is teleologically ordered by our instincts and presented as such by our incentives, a world in which we nearly always already know what to do. It is this essential homelessness that leads to the misology that Kant famously describes in the opening section of the *Groundwork*, the hatred of reason and nostalgia for instinct which he says is felt most sharply by cultivated people who try to find their happiness through reason (*G* 4:395). For now we must use intelligence and reason, both to reconstruct a picture of the world that enables us to find our way around in it, and to decide where to go and what to do in that world. That is to say, we

---

[6] The theoretical analog to this operation, one made possible by the combination of reason and intelligence, is the capacity to form a hypothesis and test it.

must resort to *science* to reconstruct a usable conception of the world, and to *ethics* to determine how to live our lives.

6.2.3

But self-consciousness introduces another, more immediate difference into the lives of human animals. It introduces what, following Plato, I will call the parts of the soul. Let me explain what I mean.

In one sense, as I have already emphasized, the soul has parts even without self-consciousness. Non-human animals experience incentives, and have instincts that tell them how to deal with those incentives, just as people have inclinations, and reason that tells us how to deal with those inclinations. But in another sense the non-human animal soul does not have parts, for what counts for a non-human animal as an incentive is settled by his instincts, and his instincts immediately tell him how to deal with the incentive: as I said in 5.6.3, in an animal soul the work of incentive and the work of instinct are not phenomenologically distinct. So in a non-human animal, the whole psychic system is closed and tightly knit. And that means that there's a sense in which self-consciousness *produces* the parts of the soul.

6.2.4

The first and most obvious way in which it does this we have already looked at. Self-consciousness is the source of reason. When we become conscious of the workings of an incentive within us, the incentive is experienced not as a force or a necessity but as a proposal, something we need to make a decision about. Cut loose from the control of instinct, we must formulate principles that will tell us how to deal with the incentives we experience. And the experience of decision or choice, the work of these principles, is a separate experience from that of the workings of the incentive itself.

One effect of this division is to make the distinction between action and mere reaction sharper and crisper in humans than it is in the other animals, although it is important to admit that even in our case it is not always sharp and crisp. The fact that human actions involve a distinct moment of choice sharpens up the distinction. Earlier I said that we could see a kind of continuum from salivating at the smell of food, to blinking when an object comes close to your eye, to ducking when something is hurled in your direction, to running when you see a predator (6.1.3). In the human case there are sharper divisions. We normally cannot choose whether to salivate or not, so usually that counts as pure reaction. We normally can choose whether to run. The reflective distance between the experience of the proposal, the incentive, and the decision to adopt it as a reason sharpens up the difference between reaction and action, making the latter case clear. But we are talking about nature, so there are still unclear cases. Ducking, for instance, is still somewhere in the middle—often it occurs without a decision like a reaction, yet it is a reaction that can be resisted if you have some powerful reason to resist it. If I say "you must hold absolutely still, or the children will die" and you duck, then it will have been an action.

6.2.5

Self-consciousness creates the need for the principles of reason, which are then more firmly separated from the associated incentives than their instinctual predecessors were. But self-consciousness also transforms the other side of the equation—it transforms incentives into what Kant calls *inclinations*. To see how this works we must look a little more closely at the relationship between incentives and inclinations.

Strictly speaking incentives are, as I said in 5.6.1, features of the represented object that make it, from some point of view, attractive or aversive. When we say that a person has an inclination for something, what we mean is that he is responding to the incentive that makes that thing attractive. For instance if dancing is pleasant, that means there is a natural incentive to dance, and if a person's awareness of that incentive is drawing him towards dancing, then we say that he has an inclination for dancing.

Now there are two important points to notice about this kind of case. One is a standard admonition. We should not say, in this kind of case, that pleasure is really the object of the inclination, rather than dancing. Dancing is the object of the inclination; to say it is pleasant is just to say that there is a natural incentive for dancing. In fact it is not even quite right to say that pleasure is the incentive: the incentive has no name, but is simply whatever it is about dancing that, given the psychological and physical characteristics of human beings, draws us to dancing. To say that dancing is pleasant is not to say exactly what the incentive is: "pleasure" is just a kind of dummy word that indicates that there is one.[7] Given our nature as physical and animal beings, we need to move our muscles in certain controlled ways and we experience that movement as welcome. The arousal of our erotic capacities may also come into it, and that is welcome too. You can explain the incentive, sometimes, but at bottom it is not something articulable. We just gesture at the fact that there is an incentive, a positive attraction, a suitableness of the object to our nature, when we say that the object is pleasant.

[7] For the parallel position about pain, see SN 4.3.1–11, pp. 145–55.

Having said that, let's nevertheless call the incentive, for short, "pleasure." Then the point of saying that pleasure is the person's incentive is not to say that he likes the pleasure rather than the dancing, but rather that the pleasure, the sheer joy of the movement, is what he likes about the dancing. Or we may even say that pleasure is what makes him like it, for there is nothing inconsistent with the concept of action in the fact that incentives operate on us causally. All we need for the concept of action is that neither incentives, nor the inclinations to which they give rise, cause the actions directly, without the intervention of principles.

The second and more complicated point is that inclinations themselves are in a sense the *products* of self-consciousness. And now I'm going to tell you, as I promised earlier, how Eve came to say to herself, "I have an inclination to eat some pears." When we are talking about the actions of a non-human animal, we may *attribute* an inclination to her—we may say that the cat *wants* some food, for instance. But this attribution is really completely third-personal, in the sense that it is just a way of describing the fact that the cat is responding to an incentive, viz., hunger—or more precisely, since an incentive is a feature of the represented object, to the fact that the food would satisfy her hunger. We don't need to say that the incentive causes an inclination, and the cat then acts from the inclination, as if the inclination were some *additional* and separate mental state. The cat does not *entertain* a desire for some cat chow: saying she has the inclination to eat is just a way of saying she experiences the incentive to eat. In fact in one way it is better not to talk about the cat's inclination, for when we mention the cat's reasons, or indeed our own, we do not mention the inclination, but rather the incentive. We say that the cat seeks food "because she is hungry" and you dance "because it is pleasant"—not "because you want to." Saying that the cat has the inclination is just a way of *naming* the fact that the cat is responding to the incentive.[8]

But there is a sense in which self-consciousness moves this attributive operation indoors, and does make our inclinations into mental items. For when we are conscious of the fact that an incentive is working upon us, our self-consciousness of our state does reify it into a kind of mental item. And that's when we say of ourselves that we "have an inclination," something we now have to decide whether to satisfy or not. So self-consciousness is the source of inclinations as well as of reason. Self-consciousness produces the parts of the soul.

---

[8] Occasionally in earlier essays I have described desires and inclinations themselves as incentives (e.g. "The Normativity of Instrumental Reason" (CA essay 1), p. 46, and "The Myth of Egoism" (CA essay 2), p. 87). Strictly speaking, I now think that is wrong.

6.3 Inside or Outside?

6.3.1

This is as good a place as any to explain my stance on a point of current discussion. A moment ago I said that when we tell others the reasons for our actions, we mention the incentive, the attractive or aversive feature of the object, not the inclination, our reaction to that feature. You say you dance "for the sheer joy of dancing," say, not that you dance "because you want to." But if it is the inclination you decide whether to act on or not, does that mean that it is the inclination that provides the reason? And is the reason then after all "because you want to"?

Some philosophers suppose that the fact that we mention the incentive rather than the inclination favors a realist account of value.[9] According to these philosophers, desires and inclinations are simply responses to the good-making properties of objects, and it is only the good-making properties of objects that we need to talk about when we talk about our reasons, not the desires and inclinations themselves. When we say why we pursue various objects, we mention the attractive features of those objects, rather than our own psychological states, and so—these philosophers conclude—it must be in virtue of the attractive features of the objects that the objects have value.

As a Kantian, I disagree with this realist picture in two ways. The picture of a desire or inclination as a response to the good-making features of its object is too cerebral, making our own desires and inclinations essentially epistemic, and too unlike the incentives of our fellow creatures. In Kant's view, the features of the objects of desire that we mention when we explain why we value those objects would not give those objects value, if it were not for the way in which those features are related to human physiology and psychology. At the basis of every desire or inclination, no matter how articulately we can defend it, is a basic suitableness-to-us that is a matter of nature and not of reason. Value is relational and what it is related to is our nature. The fact that when we run out of other ways to articulate what attracts us to an object we can just say that it is "pleasant" tends to obscure this fact, for "pleasant" seems to name a good-making property of an object. But as I said before, it does not—"pleasure" is just a dummy word that indicates that some positive form of this basic suitableness-to-us is in place.

---

[9] See for instance, Scanlon, *What We Owe to Each Other*, 37–55; Raz, *Engaging Reason*, chapter 3.

The second difference follows. As a Kantian, I believe that it is our own choices that ultimately confer value on objects, even though our choices are responsive to certain features of those objects. In choosing objects, in conferring value on things that answer to our nature in welcome ways, an agent is affirming her own value. She takes what matters *to her* to matter *absolutely* and so to be worthy of her choice. But even if the agent herself believes this Kantian theory, it doesn't follow that she must think of herself as choosing objects simply because she wants or likes them. She can still talk to herself, and to others, about what she likes about them, and why. So even though there *is* a sense, on my account, in which we choose things "because we want them," a sense in which the inclination provides the reason, it doesn't follow that, when someone asks you why you chose something, "I wanted it" is the right answer. In fact the Kantian theory of value puts us in a position to offer an alternative account of the fact that we talk about the incentive rather than the inclination when we want to convey our reasons to another. In the sense I am using the term here, an inclination just is the operation of a natural incentive upon you, as viewed through the reifying eye of self-consciousness. In that quite general sense all of our non-moral values depend on inclinations. So when you are explaining your values to another person, it is quite uninformative to mention the fact that you have an inclination for the object as the basis of the value. He knows that; or if he doesn't know it, what he doesn't know is a thesis in value theory, and that isn't what he wants to know. He wants to know why you value *this*, what you find attractive about it, not what the structure of human valuing consists in. To put it another way, he wants to know *which* inclination you are having, what is drawing you to the object. And you specify that by describing, as far as you can, the incentive.[10]

So which provides the reason, the incentive or the inclination? I don't think there's a straightforward answer to this question. At the moment, so to speak, just prior to choice, you have reflective distance from the incentive, and therefore do not take it for granted that it provides a reason. The pleasure of the dancing is what is calling out to you, but you do not, just then, take it that that pleasure provides a reason to dance: that is what you have to decide about, whether in this case you are going to take it for a reason. So for now, viewing the incentive with the questioning eye of reason, you regard the incentive's effect on you as a mere psychological state, something normatively undecided—you regard it, that is, as just an inclination. If you do decide to act as the incentive bids, you are endorsing the incentive as providing a reason,

---

[10] See also my "Acting for a Reason" (CA essay 7).

and then it becomes more natural to mention the incentive in its character as a feature of the object rather than in its character as the source of your own psychological states. This means that before the decision you seem to be asking whether the inclination provides a reason, while, after you make it, it seems to be the incentive that has provided it after all.

6.3.2

Realists, I said a moment ago, take the fact that when we talk about our reasons we talk about the attractive features of objects, rather than about our psychological states, to favor a realist conception of value. But some anti-realist philosophers, such as Simon Blackburn, take the very same facts to show that the Kantian account of deliberation involves the "fundamental mistake" of thinking that deliberation looks inward to the self rather than outward to the world. According to Blackburn, the inner act of choosing to satisfy the inclination is just an unnecessary mental duplicate of the outer act of choosing the object. To suppose such a duplicate is necessary is to make a mistake analogous to that of sense-data theorists who think perceptions are mental copies of the objects we perceive.[11]

What I've just said about the relation between incentives and inclinations responds to this point. Reasons arise within the space of reflective distance; to that extent an inward glance is essential to generating them. But it is also important to keep in mind that the question of deliberation is neither whether a certain object or state of affairs would be good, nor whether to satisfy a certain inclination, but rather whether to do a certain action: to do an act for the sake of an end. No sense can be attached to the question whether that decision looks inward or outward. Actions are not inward or outward; they are, like utterances, intelligible objects in the public world whose very nature it is to bridge the gap between inner and outer. They are acts of thinking performed by the body, mental states in the flesh: there is no need to imagine something inner behind them that causes them.

There *is* an error of the sort Blackburn describes. It's the mistake made by philosophers who deny Aristotle's dictum that the conclusion of a practical syllogism is an action (MA 7 701a10–12). These philosophers think that deliberation leads instead to the formation of an intention, a mental object that in turn causes an action which is in itself a mere outer movement. That amounts to *denying* that the gap between inner and outer can be bridged, and that is exactly the problem with sense-data theory: it adds extra

---

[11] Simon Blackburn, *Ruling Passions*, pp. 250–6.

entities, endless copies, in a fruitless attempt to bridge a gap it conceives as unbridgeable. Intentions so conceived are unnecessary mental duplicates of actions.

Why do philosophers suppose we need these mental objects, these intentions? One source of the temptation rests in the fact that, being prudent, we often think about what we are going to do in advance. So I decide, for instance, now, that I am going to go to Rome next summer. And since I can't act on my decision immediately, I form an intention, and I store it somewhere until I'm ready to use it.

But that's not what I do. As soon as my decision is made the action begins, and I start taking the means. For now every move I make must be guided by the decision I have taken. I must learn Italian, or buy a suitcase, or even if all these things are done, I must be careful not to do things that would obstruct or prevent my going to Rome, like spending all my money so I can't buy a ticket, or promising a friend I will spend the summer with him in Antarctica, or whatever it might be. And when I decide to go to Rome next summer, I am deciding that the end makes all of this, all of the relevant parts of the act I take to achieve it, worth doing. So there is never any gap between decision and action. The conclusion of a practical syllogism is an action; Aristotle was right.[12]

6.4 Pull Yourself Together

6.4.1

Self-consciousness opens up a space between the experience of the incentive and what previously had been the instinctive response, and that space transforms incentives into inclinations and governing instincts into free reason. Self-consciousness is therefore the source of a psychic complexity not experienced by the other animals, and it transforms psychic unity from a natural state into something that has to be achieved, into a task and an activity. Once we are self-conscious the soul has parts, and then before we can act it must be unified. At the very same time, and for the same reason, practical deliberation becomes necessary, for free reason need not follow inclination. We must now decide what to do. These conditions—the need to work at being unified and the need for practical deliberation—are brought about together. And this means that the function of deliberation is not merely to determine how you will act, but also to unify you. Or rather, to put the point more correctly, those are not two different things, for your movement will not be an action unless

---

[12] I am indebted to discussions with Luca Ferrero on this point.

it is attributable to you—to you as a whole or a unified being—rather than merely to something in you. And the task of deliberation is to determine what you—you as a whole or a unified being—are going to do.

6.4.2

The phenomenology of deliberation, especially in hard cases, bears this out. Suppose we are dealing with a case where you have to choose between two options, two courses of action, for both of which you experience some incentive. When you choose, as I've said before, it is as if there were something over and above your incentives, something which is you, and which chooses which incentive to act on. That much just follows from the fact of self-consciousness. You must decide whether to act on the incentive, and in effect that means you must decide whether to identify your will with it or not (4.4.3). But it is not as if the incentive itself appears in consciousness as something that is *not* you, but just something you might pick up, the way you might pick up a stone off the ground. The incentive arises from your nature and it appears in consciousness as something that wants to *be* you. As I argued in 1.4.6, our incentives, at least many of them, arise from our conceptions of our practical identity, from the various roles and relationships that we think of as giving our lives and actions value. The work of pulling ourselves back together is also the work of pulling those identities into a single practical identity, choosing among them when we have to, deciding which is to have priority, harmonizing them when we can.[13] But the incentives that spring from these forms of identity are incentives to *act*, and on any given occasion, we can only do one thing. So what we feel in a hard case of the sort I have described is that we ourselves are being pulled in both directions. That's what we say in such cases: *I feel so torn*. And I think in such a case this is literally true—it is you, your will, your agency, that is in danger of tearing. Earlier I mentioned that Socrates says that phrases like "self-control," "self-mastery," or "self-command" are like "tracks or clues" that virtue has left in the language (R 430e). So are the things we say to people when it is time for them to stop dithering and bring deliberation to an end: *Make up your mind*, or even better, *Pull yourself together*. The work of practical deliberation is reunification, reconstitution: and the function of the principles that govern deliberation—the principles of practical reason—is the unification of the self. So we arrive again at the conclusion of Chapter 4—the function of practical reason is to unify us into agents who can be the authors of our actions.

---

[13] I am indebted here to discussions with Tamar Schapiro.

6.4.3

I'll come back to the parts of the soul, and the way that we unify them, or fail to, in Chapters 8 and 9. Here I want to notice another important difference all this makes to the distinctive character of human action. As we have seen, liberation from the government of instinct means that it is up to us to decide what justifies what, what counts as a reason for what, what is worth doing for the sake of what. We don't need to think of this, and in fact we shouldn't think of it, as a decision made *prior* to action: as often as not, it is a decision embodied in the action. Action involves an incentive and a principle; the principle describes the agent's contribution to the action. In our case, that contribution takes the form of deciding *whether* to act as the incentive bids. And that decision may be *described* as your principle. If you choose to run in order to escape your predator, to stand your ground in order to protect your offspring, or to dance for the sheer joy of dancing, then those are your principles, your conception of what is worth doing for the sake of what. Human action is in that further sense autonomous; that is the sense in which we choose our principles.

I could put the conclusion of Chapter 5 this way: an animal acts when he consciously determines himself to be the cause of a change in the world. I do not mean that the animal is conscious *of* his causality—that he forms an intention or adopts a maxim—but rather that he exercises his causality by way of his consciousness, that his movements are guided by his representations. A human being acts when she *self*-consciously determines herself to be the cause of a change in the world. Unlike the other animals, we *are* conscious of our causality, and it is therefore up to us how we exercise it. We choose the laws or principles of our own causality. And this means, to switch back now to Aristotle's terms, that there is a sense in which we choose our own forms.

6.4.4

In 2.4.1, I mentioned that in his book *On the Soul*, Aristotle asserts that there are three forms of life, corresponding to what he called three parts of the soul. At the bottom is a life of basic self-maintenance, a vegetative life of nutrition and reproduction, common to all plants and animals. Animals are distinguished from plants in being alive in a further sense, given, as we have seen, by the power of action. The third form of life described by Aristotle is distinctive of human beings—the life of rational activity, the life of choice.

Each part of the soul, and each corresponding form of life, supervenes on the one below it. The addition of each new part of the soul changes the sense in which the thing lives, *both* by influencing the way the "lower" functions are carried out and by adding a new kind of activity and so a new form of life. Because she has the powers that make agency possible, an animal *lives* in a sense that a plant does not: an animal is conscious; she is active in the sense that she *does* things; she pursues what she desires and flees what she fears; in some cases she builds a home and raises a family; if she is a "higher" animal she may even know how to love and to play. But these are not just powers added, so to speak, on top of the animal's nutritive and reproductive life: they also change the way the animal carries out the tasks of nutrition and reproduction. The animal uses her capacity for action to get her food and raise her family. But she also may do things a plant doesn't do at all, like love and play. These things make the "life" of an animal a different sort of thing than the "life" of a plant.

A human being in turn has a "life" in a sense in which a non-human animal does not. For a non-human animal's life is mapped out for him by his instincts; and any two members of a given species basically live the same sort of life (unless the differences are biologically fixed, as by age and gender, or by kinds, as among bees). Two members of the same non-human animal species may indeed have very different personalities, but these do not make much difference to the way that they live. A human being has a life in a different sense from this, for a human being has, and is capable of choosing, what we sometimes call a "way of life" or, following Rawls, a "conception of the good."[14] Where her way of life is not completely fixed by some sort of cultural regulation, a human being decides such things as how to earn her living, how to spend her afternoons, who to have for friends, and in general, how she will live and what she will live for. She decides what is worth doing for the sake of what. And again, we find a double result. Choice changes the way we carry out the activities we share with the other animals, such as house-building, child-rearing, hunting or collecting food, playing, and sexual activity. Human beings approach these activities creatively and develop various ways of going about them among which we then choose. But we also do things the other animals don't do at all, like tell jokes and paint pictures and engage in scientific research and philosophy. Choice introduces a whole new sense of *life*, a new sense in which a person can be said to "have a life." So personhood is quite literally a form of life. (By the way, in case you didn't recognize it, what I just said was a rendering of Aristotle's function argument from *Nicomachean Ethics* 1.7.[15]) Since being a person, like being a living thing or an animal, is a form of life, being a person is being engaged in a specific

---

[14] Rawls, *Political Liberalism*, p. 19.
[15] See my "Aristotle's Function Argument" (CA essay 4), pp. 142–3.

form of the activity of self-constitution. Our chosen actions constitute us as persons.

6.4.5

And so with this new form of life comes a new form of identity: what I have been calling "practical identity." For each of the Aristotelian "parts" of the soul also adds a new sense in which the creature may be said to have an identity. A plant, although alive, is basically just a substance. But an animal has a kind of identity that a plant lacks. Her consciousness gives her a point of view; she's also an agent, and she does things; she's not just a substance, she's a subject, she's a someone. If she is also fairly intelligent, you can interact with her, play with her, get annoyed at her, or adore her. You're not alone when she's with you in the room. Even if she is not very intelligent you can sympathize with her and enter into her concerns, or be hostile to her and regard her as the enemy. In other words, she's the proper object of some of what Strawson called the reactive attitudes, or Hume called the indirect passions, because she is a someone.[16]

Because he is alive in a further sense, then, a person has an identity in a further sense. He has an identity that is constituted by his choices. This kind of identity is in a deeper way the person's own than an animal's identity, because he is consciously involved in its construction. And it is more essentially individual than a non-human animal's, because he is free. Constructing, creating, shaping, reshaping, maintaining, improving, in all these ways constituting this kind of identity is the everyday work of practical deliberation. And it is because we are characterized by this special kind of identity that a further stretch of the reactive attitudes is appropriate to us. It is because we have this kind of identity that we hold one another responsible, answerable, for what we do and what we are. It is this kind or level of identity I am talking about when I say we choose our own forms—the laws of our own causality.

6.4.6

Aristotle thought only God, or maybe the gods, had individual forms, but I've just claimed that it follows from his view that every human being has an individual form. Let me be clear about this. Your identity as a human animal, your human form, is given to you by nature, and you share it with the species.

---

[16] For Strawson, see "Freedom and Resentment," in *Freedom and Resentment and Other Essays*; for Hume see Book 2, parts 1 and 2, of the *Treatise*.

But the form of the human is precisely the form of the animal that must create its own form. For nature sets each human being a task: self-consciousness divides his soul into parts, and he must reconstitute his agency, pull himself back together, in order to act. And that need to reconstitute yourself introduces the necessity of exercising your freedom, and the opportunity of doing so creatively. In other words, every person must make himself into a particular person. So someone who says, "I want to make something of myself" is just describing the human condition. And it is because he makes himself into the particular person who he is that we hold him responsible for being who he is (1.4.3).

6.4.7

Yes, I did just say that. Sometimes you hear philosophers say that the idea of responsibility is incoherent, because we could not be responsible for what we do unless we are responsible for what we are, and we could not be responsible for what we are unless we created ourselves. I think it is true that we could not rightly be held responsible unless we created ourselves, but false that that makes the idea of responsibility incoherent. Philosophers who suppose that responsibility is incoherent are thinking of it this way: our actions spring from our nature, so we could not be responsible for the specific character of our actions unless we were responsible for our nature, and we could not be responsible for our nature unless we produced ourselves. And that makes no sense. But the sense in which we must create ourselves in order to be responsible is not that we must literally bring ourselves into being. Rather, we are responsible because we have a form of identity that is *constituted* by our chosen actions. We are responsible for our actions not because they are our products but because they are us, because we are what we do.

6.4.8

I don't intend to linger over this topic, interesting as it is, but I want to avert a possible misunderstanding of what I have just said. You might think I've just committed myself to the view that everyone is to be held completely responsible for every move he makes on the grounds that, after all, it's him. But I don't in the least mean to suggest either that we can *never* excuse someone for the performance of some particular action, or that we might not in general be hesitant about judging someone who has formed his identity under particularly disadvantageous conditions. I'm not really talking, at this point, about blaming people or punishing them or throwing them into jail. Behind those practices is something deeper and simpler, a basic condition of holding one another answerable, accountable in the most literal sense of the term, without which human relationships would not be intelligible at all.[17] It is because our actions are expressive of principles we ourselves have chosen, principles we have adopted as the laws of our own causality, that it makes sense for us to hold one another answerable in this way: to demand one another's reasons, and to take it, as we say, *personally*, when we hear what they are. As I've said before, actions are intelligible objects; our actions are no more just our products than our words are. And it makes no more sense to think that we might in general cease to hold people answerable for their actions than it does to think that we might in general cease to hold people answerable for their words.[18]

6.4.9

So we choose the principles of our own causality, and in doing so we constitute our identities as individual human agents. This doesn't mean, of course, that we choose the hypothetical and categorical imperatives themselves. The Kantian imperatives are principles that instruct us in *how* to formulate our maxims; autonomy and efficacy set standards for the form of our maxims. It is because for us constructing the will is in this way a *task*, that for us the standards of efficacy and autonomy take imperative form. And this shows both why and how the Kantian imperatives are normative for the human will. In 2.1.3, I said that a house-builder cannot completely ignore the normative standards inherent in the very idea of a house and still recognizably be building a house, because what it *means* to build a house is to be guided by those standards. In the same way, an agent who is deliberating about what to do cannot completely ignore the Kantian imperatives and still recognizably be deliberating about what to do, because what it *means* to deliberate is to be guided by those imperatives. Someone who is deliberating about what to do is deliberating about *how* to exercise his own causality, what the law of his own causality is to be. The hypothetical imperative directs him insofar *what* he is exercising is causality, and the categorical imperative directs him insofar as it is to be *his own*.

Of course an agent may not attend with much care to the standards set by the Kantian imperatives, just as a shoddy builder may not attend with much care to the standards set by the very idea of a house. But this does not show that one can intelligibly reject the normative standards expressed by those

---

[17] See my "Creating the Kingdom of Ends: Reciprocity and Responsibility in Personal Relations" (CKE essay 7).

[18] I'll have more to say about responsibility in 8.5.1.

imperatives. It only shows that one can deliberate badly. The kind of practical deliberation that issues in bad action is not a different activity from the kind of practical deliberation that issues in good action. *It is the same activity, badly done.*

6.4.10

But then what exactly does happen when an agent acts badly? Before we can answer that question, we need to look more closely at the kind of unity that deliberation maintains in the soul. That will be the task of the next chapter.

7

The Constitutional Model

7.1 Two Models of the Soul

7.1.1

In 6.2, I argued that self-consciousness produces the parts of the soul. It requires us to substitute principles of reason for our instincts, and it transforms our incentives into inclinations. At the same time, it makes it necessary for us to deliberate about what we are going to do. Since actions must be assignable to the person as a whole, the work of practical deliberation, the work that leads to action, is also a kind of reunification.

7.1.2

But there are different views about how this happens. One of the most famous sections of Hume's *Treatise* begins with these words:

Nothing is more usual in philosophy, and even in common life, than to talk of the combat of passion and reason, to give the preference to reason, and to assert that men are only so far virtuous as they conform themselves to its dictates. Every rational creature, 'tis said, is oblig'd to regulate his actions by reason; and if any other motive or principle challenge the direction of his conduct, he ought to oppose it, 'till it be entirely subdu'd, or at least brought to a conformity with that superior principle. (T 2.3.3,413)

As Hume understands these claims, reason and passion are two forces in the soul, each of them a source of motives to act, and virtue consists in the person following the dictate of reason. Why should the person do that? Hume tells us that in philosophy:

The eternity, invariableness, and divine origin of [reason] have been display'd to the best advantage: The blindness, unconstancy, and deceitfulness of [passion] have been as strongly insisted on. (T 2.3.3,413)

Hume proposes to show us "the fallacy of all this philosophy," but in his demonstration he does not exactly deny what I am going to call the "Combat Model" of the soul. He simply argues that reason is not after all a force, and therefore that there is no combat.

According to the Combat Model, the difference between reason and passion is pretty much the same as the difference between one passion and another: they are two forces, each urging a certain action upon the soul. Deliberative unification takes place when one side wins. There are actually two versions of the Combat Model, but neither of them enables us to make any sense of the idea of action. According to the first version, the person's actions are just the result of the play, or rather of the combat, of these forces within her. But as we have seen before, action cannot just be the result of forces working in or on an agent. If the movement is to be assignable to the agent in the way that the idea of action requires, then the agent must be something over and above the forces working in her and on her, something that can intelligibly be said to determine herself to action.

Now it may seem as if the obvious way to solve this problem is to bring the person, the agent, back into the picture, and to say that she chooses between reason and passion. And Hume's description suggests this—the person, he says, "gives the preference" to reason. But this second version of the Combat Model is even more perplexing than the first. For what is the essence of this person, in whom reason and passion are both forces, *neither* of them identified with the person herself, and between which she is to choose? And if the person identifies neither with reason nor with passion, then how—on what principle—can she possibly choose between them? The philosophers Hume describes here seem to be imagining that the person chooses between reason and passion by assessing their merits—reason is divine and reliable, passion blind and misleading. But surely that presupposes that the person *already* identifies with reason, since that is the part of us that assesses merits. How then could the person ever choose passion over reason? The Combat Model does not enable us to form any picture of this agent who supposedly chooses between reason and passion. And this is not surprising, for on the first version of the Combat Model there is no agent, while the second version presupposes an agent who can have no essence and who must always already exist.

7.1.3

The tradition supplies us with another model of the interaction between reason and passion in the soul, which makes better sense, because it assigns them functional and structural differences. I call it the Constitutional Model, because its clearest appearance is in Plato's *Republic*, where the human soul is compared to the constitution of a *polis* or city-state. The Constitutional Model, unlike the first version of the Combat Model, conceives the agent as something over and above her parts. But the agent is not, as in the second version of the Combat Model, a separately existing entity who chooses to identify with one of those parts. Instead, the agent is something over and above her parts in the way that the constitution of a city is something over and above the citizens and officials who live there. If the agent conforms to the dictate of reason, it is not because she identifies with reason, but rather because she identifies with her constitution, and it says that reason should rule. Following Plato, in this chapter I will argue that using this model we can explain action, because we can explain how an agent achieves the kind of unity that makes it possible to attribute her movements to her as their author.

7.2 The City and the Soul

7.2.1

Let me start by reminding you how the Constitutional Model gets on the table. In Book 1 of the *Republic*, Socrates and his friends discuss the question what justice is. The discussion is interrupted by Thrasymachus, who asserts that the best life is the unjust life, the life lived by the strong, who impose the laws of justice on the weak but ignore those laws themselves. The more completely unjust you are, Thrasymachus says, the better you will live, for pickpockets and thieves, who commit small injustices, get punished, while tyrants, who enslave whole cities and steal their treasuries, lead a glorious life, and are the envy of everyone. Socrates, distracted by these claims, drops the discussion of what justice is, and takes up the question whether the just or the unjust life is the best (R 336b–348e).

7.2.2

Socrates proceeds to construct three arguments designed to show that the just life is best. The one that is important to us goes like this: Socrates asks Thrasymachus whether a band of robbers and thieves with a common unjust purpose would be able to achieve that purpose if they were unjust to each other. Thrasymachus agrees that they could not do that. Justice, as Socrates says, is what brings a sense of common purpose to a group, while injustice causes hatred and civil war, and makes the group "incapable of achieving anything as a unit." Thrasymachus is then induced to agree that justice and injustice have the same effect wherever they occur, and therefore, the same effect within the individual human soul as they have in a group. Injustice, therefore, makes an individual "incapable of achieving anything, because he is in a state of civil war and not of one mind." The more complete this condition is the worse it is, for as Socrates tells us "those who are all bad and completely unjust are completely incapable of accomplishing anything" (R 351b–352c).[1]

7.2.3

Now, there's nothing obviously wrong with this argument, except of course that it flies in the teeth of the fact that we seem to see unjust people all around us, doing and accomplishing things right and left. So what can Socrates be talking about? The argument leaves his audience puzzled and dissatisfied. So Plato's brothers, Glaucon and Adeimantus, demand that Socrates return to the abandoned question, what justice is, and what effect it has in the soul. It is this demand that sets Plato off on his attempt to identify justice in a larger and more visible object, the ideal city, and his famous comparison between the city and the soul.

7.2.4

Let me review the main elements of that comparison. Plato identifies three classes in the city. First there are the rulers, who make the laws and policies for the city, and handle its relations with other cities. Second, there are the auxiliaries, a kind of combination of soldier and police force, who enforce the laws within the city and also defend it from external enemies, following the orders of the rulers. The rulers are drawn from the ranks of these auxiliaries, and the two groups together are called the guardians. And finally there are the farmers, craftspeople, merchants, and so forth, who provide for the city's needs.

The virtues of the ideal city are then identified with certain properties of and relations between these parts. The wisdom of the city rests in the wisdom of its rulers (R 428b–429a). We aren't told much about this at first, except that the rulers of the ideal city, unlike Thrasymachus's rulers, rule with a view to the good of the city as a whole, and not just for their own good (R 342e, 412d–e). The courage of the city rests in the courage of its auxiliaries, which is identified with their capacity to preserve certain beliefs, which are instilled in them by the rulers, about what is to be feared—to preserve them in the face of temptation, pleasure, pain, and fear itself (R 429a–430d). The

---

[1] The other two arguments are the "outdoing" argument used to establish that justice is a form of virtue and knowledge (R 349a–350d), and the function argument used to establish that the just person is happiest (R 352d–354a).

auxiliaries are able to hold onto their belief, for instance, that nothing is more to be feared than the loss of the city's freedom, even in the face of danger to themselves. The city's *sophrosyne*—its moderation or temperance—rests in the agreement of all the classes in the city about who should rule and be ruled (R 430d–432b). And its justice rests in the fact that each class in the city does its own work, and no one tries to meddle in the work of anyone else (R 433a–434d).

7.2.5

Plato then undertakes to find the same three parts in the human soul. The Constitutional Model, like the Combat Model, starts off from the experience of inner conflict. Socrates puts it forth as a principle that "the same thing will not be willing to do or undergo opposites in the same part of itself, in relation to the same thing, at the same time" (R 436b–c). So if we find in the soul opposite attitudes or reactions to a single object at a single moment, we must suppose that the soul has parts. Accordingly, what alerts us to the distinction between reason and the appetites is the experience of refusing to satisfy our own appetites even as we experience them. For example, Socrates tells us, the soul of a thirsty person wishes to drink and is impelled towards drinking (R 439b). If the soul at the same time draws back from drinking, it must be with a different part. And this is an experience people have—as Socrates says, there are thirsty people who don't wish to drink. It happens, for instance, when they judge that the drink will be bad for them. So Socrates concludes:

> Isn't it that there is something in their soul, bidding them to drink, and something different, forbidding them to do so, that overrules the thing that bids? . . . Doesn't that which forbids in such cases come into play . . . as a result of rational calculation? (R 439c–d)

So reason and appetite must be two different parts of the soul.

7.2.6

As Socrates points out, there is a tempting way to try to block this division of the soul into parts. We could try to claim that the thirsty soul that refuses the bad drink actually only wanted a *good* drink, so that the rejected drink was not the object of its appetite after all. In this way, the appearance that the soul is wholehearted is restored, and we need not conclude that the soul has parts. But Socrates has already laid the ground against this sort of move, by making an argument against the existence of what we might call "essentially qualified appetites" (R 436c–439a). If an appetite is qualified—so that if what one wants is specifically a *hot* drink or a *cold* drink or a *good* drink—then something complicated is going on, either some calculating or some compounding—which is not simply part of the appetite itself.[2] Thirst itself, Socrates says, is not for a cold drink or a hot drink, but simply for a drink, and if it is qualified, say if one would prefer a cold drink, this must be the result of "additions," as for instance when you are hot as well as thirsty. So Socrates proposes that we shouldn't let his argument be derailed by someone who suggests that the apparently conflicted person really only wanted a good drink, on the grounds that people always desire the good. Quite apart from this move being false to the experience of conflict, it is a cheat, for it effectively tries to conceal the operations of "rational calculation"—the quest for the good—within the appetite itself.

7.2.7

Socrates says that he makes this argument "in order to avoid disputes later on" (R 436c), but the precaution didn't take, for the same sort of move that Socrates is warning us against here is a commonplace in the theory of rationality popular in economics and the social sciences, and we've actually come across it before (3.3.3). According to the economic theory of rationality, it is rational for each person to try to maximize his own welfare. Many economists who believe this theory of rationality *think* that they also believe the theory that the only form of practical reason is instrumental reason. Yet as I argued before, this combination of ideas is incoherent on its surface, for the principle of taking the means to our ends of course says nothing whatever about what our ends should be, and therefore cannot say that we ought to pursue our maximum welfare, and prefer it to more immediate or local satisfactions. The economic theory of rationality has to involve some principle of reason that goes beyond the instrumental, some principle that assigns us our maximum welfare as an *end*. How do the defenders of this theory of rationality manage to avoid acknowledging this? They simply *assume* that everyone wants *good* things, and therefore that people's real desires are for things that count by this standard as "good"—things that are consistent with their maximum welfare. Quite

---

[2] By "compounding," I mean the phenomenon Socrates describes in these words: "where heat is present as well as thirst, it causes the appetite to be for something cold as well" (R 437d–e). That might be one reason why the thirsty soul refuses a drink, but the appetite may also be misnamed, as Socrates goes on to explain. For instance, there might be a particular appetite which we call being thirsty-for-a-hot-drink, which is misnamed because it is actually not a version of thirst at all, but just a desire for a certain internal warming sensation.

apart from this move being false to the experience of conflict, it is a cheat, for it effectively tries to conceal the operations of rational calculation within the appetite itself.

7.2.8

In fact, however, Socrates's emphasis on conflict is slightly misleading, for even if there is no conflict, two parts of the soul can be discerned. Suppose instead that the drink has nothing wrong with it, and the person who is thirsty does drink. In this kind of case, Socrates says,

> the soul of someone who has an appetite for a thing wants what he has an appetite for and takes to himself what it is his will to have, and . . . insofar as he wishes something to be given to him, his soul, since it desires this to come about, nods assent to it as if in answer to a question. (R 437c)

The complexity of this passage is not an accident or a mistake. The soul that drinks in response to thirst does so not merely because it has an appetite to drink, but because it "nods assent to [the appetite] as if in answer to a question." Having an appetite for something and giving that appetite the nod are not the same thing. The soul does not act from appetite, but from something that endorses the appetite and says yes to it. Even when conflict is absent, then, we can see that there are two parts of the soul. To put it Kant's way: in the human soul, the experience of choosing to act on an incentive—the experience of adopting a principle—is distinct from the experience of the incentive itself (6.2.4). That's what Socrates is talking about here.

7.2.9

Socrates also argues, less familiarly to the modern reader, that there is a third part of the soul, *thymos* or spirit, which is distinct from both reason and appetite, although it is the natural ally of reason. That it is distinct from appetite shows up in the fact that anger and indignation, which are manifestations of spirit, are often directed against the appetites themselves. This is illustrated by the story of Leontius, who was disgusted at himself for wanting to look at some corpses, and berated his own eyes for the evil appetites which they harbored (R 439e–440a). The story also shows, according to Socrates, that spirit is the ally of reason. He says:

> don't we often notice in other cases that when appetite forces someone contrary to rational calculation, he reproaches himself and gets angry with that in him that's doing the forcing, so that of the two factions which are fighting a civil war, so to speak, spirit

allies itself with reason? But I don't think you can say that you've ever seen spirit, either in yourself or anyone else, ally itself with an appetite to do what reason has decided must not be done. (R 440a–b)

Spirit, as Socrates brings out more clearly in Book 8, is the sense of honor (R 548c), protective of the dignity and value of the self—and Plato's claim here is that the sense of honor is the natural ally of reason. Although spirit always fights on reason's side, it is distinct from reason, for it is present in small children and animals who don't have reason; and, furthermore, it may need to be controlled by reason. Socrates establishes this last point by invoking a quotation from Homer: *He struck his chest and spoke to his heart.* Socrates comments that, "here Homer clearly represents the part that has calculated about better and worse as different from the part that is angry without calculation" (R 441b–c).

7.2.10

Socrates does not, however, make any comment on the important assumption that has quietly slipped in here, namely, that the person speaks when his reason speaks. For the *"He"* in that Homeric quotation refers to both the person and to his reason. Is the person then to be identified with his reason? And does that mean he fails to identify with his appetites and his spirit, regarding them merely as forces at work within him, which he, being identified with his reason, must control? How different would that be from the Combat Model after all? But the analogy to the city shows that this cannot be right. For the rulers in the city, since they are supposed to govern for the good of the whole, are chosen partly by determining which of the auxiliaries most thoroughly identify with the city as a whole. As Socrates explains:

someone loves something most of all when he believes that the same things are advantageous to it as to himself and supposes that if it does well, he'll do well, and that if it does badly, then he'll do badly too. . . . Then we must choose from among our guardians those men who, upon examination, seem most of all to believe throughout their lives that they must eagerly pursue what is advantageous to the city and be wholly unwilling to do the opposite. (R 412d–e)

The rulers identify with the city as a whole; by the analogy, then, reason identifies with the person as a whole. If reason identifies with the person as a whole, then the person, in identifying with reason, cannot be distancing himself from his appetites and his spirit. Why then is the *"He"* in that Homeric quotation attached at once to reason and to the person, while spirit stands as the thing addressed? The Constitutional Model again supplies the answer. A city is not identical to its rulers, and yet its rulers do speak for it. They do so because the constitution gives them that role. So the answer is that a person does not, except indirectly, identify with his reason. Rather, he identifies with his constitution, which assigns to reason his voice. It is because of this, not because of an identification with reason, that we say of the imprudent person that his passion got the better not just of his reason but of *him*.

7.2.11

By these arguments Socrates establishes that the soul has the same three parts as the city. Reason corresponds to the rulers and its function is to direct things, for the good of the whole person. Spirit corresponds to the auxiliaries and its function is to carry out the orders of reason. The appetites correspond to the rest of the citizens, whose business is to supply the whole person with whatever he needs.

Now if the soul has parts the question is going to arise what makes them one, what unifies them into a single soul. And part of the answer is that the parts of the soul must be unified—they *need* to be unified, like the people in a city—in order to act. Specifically, we can see the three parts of the soul as corresponding to three parts of a deliberative action. Deliberative action begins from the fact we have certain appetites and desires. We are conscious of these, and they invite us to do certain actions or seek certain ends. Since we are self-conscious, however, we do not act on our appetites and desires automatically, but instead decide whether to satisfy them or not. And then finally there is carrying the decision out—actually doing what we have decided to do. For of course we don't always do what we have decided to do, but are sometimes distracted by temptation, pleasure, pain, and fear from the course we have set for ourselves. So we can identify three parts of a deliberative action corresponding to Plato's three parts of the soul, namely:

Appetite makes a proposal.
Reason decides whether to act on it or not.
Spirit carries the decision of reason out.

This line of thought supports Plato's analogy between the city and the soul. For a city also engages in deliberative action: it is not just a place to live, but rather a kind of agent that performs actions and so has a life and a history. And we can see the same three parts in a political decision. The people of the city make a proposal: they say that there is something that they need. They ask for schools, or better health care, or more police protection. The rulers then decide whether to act on the proposal or not. They say either "yes" or "no" to the people. And then the auxiliaries carry the decision of the rulers out. And it is only when this happens, when these procedures are followed, that we attribute the action to the city. If a Spartan attacks an Athenian, for instance, we do not conclude that *Sparta* is making war on Athens, unless the attack was made by a soldier acting under the direction of the Spartan rulers: that is, unless it issues from Sparta's constitutional procedures. According to the analogy, we will only attribute an action to a person, rather than to something in him, if it was the result of his reason acting on a proposal from his inclination—or, to put it in Kant's terms, if it is the result of an incentive having been adopted in accordance with a principle.

7.2.12

In fact, the main purpose of a literal political constitution is precisely to lay out the city's mode of deliberative action, the procedures by which its collective decisions are to be made and carried out. A constitution defines a set of roles and offices that together constitute a procedure for deliberative action, saying who shall perform each step and how it shall be done. It lays out the proper ways of making proposals (say by petition, or the introduction of bills, or whatever), of deciding whether to act on these proposals (that's the legislative function), and of carrying the resulting decisions out (the executive function). And it says who is supposed to carry out the various steps in the procedures it has specified. The constitution in this way makes it possible for a group of citizens—who without the constitution would be a *mere heap* of individual people—to function as a single collective agent.

7.3 Platonic Virtues

7.3.1

What Plato says about the specific nature of the virtues—wisdom, courage, temperance, and justice—supports this picture. As I've already mentioned, at this point in the *Republic*—we are in Book 4—Plato has not said anything substantive about the nature of wisdom. He has told us only that it rests in the rulers of the city or the rational and calculative part of the soul, and that it is concerned with the good of the whole. The focus of the discussion here will be on the other three virtues: courage, temperance, and justice itself.[3]

---

[3] I won't be discussing Platonic wisdom, but Plato's view of it is given in the quotation in 9.1.4 (R 443d–444a); it is the knowledge that "oversees" just action, where just action is action that unifies the soul.

7.3.2

Socrates claims that the courage of the city is found in the auxiliaries and consists in:

> preservation of the belief that has been inculcated by the law through education about what things and sorts of things are to be feared. And by preserving this belief "through everything," I mean preserving it and not abandoning it because of pains, pleasures, desires, or fears. (R 429c–d)

Since courage rests in the auxiliaries, who carry out the orders of the rulers, Socrates seems to have in mind something like this. Suppose the rulers go to the auxiliaries and say:

> We have learned that the Spartans are planning to invade our republic. You must keep them outside of the walls at any cost. As we have always taught you, nothing is more to be feared than the loss of our liberty to a foreign power. A Spartan takeover is a worse thing, and more to be feared, than your own death or injury.

If the auxiliaries have absorbed these beliefs thoroughly and permanently, then they will fight to the death to keep the Spartans outside of the gates. Indeed, it will seem to them to be obviously worth it to die for this goal, so they will fight with conviction and determination. And in that case, the city will be courageous.

There are several interesting things to notice about this account. First, Socrates' definition does not imply that the soldiers are not afraid of injury and death. The important thing is that they are *more* afraid of losing the city to the Spartans. To them, the thought of failing in their mission is of a thing so terrible that it is worth dying to avoid it. So the definition does not require them to be unafraid. It requires them to fear the right things, in the right order, so that they will keep hold of the city's beliefs about *what is worth what*. In other words, courage is a virtue that supports *actions*, and not merely acts, in the sense I described in 1.2.

It is also worth noting the special role that fear plays in this definition, which is rather different than what we might have expected. We might have expected Socrates to say that *fear* is the force that causes us to lose hold of our belief about what is to be *done*, and that courage is the virtue that prevents this from happening. But that's not what he says: what he says is that pleasures, pains, desires, and fears *all* cause us to lose hold of our belief about what is to be *feared*. In including these different causes of the loss of belief, Socrates seems to broaden the definition of courage to the point where it hardly seems different from will-power in general. Nearly all of the forces that tend to undermine our ability to carry out our decisions are included here. Yet, in saying that the preserved belief concerns not what is to be *done* but more specifically what is to be *feared*, Socrates brings us back to the fact that he is focusing on a property of *spirit* in particular. In making it a *belief* about what is to be *feared*, I think Plato is trying to capture the idea that spirit is something with both a cognitive and an affective aspect. There is an affective dimension to courage: spirit *recoils* from the loss of the city's liberty, regarding that as something to be feared. The courageous person, in other words, does not merely *believe* that the loss of the city is something to be feared—he *perceives* it that way (6.1.4). The structure of courage is complex: the city or person as a whole is able to retain its belief about what is to be *done* in the face of fear and temptation *because* the spirited part retains its belief about what is to be *feared* in the face of those forces. In this way, courage, or the sense of honor, is the guardian of deliberative action.

7.3.3

There does not seem to be anything corresponding to spirit in Kant's account of the divisions of the soul, and in the *Groundwork* Kant, rather oddly, characterizes honor as the object of an inclination (G 4:398). Yet Kant, like Plato, sometimes emphasizes the role of the sense of honor as a natural ally of reason. In his "Idea for a Universal History with a Cosmopolitan Purpose," Kant calls the love of honor a "semblance" of morality. He says that those who are moved by it are not yet "morally mature" and the stage when it prevails is "merely civilized" rather than really good (IUH 8:26). Yet the stage is one that humanity has to pass through on its way to being good, just as a Platonic ruler must be educated first as an auxiliary. In the discussion of punishment in *The Metaphysics of Morals*, Kant suggests that people who commit murder from motives of honor, such as young officers who become involved in duels, should perhaps not be subject to capital punishment. Legislation itself, Kant urges, is responsible for the fact that these people are still morally backwards, so that the incentives of honor are not yet attached to the measures that are "suitable for its purpose" (MM 6:337). In this passage Kant again seems to regard honor as something more primitive and immature than reason, but there is no suggestion here that it can be dispensed with altogether. The discussion of courage and honor in Kant's *Anthropology* is startlingly Platonic, and with an interesting wrinkle. Courage is defined as "the mind's self-control by which it takes charge of the danger with reflection" (ANTH 7:256). To Plato's list of the forces that can cause us to lose hold of our beliefs about what is to be feared—pains, pleasures, desires, and fears—Kant is especially concerned to add humiliation. He says:

courage as an affect (and so as belonging, on one side, to sensibility) can also be aroused by reason and, accordingly, be true fortitude (strength of virtue). If, when we are doing something worthy of honor, we are not intimidated by taunts and by caustic derision of it, which is all the more dangerous for being sharpened by wit, but pursue our course resolutely, we show a moral courage not to be found in many who cut brave figures on the battlefield or in a duel. In other words, the fixity of purpose by which we venture something that duty commands, even at the risk of being ridiculed by others, requires an even higher degree of courage; for *love of honor* is the constant companion of virtue, and even a man who is, otherwise, sufficiently composed in the face of *violence* seldom feels equal to the derision that jeeringly denies his claim to honor. (ANTH 7:257)

Facing humiliation requires a higher degree of courage than facing violence because the threat to one's resolution—or in Socrates' terms, to the ability to preserve your belief about what is to be feared—originates not in fears and appetites but in the sense of honor *itself*.

7.3.4

That actually gives rise to a question. Spirit controls appetite in the face of temptation, pleasure, pain, and fear, according to Plato; if spirit has to control *itself* in the face of humiliation, as Kant's view suggests, must there then be parts to spirit? For Plato's rule, that "the same thing will not be willing to do or undergo opposites at the same time" seems to apply to spirit as well, and so to require a division. Later, as we will see, Plato says of the just person that, "He binds together [the three] parts *and any others there may be in between . . .*" (R 443d; my emphasis). Surprisingly, after what seemed like a lot of bother over the question just how many parts there are in the soul, it turns out that there could be more. The truth is that self-consciousness can ramify the number of parts that there are in the soul as much as you like. *It does not matter to the argument how many parts there are.*

7.3.5

Socrates next discusses *sophrosyne*—moderation or temperance. It is here that he remarks, as I mentioned before (1.1.3) that phrases like "self-control" or "self-command," which people use in connection with this virtue, seem absurd on their surface, since the same person who is doing the controlling is also the one who gets controlled. More specifically, he says these phrases are like "tracks or clues" that the virtue has "left behind in language" (R 430e) to show us that the soul has both a ruled and a ruling part.

There's a parallel but slightly more complicated argument in Kant, in the *Metaphysics of Morals*, where he discusses the question of duties to the self.

He first argues that the idea of a duty to oneself seems like a contradiction. He says:

> If the I *that imposes obligation* is taken in the same sense as the I *that is put under obligation*, a duty to oneself is a self-contradictory concept. For the concept of duty contains the concept of being passively constrained (I am *bound*). But if the duty is a duty to myself, I think of myself as *binding* and so as actively constraining (I, the same subject, am imposing obligation). (MM 6:417)

We could put his argument in exactly Plato's terms. If "the same thing will not be willing to do or undergo opposites at the same time" then I cannot all at once and in the same part of myself be both actively constraining and passively constrained. And yet, Kant goes on to argue, there *must* be duties to the self, for if duties spring from autonomy then all duties are ultimately self-imposed. Good arguments for opposite conclusions leave us with an antinomy, which like all antinomies must be solved by the distinction between noumena and phenomena—the active and passive aspects of the self (MM 6:418). So the self has aspects or parts. In the course of this discussion Kant also finds a track or clue in the language. "So when it is a question, for example, of vindicating my honor or of preserving myself, I say, 'I owe it to myself'" (MM 6:418 n.).

7.3.6

In a city that has *sophrosyne*, "the desires of the inferior many are controlled by the wisdom and desires of the superior few" (R 431c–d). In the corresponding person, the appetitive part is controlled by the wisdom and desires of reason. As I said before, we haven't yet seen what wisdom consists in, but reason's desire is, or at least includes, the good of the whole. The control Socrates is talking about here is not forceful constraint or repression, however, for he says that the virtue consists in an *agreement*, a belief *shared* by all the classes in the city, about which class should rule (R 431d–e; 442c–d). In general, the tradespeople and auxiliaries accept the rule of the rulers, and identify with their edicts. And the rulers also identify with the appetites and passions of the tradespeople and auxiliaries, for as Plato explains later, the best city is the one in which "as far as possible, all the citizens rejoice and are pained by the same successes and failures" (R 462b). It is "the city that is most like a single person":

> For example, when one of us hurts his finger, the entire organism that binds body and soul together into a single system under the ruling part within it is aware of this, and the whole feels the pain together with the part that suffers. That's why we say that the man has a pain in his finger. (R 462c–d)

In the same way, in a moderate or temperate person, all parts of the soul "agree" that reason should rule and the other parts should be ruled.

The kind of self-command or self-control that Socrates is describing here is not that of the Reformed Miserable Sinner, whose desires must be repressed in the name of duty (1.1.3). Yet neither is there any implication that the desires by themselves could be so perfectly orderly, so spontaneously aimed at the good, that they don't need to be ruled at all. Recall once again the argument against essentially qualified appetites—desires by their nature are not *for the good*, but for various particular objects.[4] Generally speaking, in the temperate or moderate person, if reason does not accept the proposals of appetite, then the appetites back off gracefully. Yet should the appetites from time to time rebel, the auxiliaries are armed: constitutional rule is still essentially coercive, as all government must be. The presence of the sense of honor in the soul is a standing reminder to the appetites that after all they must obey. So *necessitation* does exist in the Platonic soul, but it does not take the form of active, forcible repression. It is simply the *work* of government—the constant and everyday fact of coercive constitutional rule.

7.3.7

So the function of appetite is to propose and obey, of reason to rule, and of spirit to ensure that reason's decisions get carried out. The parts of the soul are not—at least not when the soul is in order—contenders for power, but rather each has its own work to do, and together they make collective action—that is to say, action—possible. And this explains Socrates' puzzling definition of justice. Justice, he says, is "doing one's own work and not meddling with what isn't one's own" (R 433a–b). When Socrates first introduces this principle into the discussion (R 369e–370d), he's talking about the specialization of labor, and that's what the principle sounds like it's about.[5] But if we think of the constitution as laying out the procedures for deliberative action, and the roles and offices that constitute those procedures, we can see what Socrates' point is. For usurping the office of another in the constitutional procedures for collective action is *precisely* what we mean by injustice, or at least it is one thing

---

[4] This point play an essential role in many of the arguments advanced by Joseph Butler, the 18th-century philosopher who made most explicit use of the Constitutional Model, in his *Fifteen Sermons Preached at the Rolls Chapel*. Butler uses it to argue that both self-love and conscience have a kind of natural authority over the particular passions (they direct the particular passions towards good) in Sermons 1–3, and in an effective argument against egoism in Sermons 11–12 (4–5 of the Darwall edn.).

[5] Socrates not only openly acknowledges this oddity later on, but actually suggests that the principle of the specialization of labor is "beneficial" because it is "a sort of image of justice" (R 443c).

we mean. For instance if the constitution says that the president cannot make war without the agreement of the congress, and yet he does, then he has usurped the congress's role in this decision, and that's unjust. If the constitution says that each citizen gets to cast one vote in the election, and through some fraud you manage to vote more than once, you are diminishing the voice of others in the election, and that's unjust. So injustice, in one of its most familiar senses, is usurping the role of another in the deliberative procedures that define collective action. It is meddling with somebody else's work.

7.4 Justice: Substantive, Procedural, and Platonic

7.4.1

I said "in one sense," for this is very much what is sometimes called a *procedural* conception of justice, as opposed to a *substantive* one. This distinction represents an important tension in our concept of justice, and a standing cause of confusion about the source of its normativity. On the one hand, the idea of justice essentially involves the idea of following certain procedures. In the state, as I have been saying, these are the procedures which the constitution lays down for collective deliberative action: for making laws, waging wars, trying cases, collecting taxes, distributing services, and all of the various things that a state does. According to the procedural conception of justice, an action of the state is just if, and only if, it is the outcome of actually and correctly following these procedures. That is a *law* which has been passed in form by a duly constituted legislature; this law is *constitutional* if (say) the supreme court says that it is; a person is *innocent* of a certain crime when he has been deemed so by a jury; someone is *the president* if he meets the legal qualifications and has been duly voted in, and so forth. These are all normative judgments—the terms *law, constitutional, innocent,* and *president* all imply the existence of certain reasons for action—and their normativity *derives from* the carrying out of the procedures that have established them.

On the other hand, however, there are certainly cases in which we have some idea of what outcome the procedures ought to generate. These ideas serve as the criteria for our more substantive judgments—in some cases, of what is just, in other cases, simply of what is right or best. And these substantive judgments can come in conflict with the actual outcomes of carrying out the procedures. Perhaps the law is unconstitutional, although it has been passed by the legislature or even upheld by the supreme court; perhaps the defendant is guilty, though the jury has set him free; perhaps the candidate elected is not the best person for the job, or even the best of those who ran, or perhaps due to the accidents of voter turnout he does not really represent the majority will.

As this last example shows, the distinction between the procedurally just and the substantively just, right, or best, is a rough and ready one, and relative to the case under consideration. Who should be elected? The person who best represents the general will, the person who comes closest to this of those who actually run, the person preferred by the majority of the citizens, the person preferred by the majority of the registered voters, the person actually elected by the majority of those who turn out on election day . . . As we go down that list, the answer to the question becomes increasingly procedural; the answer above it is, relatively, more substantive. We may try to design our procedures to secure the substantively right or best outcome. But—and here is the important point—according to the procedural conception of justice, the normativity of these procedures nevertheless does not spring from the goodness, rightness, or even the substantive justice of the outcomes they produce. The reverse is true: it is the procedures themselves—or rather the actual carrying out of the procedures—that confers normativity on those outcomes. The person who gets elected holds the office, no matter how far he is from being the true representative of the general will. The jury's acquittal stands, though we later come to believe that after all the defendant was guilty.

Now if the normativity of the outcomes springs from the carrying out of the procedures, where, we may ask, does the normativity of the procedures themselves come from? Why must we follow them? And here we run into the cause of confusion I mentioned at the outset, for there is a standing temptation to believe that the procedures themselves must derive their normativity from the substantively good quality of their outcomes. That cannot be right, as I've just been saying, since if the normativity of our procedures came from the substantive quality of their outcomes, then we'd be prepared to set those procedures aside when we knew that their outcomes were going to be poor ones. And as I've also just been saying, we don't do that. Where constitutional procedures are in place, substantive rightness, goodness, or even justice is neither necessary nor sufficient for the normative standing of their outcomes: all that is necessary is that the procedures have actually been followed.

Perhaps you may now be tempted to say that what makes the procedures normative is the *usual* quality of their outcomes, the fact that they get it right most of the time. After all, even if we do stand by the outcomes of our procedures though in this or that case they are bad, we would certainly change those procedures if their outcomes were bad *too often*. But this cannot be the whole answer, not only because it isn't always true—think of the jury system—but also because, as act utilitarians have been telling us for years, it is irrational to follow a procedure merely because it usually gets a good outcome, when you know that this time it will get a bad one. So perhaps we should say instead that the normativity of the procedures comes from the usual quality of their outcomes *combined* with the fact that we must have some such procedures, and we must stand by their results. But *why* must we have some such procedures? Because without them collective action is impossible. And now we've come around to Plato's view. In order to act together—to make laws and policies, apply them, and enforce them—in a way that represents, not some of us tyrannizing over others, but all of us acting together as a unit—we must have a constitution that defines the procedures for collective deliberative action, and we must stand by its results.

7.4.2

It may seem as if I am suggesting that we just have two separate conceptions of justice, substantive and procedural, but that is not the case, as I will now try to make clear. As I have already suggested, the procedural conception of justice comes from the need to have procedures that constitute the state's deliberative processes and so its agency. So where does the substantive conception come from? Here there are different kinds of cases. It is easiest to explain this point by starting from a slightly different view.

In *A Theory of Justice*, Rawls distinguishes three cases of procedural justice. First there is perfect procedural justice, where we know the desired outcome and can design a procedure that achieves it. Rawls's example involves a bunch of people dividing a cake—assuming that everyone wants as large a share as possible, and that the desired outcome is equal shares, the procedure is to give the person who cuts the cake the last piece after the others have chosen. Assuming the person chosen is not too clumsy to cut evenly, this will work. Imperfect procedural justice is where we know the desired outcome but cannot design a procedure that guarantees the outcome: Rawls's example is a criminal trial. Assuming that the desired outcome is conviction of the guilty and exoneration of the innocent, we cannot design a flawless procedure, but do our best. Pure procedural justice exists in a case where the desirability of the outcome depends entirely on the carrying out of the procedures; there is no independent criterion. Rawls's example is gambling. Prior to the game there is nothing we can say about who ought to win; supposing that the table isn't rigged and that nobody cheats, any outcome of the play is equally good.[6]

Now this is obviously very plausible; and yet, as we have already seen, I have claimed that in the political context all of these cases must be treated like

---

[6] Rawls, *A Theory of Justice*, section 14.

the third case, the case of pure procedural justice. That is, in all cases, even the heartbreaking case of the criminal trial, the *normative* outcome, the one we must stand by, is the one that follows from the procedures, even when there is an independently defined *desirable* outcome and we know what it is. Why is that? The function of justice is to enable the state to function as a unified agent, and here again it helps to recall that the object of an agent's choice, and the bearer of moral value is what, in 1.2.5, I called an "action," not a mere "act". This means that the talk of knowing which outcomes would be just is a little misleading, because strictly speaking justice itself is a property of actions, not of outcomes. So it is not quite right to say that what justice requires is that *the guilty should be punished*; rather, what justice requires is that *the state should punish the guilty on account of his guilt*. This is why a lynching does *not* count as the next best thing. This is not of course to say that the state, as a state, shouldn't design the best possible procedures for identifying guilt and innocence: the instrumental principle is an aspect of the law that governs action, and the state is bound by it like any other agent.

But the cases where there is a substantive notion of *justice* are a little different. As I mentioned earlier, in many cases the distinction between procedural and substantive justice seems rough and essentially comparative. When we compare "the candidate preferred by the majority of registered voters" to "the candidate actually elected," the first seems more substantive and the second more procedural. But when we compare "the candidate preferred by the majority of registered voters" to "the candidate preferred by the majority of the citizens," then the first seems more procedural compared to the second. And when we compare all of these to "the candidate who best represents the will of the people," they all seem procedural, and like very imperfect procedures indeed. This may seem to suggest that a substantive notion of justice is, so to speak, at the top of the hierarchy, and all procedures are mere imperfect attempts to realize or embody it. But I think that exactly the opposite is true. For we do not really have an independent notion of the will of the people, or, rather, to the extent that we do it is a procedural, if somewhat fuzzy, notion: the will of the people is something we know we must arrive at by somehow consulting each citizen and making sure his or her point of view is fairly represented in the final decision. So it turns out that what we mean by "the more substantive notion of justice" is "whatever would result from applying a more ideal procedure" and what we mean by "the most substantive notion of justice" is "whatever would result from applying the most ideal procedure." The most ideal procedure, according to Plato, as we are about to see, is the procedure that really makes the city one, the procedure that unifies its agency completely. But that's not an independent goal that the most ideal procedure achieves as a kind of result. That is just what it *means* to have the most ideal procedure. So as we move towards the top of the hierarchy the two notions simply come together, or if we privilege either, it must be the procedural notion.[7]

7.4.3

So according to Plato, the normative force of the constitution *consists* in the fact that it makes it possible for the city to function as a single unified agent. For a city without justice, according to Plato, above all lacks unity—it is not one city, he says, but many (R 422d–423c; see also R 462a–e). When justice breaks down, the city falls into civil war, as the rulers, the soldiers, and the people all struggle for control. The deliberative procedures that unify the city into a single agent break down, and the city *as such* cannot act. The individual citizens and classes within it may still perform various actions, but the city cannot act as a unit.

And this applies to justice and injustice within the individual person as well. Socrates says:

> One who is just does not allow any part of himself to do the work of another part or allow the various classes within him to meddle with each other. He regulates well what is really his own and rules himself. He puts himself in order, is his own friend, and harmonizes the three parts of himself like three limiting notes in a musical scale—high, low, and middle. He binds together those parts and any others there may be in between, and from having been many things he becomes entirely one, moderate and harmonious. *Only then does he act.* (R 443d–e; my emphasis)

But if justice is what makes it possible for a person to function as a single unified agent, then injustice makes it impossible. Civil war breaks out between appetite, spirit, and reason, each trying to usurp the roles and offices of the others. The deliberative procedures that unify the soul into a single agent break down, and the person *as such* cannot act. So Socrates's argument from Book 1 turns out to be true (7.2.2). Desires and impulses may operate within the unjust person, as individual citizens may operate within the unjust state. But the unjust *person* is "completely incapable of accomplishing anything" (R 352c) because the unjust *person* cannot act at all. Platonic justice is a constitutive principle of action.

---

[7] My thanks to David Dick for prompting me to clarify this point.

7.5 Kant and the Constitutional Model

7.5.1

One of the prevailing misconceptions about Kant is that he espouses the Combat Model of the soul. To see that Kant uses the Constitutional Model, we need only consider the argument he uses in the third section of the *Groundwork* to establish that the categorical imperative is the law of a rational will (G 4:446–8). Kant argues that insofar as you are a rational being, you must act under the idea of freedom. And a free will is one that is not determined by any alien cause—not determined by any law that it does not choose for itself. If you have a free will, then you are not, as Kant puts it, heteronomous. But Kant claims that the actions of a free will must be determined by some law or other. We have already looked at the argument for this in 4.4, the argument against particularistic willing, which shows that the will must always determine itself in accordance with some universal law. Since, if you have a free will, you cannot be heteronomous, and yet you must have a law, then you must be autonomous—you must act on a law that you legislate for yourself. And Kant says that this means that insofar as you are rational the categorical imperative *just is* the law of your will.

To see why, we need only consider how a person with a free will must deliberate. So here you are with your free will, completely self-governing, with nothing outside of you giving you any laws. And along comes an incentive, let us say, a representation of a certain object as pleasant. Being aware of the workings of that incentive upon you, you have an inclination for the object. And that inclination takes the form of a proposal. So the inclination says: end-E would be very pleasant. So how about end-E? Doesn't that seem like an end worth pursuing? Now what the will chooses is, strictly speaking, actions, so before the proposal is complete, we need to make it a proposal for action. Instrumental reasoning determines that you could produce end-E by doing act-A. So the proposal is: that you should do act-A in order to produce this very pleasant end-E.

Now if your will were heteronomous, and pleasure were a law to you, this is all you would need to know, and you would straightaway do act-A in order to produce that pleasant end-E. But since you are autonomous, pleasure is not a law to you: nothing is a law to you except what you make a law for yourself. You therefore ask yourself a different question. The proposal is that you should do act-A in order to achieve pleasant end-E. Since nothing is a law to you except what you make a law for yourself, you ask yourself whether you could take *that* to be your law. Your question is whether you can will the maxim of doing act-A in order to produce end-E as a universal law. Your question, in other words, is whether your maxim passes the categorical imperative test. The categorical imperative is therefore the law of a rational will.

Inclination presents the proposal; reason decides whether to act on it or not, and the decision takes the form of a *legislative act*. This is clearly the Constitutional Model.

7.5.2

Recall now the conclusion we derived from Plato. The dictates of reason are the dictates of the person, but this is not because the person is identified solely with his reason, and so regards his appetites as alien things. It is rather because the person is identified with his constitution, and his constitution says that reason should rule. Could Kant have held this view? You may think not, for in the *Groundwork*, Kant famously and rather morosely says that "inclinations themselves, as sources of needs, are so far from having an absolute worth . . . that it must instead be the universal wish of every rational being to be altogether free from them" (G 4:428). Kant appears to disagree with Plato's ratification of the view that the man has a pain in his finger, and to suppose instead that it is only the finger that has the pain.

But in the more considered view of *Religion within the Limits of Reason Alone*, Kant took this back, and even apparently took himself to task for having said it: "*considered in themselves*," he says there, natural inclinations "are *good*, that is, not a matter of reproach, and it is not only futile to want to extirpate them but to do so would also be harmful and blameworthy" (REL 6:58).

7.5.3

In any case, Kant is absolutely committed to the conclusion that I have just mentioned: that the person identifies, not directly with his reason, but with his constitution. Kant is committed to this by what he says in his political philosophy about the nature of the state. This will be a bit of digression, but I want to explain why this is so.

According to Kant, the purpose of the state is the coercive enforcement of human rights. Rights by their very nature admit of coercive enforcement, and indeed they are the only things that do that, for our freedom is embodied in our rights, and the only legitimate use of coercion is in defense of freedom—coercion may be used against coercion itself. But in order to be in this way legitimate, the use of coercion must be reciprocal rather than unilateral. I force you to give way to my right on the implicit understanding that you would be justified in forcing me to give way to yours. Coercive action must be governed by a law that holds for both of the parties who are involved in it. In other words, for the use of coercion to be legitimate, everyone collectively must compel each one individually to respect the freedom of each other one. So the political state more generally must embody the general will of its people to the reciprocal enforcement of rights. And in order to do this, Kant argues, the state must be a *republic*, characterized by a constitution and by the separation of powers, in which legislation is carried on by the representatives of the citizens.

To see why, we must look at Kant's complex account of the nature of political authority. Kant asserts that "legislative authority can belong only to the united will of the people" (MM 6:313). This is clear enough from what we have already said—the laws are coercive, and so must be grounded in the general will to the reciprocal enforcement of rights. When a state is formed, this legislative authority is invested in what Kant calls a *sovereign* authority or *ruler*, which may be constituted by all, some, or one of the people, making the form of sovereignty democratic, aristocratic, or autocratic respectively (MM 6:338–339; PP 8:352).

Now the sovereign or ruler in a sense has the right to govern, but it isn't exactly, or necessarily, the government yet. The sovereign is rather the voice of the legislative authority of the people. But the sovereign or ruler is responsible for setting up the government. This may make the first step—the determination of the form of sovereignty—seem like an extra step, but it is not, and it is important to see why it is not. Kant does not assume, the way that, say, Locke does, that the united will of the people is automatically expressed by a majority vote.[8] Majority voting is just one way to unify the people into a collective legislative authority—that is, a collective agent—and it is not a privileged way. Speaking strictly, only the unanimous choice of all of the people could determine the form of sovereignty, and the people could unanimously just as well choose autocracy as democracy.

Of course it is unlikely that any real group of people would spontaneously reach a unanimous decision about how to make their decisions, but this doesn't show that the determination of the form of sovereignty is an extra step. It only shows that there is usually no legitimate way to *make* this step. Let me illustrate the point. Suppose you've got a hundred people, and each of them agrees that he wishes to compound with the others, and form a collective agent, a state. The next thing they must do is to decide how their collective decisions are to be made. If each of them, individually, wants to use majority voting, then they have a democratic form of sovereignty, and it's perfectly

---

[8] John Locke, *The Second Treatise of Government*, section 96.

legitimate. But in exactly the same way, if each of them, individually, wants to have an autocracy, with Solomon in charge, then they have an autocratic form of sovereignty, and it's perfectly legitimate. Democracy and autocracy are exactly on a footing, so far as legitimacy goes. Democracy may be better in all sorts of ways, but its claims to *legitimacy* are not superior. Actually, what I've just said oversimplifies the problem, for I'm ignoring the fact of future generations, whose agreement is also needed for legitimacy. That's so much the better for the argument, for I am trying to show that there is a problem here. But even if we set aside the problem posed by future generations, a unanimous choice isn't going to happen—I mean, they aren't all going to agree on a form of sovereignty. So now suppose they don't. Suppose that ninety-eight of them want democracy, but two of them want autocracy, with Solomon in charge. (Probably one of them is Solomon, but that doesn't matter to the argument.) Now we are at an impasse. Since democracy has no prior claims to legitimacy, we obviously cannot say that the ninety-eight may legitimately prevail because they are the majority. Exactly what's in question is whether the majority is to rule or not. So if the majority does prevail, it is not legitimately, but merely as a tyranny of the majority. And if the two prevail, and manage to put Solomon in charge, of course that is tyranny too. So if, as seems likely, there is any disagreement about the form of sovereignty, then there is *no* way to determine what it should be. And of course, even if there were an original agreement, new generations are going to be born, and they might not agree.

So, since that step can't be made, let's just skip it, for now anyway, and suppose that somehow or other the form of sovereignty has been determined, not necessarily legitimately, and there is a ruler, under whom these people are able to function as a collective agent. Now as I said, the sovereign or ruler's job is, strictly speaking, to set up the government. Suppose the sovereign "itself," as Kant puts it, simply proceeds to govern—it carries out all three functions of government directly. In this case, the government is *despotic.* Even if the *de facto* form of this sovereignty is democratic, the direct rule of the minority by the majority is despotic, for as we've just seen, the democratic form is not privileged, and we can't just assume that everyone agrees to democracy. Suppose instead, however, that the sovereign in Kant's strange words "lets itself be represented" (MM 6:341). That is to say, the sovereign adopts a constitution that sets up the offices of various magistrates who perform the three functions of government separately, and all government takes place through this constitution. In this case, the government is *republican* (MM 6:341). A republican constitution, Kant says, is the "the only constitution that accords with right" (MM 6:340) because it is "the only constitution of a state that lasts, the constitution in which *law* itself rules and depends on no particular person" and in which therefore "each can be assigned *conclusively* what is his [his rights]" (MM 6:341). In a republican constitution, Kant is saying, every person is bound by the law and so nobody's rights are dependent on anyone's will—not even on the majority's will. Kant puts it this way:

Any true republic is and can only be a *system representing* the people, in order to protect its rights in its name, by all the citizens united and acting through their delegates (deputies). But as soon as a person who is head of state (whether it be a king, nobility, or the whole of the population, the democratic union) also lets itself be represented, then the united people does not merely *represent* the sovereign: it *is* the sovereign itself. (MM 6:341)

The point is that once such constitutional forms are established, the united people no longer have to invest the sovereignty in any "person," not even the majority. Instead the people govern themselves *directly* through their constitutional forms. This means that, once this form of government is in place, it does not matter that there was no legitimate way to establish the form of sovereignty. We don't have to agree on the question in whose hands we shall invest the sovereignty, because it doesn't have to be in anybody's hands. (And even if we did have initial unanimity about the form of sovereignty, only the republic constitution "lasts"—remains legitimate—since only it solves the problem of new generations.) Outwardly, of course, somebody must administer the various functions of government, but those who do so are now regarded as "delegates" who work for the people in accordance with the constitution, not as authoritative individuals in whom the sovereignty has been invested. We are unified not under a centralized authority, but under constitutional forms themselves.

Only under such a constitution can a people really rule themselves. Kant goes so far as to claim that the despotic forms of government are mere empirical appearances, of which the true Republic is the *form* (MM 6:340, 371).[9]

So if Kant does use the Constitutional Model for the soul, and the analogy holds, he is committed to rejecting the *despotism* of reason. True unity requires a constitution, which makes it possible for a whole to rule itself, and the merely apparent or empirical unity that is achieved when one part rules another is just a poor earthly substitute for that. That applies to the person as much as to the state. So for Kant, just as for Plato, reason must rule for the good of

---

[9] In the latter passages Kant says that the idea of a rightful constitution, a republican constitution, is an "idea," in the technical sense which he himself associates with Plato's forms in the *Critique of Pure Reason* (C1 A312–320/B368–377; A567–569/B595–597).

the whole, and if we identify with the voice of reason, it is only because we identify with our constitution, and it says reason should rule.

7.5.4

The Constitutional Model, I have proposed, can be used to explain the nature of action. This is because it can be used to explain how we can attribute a movement to an agent as the agent's own. At the same time, it shows us why certain formal principles—the categorical imperative, and Plato's principle of justice—are constitutive principles of action: because they bring the constitutional unity that makes action possible to the soul. If that is so, then agents must act justly and on the categorical imperative, if they are to act at all. But in that case, what happens when an agent acts badly? That will be my topic in the next chapter.

8

Defective Action

8.1 The Problem of Bad Action

8.1.1

What happens when someone acts badly? According to the Combat Model, the answer must be that the person is overcome by passion. But on the Combat Model, we could just as well say that when a person acts well, she is overcome by reason. For if reason and passion are simply two forces within a person, neither with any special right to rule within the person herself, then the two forces seem to be on a footing, and the agent is overcome either way.

According to the Constitutional Model, as we have seen, a person acts well when she acts in accordance with her constitution. If reason overrules passion, the person should act in accordance with reason. This is not because she identifies with reason rather than passion—it is because she identifies with her constitution, and it says that reason should rule. So what happens when a person acts badly? Here we run into what looks, at first, like a difficulty for the Constitutional Model.

8.1.2

The difficulty is, of course, that according to the account of Plato that I offered in Chapter 7, an unjust *person* cannot act at all, because an unjust person is not unified by constitutional rule (7.4.3). When a city is in a state of civil war, it does not act, although the various factions within it may do things. The parallel suggests that when a soul is in a state of civil war, and the various forces in it are fighting for control, what looks to the outside world like *the person's actions* are at best the actions—or rather manifestations—of forces at work within him. So it looks at first as if *nothing exactly counts as a bad action*. And of course there's an *exact* analogy to this difficulty in Kantian ethics. For a well-known problem in the *Groundwork*—indeed, one we have already considered (5.3.1)—is that Kant appears to say that only autonomous action, that is, action governed by the categorical imperative, is really free action, while bad or heteronomous "action" is behavior *caused* by the work of desires and inclinations in us (G 4:453–5). But if this is so, then it is hard to see how we can be held responsible for bad or heteronomous action, or indeed why we should regard it as action at all. So it looks at first as if for Kant *nothing exactly counts as a bad action.*

8.1.3

It's important to see that the *structure* of the problem in these two arguments is exactly the same. Each argument first identifies an essential metaphysical property of action—autonomy in Kant's argument and constitutional unity in Plato's—and then identifies this metaphysical property with a normative property: the universalizability of your maxim in Kant's argument and justice in Plato's.[1] In both arguments the identification of the metaphysical property is an attempt to capture the essential feature of action, the thing that distinguishes an action from a mere event, namely, the fact that an action is *attributable* to the person who does it. The metaphysical feature Plato and Kant are looking for is the one that makes it true that the action is not just something that happens in or to the person's body or his mind but rather is something that he as a person *does*. What makes an action *mine*, in the special way that an action is *mine*, rather than something that just *happens* in me? That it issues from my constitution, rather than from some force at work within me; that it is expressive of a law I give to myself, rather than a law imposed upon me from without.

And so we get the problem. It is the essential nature of action that it has a certain metaphysical property—autonomy in Kant's argument, constitutional unity in Plato's. But in order to have that metaphysical property it must have a certain normative property—universalizability in Kant's argument, justice in Plato's. This explains why the action must meet the normative standard: *it just isn't action* if it doesn't. But it also seems as if it explains it rather too well, for it seems to imply that only good action really is action, and that there is nothing left for bad action to be.

8.1.4

But on reflection, we will see that this is just the result we should have expected. For of course what we have just observed is that, according to Kant and Plato, moral standards are constitutive principles of action, in the sense introduced in 2.1—they are standards that actions must meet in virtue of what they are.

---

[1] I haven't yet made good on the claim that these formal properties are identical to their ordinary moral counterparts. That will be the work of the next chapter.

Just actions, according to Plato, actions on universalizable maxims, according to Kant, are actions that are good *as* actions, in the way a house that shelters successfully is good *as* a house. Bad actions, actions that are contrary to justice and the categorical imperative, then, are *defective* actions, actions that are bad *as* actions (2.1.6).

What does it mean for an action to be defective? The function of a house is to serve as a shelter; a house with a leaky roof tries and fails to shelter, and therefore it is a defective house. The function of a sentence is to express a thought; a sentence without a verb tries and fails to express a thought; and therefore it is a defective sentence. The function of an action is to unify its agent, and so to render him the autonomous and efficacious author of his own movements. An unjust or unlawful action therefore fails to unify its agent, and so fails to render him the autonomous and efficacious author of what he does.

To clarify this claim, it helps to remember a point I made earlier (5.1.1; 5.1.4). Efficacy is not a property you can have independently of autonomy; for efficacy is a property of agents, and agents must move under their own steam. So no matter how much stuff is happening as a result of your movements, *you* are not efficacious unless you are the author of those movements, and you are not their author unless they are expressive of your own autonomous choice. So when Plato says that "those who are all bad and completely unjust are completely incapable of accomplishing anything" (R 351b–352c), he is not denying the obvious truth that lots of stuff happens as the result of unjust people's movements—he is denying that those movements are (fully) their own. If Plato is right about this, there is after all an element of truth in Kant's idea that badness is a kind of heteronomy. The bad person is determined from outside, for he is a conduit for forces working in him and through him, and he is to that extent, internally, enslaved.

8.2 Being Governed by the Wrong Law

8.2.1

But then how is it possible for action to be defective, and still be action? The Constitutional Model here provides us with the resources for an answer. For as we saw before, the action of a city may be formally or procedurally constitutional and yet not substantively just (7.4). Indeed, nothing is more familiar: a law duly legislated by the congress and even upheld by the supreme court may for all that be substantively unjust. So it's not as if there's no territory at all between a perfectly just city and the complete disintegration of a civil war. A city may be governed, and yet be governed by the wrong law. And so may a soul. This, according to Plato and Kant, explains how bad action, defective action, is possible.

8.2.2

In Kant's work this emerges most clearly in the first part of *Religion within the Limits of Reason Alone*. There we learn that a bad person is not after all one who is pushed about, or caused to act, by his desires and inclinations. Instead, a bad person is one who is governed by what Kant calls the principle of self-love. The person who acts on the principle of self-love *chooses* to act as inclination prompts (REL 6:32–39): he takes his inclinations, without further reflection, to be reasons for action. Why is the principle of self-love the wrong law? The wrong law must be one that fails to constitute the person's agency, and so that fails to render him autonomous and efficacious. So with that in view, let me try to make it clear why Kant thinks that an action based on the principle of self-love is *defective* as an action, rather than merely bad by some external standard.

Imagine a person I'll call Harriet, who is, in almost any formal sense you like, an autonomous person. She has a human mind, she is self-conscious, with the normal allotment of the powers of reflection. She is not a slave or an indentured servant, and we will place her—unlike the original after whom I am modeling her—in a well-ordered modern constitutional democracy, with the full rights of free citizenship and all of her human rights legally guaranteed to her. In every formal legal and psychological sense we can think of, what Harriet does is *up to her*. Yet whenever she has to make any of the important decisions and choices of her life, the way that Harriet does that is to try to figure out what Emma thinks she should do, and then that's what she does.[2]

This is autonomous action and yet it is *defective* as autonomous action. Harriet is self-governed and yet she is not, for she allows herself to be governed by Emma. Harriet is heteronomous, not in the sense that her actions are caused by Emma rather than chosen by herself, but in the sense that she allows herself to be governed in her choices by a law outside of herself—by Emma's will. It even helps my case here that the original Harriet does this because she is afraid to think for herself. For as I have argued elsewhere, this is how Kant envisions the operation of the principle of self-love.[3] Kant does not envision the person who acts from self-love as actively reflecting on what he has reason to do and

---

[2] The model for my Harriet is the persuadable Harriet Smith in Jane Austen's novel *Emma*.
[3] See my "From Duty and for the Sake of the Noble: Kant and Aristotle on Morally Good Action" (CA essay 6), pp. 181–4.

arriving at the conclusion that he ought to do what he wants. Instead, Kant envisions him as one who simply follows the lead of his inclinations, without sufficient reflection. He's heteronomous, and gets his law from nature, not in the sense that it causes his actions, but in the sense that he allows himself to be governed without much thought by its proposals—just as Harriet allows herself to be governed by Emma's.

8.2.3

The analogous doctrine in Plato is much more elaborate, and this is to Plato's credit. For what Kant says here seems incomplete and confusing. Minimally, we might think, Kant ought to have distinguished between a wanton principle of self-love—the principle of acting on the desire of the moment—and a prudent principle of self-love—which seeks, say, the greatest satisfaction of desires over time. Versions of both of these characters *are* found in Plato, and others besides. In Books 8 and 9 of the *Republic*, Plato in fact distinguishes five different ways in which the soul may be governed, comparing them to five different kinds of constitutions possible for a city: the good way, which he calls monarchy or aristocracy; and four bad ones, growing increasingly worse: timocracy, oligarchy, democracy, and worst of all, tyranny. In each of these cases, some part of the soul other than reason takes over the work of reason, establishing a principle that is really for its own good rather than for the good of the whole. And this story captures something else that Kant's account seems to lack. As I said before, action, as I conceive it, is something that comes in degrees: an action can unify and constitute its agent to a greater or a lesser degree (1.4.8). And Plato's story, as we will see, traces those degrees.

In section 8.3 I'll take a look at each of Plato's bad constitutions, explain what I think he has in mind, and why they are supposed to be *defective* and not just externally bad. Since the aim of the constitution is to unify the soul, the defective constitutions must lead to disunity and to that extent must undercut agency. The good constitution—the aristocratic soul—will by contrast be that of a truly unified agent whose movements are wholly her own. That constitution will be my topic in Chapter 9.

8.2.4

But first I should note that it doesn't matter that there are *five* types of constitution, any more than it matters that there are *three* parts of the soul (7.3.4). As Plato says, "there is one form of virtue and an unlimited number of forms of vice, four of which are worth mentioning" (R 445c).

What does matter is that it doesn't matter. At bottom, bad souls are mere heaps, and different types of heaps by their nature don't have very definite criteria of identity—counting them must be something of a rough and ready business.

8.2.5

Before I sketch the four types of vice Plato thinks are worth mentioning, a word of warning is in order. The question I am considering here is the question what happens when someone acts badly—not the question how defective action could possibly come about. On the views we are discussing, that is also, at least in one way, a *very* puzzling question, even once we've ascertained that there is something left for bad action to be. If the categorical imperative is the natural law of a free will, why should a free will, noumenal and pure, that is, uninfluenced by any law of outside of itself, act on any law other than its own? Why should it allow itself to be governed by inclination? And if justice is the very form of the unified soul, why are there souls that are not just? The puzzle finds expression in both philosophers. In *Religion within the Limits of Reason Alone*, Kant invokes the biblical doctrine of the Fall as an expression of the incomprehensibility of evil choice (REL 6:39–44; see also CBHH 8:115).[4] Plato, in Books 8 and 9 of the *Republic*, provides an elaborate and rather bewildering account of how and why the just city, and with it the souls of the people in it, must inevitably decay through various stages of injustice to eventual tyranny and madness.[5] Plato's account of the four bad constitutions is embedded in this discussion, and he takes them in the order of decay, starting with the timocratic soul that falls just short of justice, and moving by steps towards the tyrannical. Although I will take them in that order too, my aim here is only to say what they are, with a view to showing what defective action is. I am not trying to explain Plato's views on how bad action comes about, or to say anything about that question myself.

---

[4] In the text I say that evil is very puzzling "in one way," because in another way it isn't hard to understand evil at all. Speaking a little roughly: when we take up the first-person point of view of the agent, and imagine her making the choice with her eyes wide open, we cannot fathom how she could choose to be anything less than a unified, free, and effective agent. On the other hand, looking at her conduct from a third-person point of view, say, as the object of a social scientific explanation, we may be able to see quite clearly why she did what she did. See my "Morality as Freedom" (CKE essay 6), pp. 171–4.

[5] Plato offers a deliberately obfuscating reason why the first step in the decay is inevitable at R 546a–e: Socrates presents an elaborate mathematical explanation of the supposed fact that people will inevitably reproduce at the wrong time, producing inferior children. One can only wonder at Plato's motive.

8.3 Four or Five Bad Constitutions

8.3.1

Nearest to the "aristocratic" soul—the soul of the good person—is the timocratic person, who, like the city he is named for, is ruled by the spirited part of his soul: by the sense of honor and the love of victory. Recall that the function of spirit, according to Plato, is to preserve a belief laid down by the rational part of the soul about what is to be feared—say, for instance, that nothing is more to be feared than the loss of the city's freedom. Now there's a character like this: he says that he's fighting for the freedom of the city, but if he keeps on with the battle at this rate, there won't be any city left to be free. The buildings are all in ruins, and the stores have all been looted, and there are so many wounded citizens that the medics can't take care of them all. And we begin to suspect that he doesn't exactly care about the freedom of the city, not really, but rather that the idea of a certain action, fighting-for-the-freedom-of-the-city, has an aesthetic character, a kind of moral glamour if you will, and he's got fixed on that, and become quite heedless of what actually is happening to the city. This is a person in whom spirit, the sense of honor, has usurped the role of reason. Most of the time, of course, the person ruled by honor does better, for he loves the outward manifestation, the beauty of goodness, just as if it were goodness itself. Indeed he cannot distinguish the two, and that is his problem: the work of spirit is to preserve a belief, not to reflect on it. Spirit is a source of incentives, and it preserves the belief by building it into the person's representation of the world; giving up the fight is dishonorable and so it *looks* wrong to him, and that's why he won't do it.

I am tempted to say that the problem with the timocratic person is that he is unable to deal with those contingencies that call for the application of what I have elsewhere called, following John Rawls, "non-ideal theory."[6] That is, to put the point roughly, he does fine, except in those moments when what the situation actually calls for is concession, compromise, a bending of the rules, or even—as for instance in a case of civil disobedience—actions that are in some formal sense wrong.[7] So in this kind of case, while fighting for the freedom of the city, he destroys the city; in this kind of case, although perhaps only here, an incoherence in his will makes its appearance, destroying his efficacy and his agency with it.

---

[6] See Rawls, *A Theory of Justice*, s. 39; and my own "The Right to Lie: Kant on Dealing with Evil" (CKE essay 5).

[7] For a case of this kind see my "Taking the Law into Our Own Hands: Kant on the Right to Revolution" (CA essay 8).

Kant, as we saw before, suggests that being governed by honor is a stage just prior in human development to the stage of morality itself (7.3.3). Kant's story of our inevitable progress is Plato's story of our inevitable decline in reverse.

8.3.2

Next comes the oligarchic person, who in Plato's account appears to be ruled by prudence, in a sense that's somewhere between the contemporary philosophical sense—someone who tries to maximize his own satisfaction—and the more everyday sense of being cautious, non-luxurious, and concerned with long-term enrichment. In describing him, Plato employs an important distinction: between the "necessary" desires, whose satisfaction is beneficial or essential to survival, and the unnecessary or luxurious desires, which are harmful and unhealthy and ought not to be indulged. The oligarchic person is attentive to the necessary desires and to money, while he represses his unnecessary desires. But he represses them because they are unprofitable, rather than because it is bad to indulge them. Socrates says that "He holds them in check, not by persuading them that it's better not to act on them or taming them with arguments, but by compulsion and fear, trembling for his other possessions" (R 554d). The breakdown of integrity sets in here, for the result of this forceful repression, according to Socrates, is that "someone like that wouldn't be entirely free from internal civil war and wouldn't be one but in some way two" (R 554d–e). His self-stinting prudence rules despotically over his appetitive part, which boils with repressed and unhealthy desires. Should some outside force—perhaps simply a sufficient temptation—strengthen and enliven his unnecessary desires, the oligarchic person may quite literally lose control of himself. The oligarchic person usually manages to hang together, because he has the sort of imitation virtue which Socrates makes fun of in the *Phaedo*—namely, the virtue of those who are able to master some of their pleasures and fears because they are in turn mastered by others (*Phaedo* 68d–69c). Socrates has in mind such arguments as the old chestnut that you should refrain from overindulging in pleasure because that way you will get more pleasure on the whole. In general, Plato seems to think that honor and prudence are principles of choice sufficiently like true virtue to hold a soul together through most kinds of stress, although in the oligarchic person the fault lines are increasingly visible.

8.3.3

Plato's oligarchic person isn't exactly like what appears to be his modern descendent—the contemporary rational egoist who, we are told, aims to maximize the satisfaction of his desires. And it's worth saying a word about him in this context, for this character seems to many people to be the primary rival to the good person. After all, he has a way of organizing his inclinations—namely maximization—into a unified goal. So it may seem to follow that he will also have a unified will.

Earlier, I argued that maximization only makes sense in light of a substantive theory of the good (3.3.3); it is time to take a closer look at what that substantive theory would be. The view that we are to maximize the satisfaction of our desires is ambiguous, because the idea of "satisfaction" is ambiguous. "Satisfaction" may refer either to an objective or a subjective state. Objective satisfaction is achieved when the state of affairs that you desire is in fact realized. For instance, you want your painting to hang in the Metropolitan Museum of Art, and it does. Obviously, you could achieve the satisfaction of your desire in the objective sense without knowing anything about it: you may never know that your dream of artistic fame has been realized. Subjective satisfaction, by contrast, is a sort of pleasurable consciousness that objective satisfaction obtains. You know that your picture has been hung in the museum, say, and you feel good about that; you reflect on the fact with pleasure. Although subjective satisfaction is pleasurable, it is important to distinguish it from pleasure in general. Rational egoism is not supposed to be the same thing as hedonism. Subjective satisfaction is a specific kind of pleasure, pleasure taken in the knowledge or belief that a desire has been satisfied. Is this what the rational egoist tries to maximize?

Someone who deliberates with the aim of achieving the maximum sense of subjective satisfaction over the whole course of his life does seem to be in a recognizable sense egoistic. His conduct is governed by the pursuit of something that will be experienced as a good by himself. But there is a problem about saying that he is rational. Subjective satisfaction is the pleased perception of objective satisfaction and so is conceptually dependent upon objective satisfaction. And so, one would think, its importance must be dependent on the importance of objective satisfaction as well. There would be something upside down about thinking it mattered that you should achieve subjective satisfaction independently of thinking that it mattered that you should achieve objective satisfaction. You can see the problem by imagining a case in which they pull apart. John Rawls used to tell the following story in his classes:

A man is going away to fight in a war, in which he may possibly die. The night before he leaves, the devil comes and offers him a choice. Either while he is away, his family will thrive and flourish, but he will get word that they are suffering and miserable; or while he is away his family will suffer and be miserable, but he will get word they are thriving and happy. He must choose now, and of course he will be made to forget that his conversation with the devil and the choice it resulted in ever took place.

The problem is obvious. The man loves his family and wants them to be thriving and happy, and this clearly dictates the first choice, where his family thrives but he believes they do not. But the goal of achieving subjective satisfaction seems to favor the second choice, where he gets to enjoy the satisfaction of believing they thrive when actually they do not. So here we have *rationality* supposedly dictating the choice of a pleasing delusion over a state of affairs which the man by hypothesis genuinely cares about. He must care about it, or he could not get the subjective satisfaction. The pursuit of subjective satisfaction in preference to objective satisfaction can lead to madness, in the literal sense of madness: you can lose your grip on *reality*.

So perhaps we should say that the rational egoist is a person who tries to maximize his objective satisfaction. But then we run into a new problem. The idea of *maximizing* objective satisfaction makes no obvious sense. Even supposing that we had some clear way of individuating and so counting our desires, nobody thinks that maximizing objective satisfaction is rational if that means maximizing the raw *number* of satisfied desires, for everyone thinks that our desires differ greatly in their importance and centrality to our lives. Maximizing satisfaction must have something to do with giving priority to the things that matter more to us. So we need some way of assigning prima facie weights of some kind to our desires or more generally to our projects before we know how to maximize their objective satisfaction. And as we saw before, the only way to get those weights is to postulate some substantive theory of the good, so that we can assign the largest "weights" to those projects that contribute the most to our good (3.3.5). But in that case the idea of maximizing *satisfaction* isn't really doing any work for us—unless, of course, the substantive good in question is subjective satisfaction. And that way, as we have already seen, madness lies.[8]

8.3.4

Next in line is the democratic person, who in contemporary jargon is kind of wanton. Socrates says that the democratic person:

puts his pleasures on an equal footing . . . always surrendering rule over himself to whichever desire comes along, as if it were chosen by lot. And when that is satisfied, he surrenders the rule to another, not disdaining any but satisfying them all equally. (R 561b)

---

[8] For further discussion see my "The Myth of Egoism" (CA essay 2), from which part of this section was lifted, especially pp. 96–8.

Democracy is a degenerate case of government, for such a person is governed only in a minimal or formal sense, just as choosing by lot is different only in a minimal or formal sense from not choosing at all. It's as if someone made it his principle to have a particularistic will. The coherence of the democratic person's life is completely dependent on the accidental coherence of his desires. To see the problem, consider a story:

Jeremy, a college student, settles down at his desk one evening to study for an examination. Finding himself a little too restless to concentrate, he decides to take a walk in the fresh air first. His walk takes him past a nearby bookstore, where the sight of an enticing title draws him in to look at the book. Before he finds it, however, he meets his friend Neil, who invites him to join some of the other kids at the bar next door for a beer. Jeremy decides to have just one, and he goes with Neil to the bar. While waiting for his beer, however, he finds that the loud noise in the bar gives him a headache, and he decides to return home without having the beer. He is now, however, in too much pain to study. So Jeremy doesn't study for his examination, hardly gets a walk, doesn't buy a book, and doesn't drink his beer.[9]

Of course the democratic life does not *have* to be like this; it is only an accident that each of Jeremy's impulses leads him to an action that completely undercuts the satisfaction of the last one. But that is the trouble, for it is also only an accident if that does *not* happen. The democratic person has no resources for shaping his will to prevent this, and so he is at the mercy of accident. Like Jeremy, he may be almost completely *incapable of effective action*.

Socrates accuses *himself* of democracy at the end of Book 1 of the *Republic* when he says:

I seem to have behaved like a glutton, snatching at every dish that passes and tasting it before properly savoring its predecessor. Before finding the answer to our first inquiry about what justice is, I let that go and turned to investigate whether it is a kind of vice and ignorance or a kind of wisdom and virtue. Then an argument came up about injustice being more profitable than justice, and I couldn't refrain from abandoning the previous one and following up on that. Hence the result of the discussion, as far as I'm concerned, is that I know nothing . . . (R 354b)

8.3.5

According to Plato, it is from the chaos resulting from this kind of life that the final type, the tyrannical soul, emerges. In a horrifying imitation of the unity and simplicity that characterize justice, this kind of soul is once again unified,

---

[9] I first used this example in "The Normativity of Instrumental Reason" (CA essay 1), p. 59 n. 52.

but not by reason looking to the good of the whole. Plato tells us the tyrannical soul is governed by some nightmarish erotic desire, which subordinates the entire soul to its purposes, leaving the person an absolute slave to a single dominating obsession (R 571a–575a).

8.4 Conceptions of Evil

8.4.1

It's a strange moment, this bit about the tyrant: a strange entry into the ongoing argument about how we are to envision evil. According to one view, the bad or evil person is pathetic, and powerless—the drunk in the gutter, the junkie, the stupid hothead who shoots a policeman and pays for it for the rest of his life, the perpetual loser who cannot hold down a job. Bad people are people without standards, without integrity, without plans even, who can be led in any direction by the desire or the suggestion of the moment. Bad people are people who cannot sustain friendships, because they would betray a friend for a few dollars in order to buy themselves a pleasure. Bad people are people who cannot pursue any larger or more spiritual ambitions, since their appetites always hold sway and are always diverting them from the course they set.

These cases come naturally to mind when we think of bad action as *defective*. For when we think of these kinds of cases we think of badness or evil as a lack, a deficiency, a psychological failure. Uncontrolled and insubstantial, the bad person cannot stay on the track of an ambition or a relationship. The good person, by contrast, is someone with standards, someone with integrity, someone who is able to govern herself. The good person is someone who can deny her appetites when it is called for by her larger purposes, and someone who can give way gracefully to the wishes of a friend or a fellow citizen when that is the reasonable thing to do. Evil is weakness and goodness is the self-confidence of efficacious power. Call that the privative conception of evil: evil is a privation, a lack.

But then there is that other vision, isn't there? Thrasymachus's vision. According to this view, the bad or evil person is powerful, ruthless, unconstrained. The evil person is prepared to do *whatever is necessary* to get what he wants, and determined to let nothing stand in his way. He is clever enough to circumvent the law, and both able and willing to outwit, outsmart, or if necessary outshoot whoever and whatever comes between him and the satisfaction of his desire. The tyrant of the ancient Greek imagination is the glamorous mafia kingpin of our own. So far from being *unable* to sustain relationships or projects, the evil person is more than anybody else able to stay on the track of them. For he is the one who is prepared to do *whatever is necessary*, whatever it takes. And this is where the doubt about morality comes in. Compared to the evil or ruthless person, the just and good person seems to be a kind of weakling. Hedged around by rules and restrictions, the good person cannot take a single step forward without asking God or Society for permission; and the moment these forces seem to him to say "no," he desists immediately. Moral rules and restrictions trap and constrain him; they impose limits on what he can do, they make him suffer agonies of guilt on the rare occasions when he does as he pleases. The good and just person is docile, tame, there to be taken advantage of by those who are stronger and more ruthless, a lamb to be led to the slaughter. Evil is power and goodness is weakness. Call that the positive conception of evil; evil is a positive force.

8.4.2

It may be said—and not I think exactly wrongly—that the work of the *Republic* is to show that the privative conception of evil is the true one. But it isn't quite that simple, for, as I said earlier, the mere privation of self-government is the democratic state. And Plato's story does not end there. The tyrannical soul is consistently ruled and unified, though it is not self-governed. The tyrannical person is a slave, a terrified and captive soul, in thrall to erotic obsession; but slavery is not the mere privation of government—it's a positive state. For the modern reader, it's hard not to think of the addict, with his dominating obsession, or even more, given Plato's reference to erotic desire, of a figure of horror from the modern landscape, the serial sex killer, condemned to the eternal reenactment of some horrifying sexual scene. So Plato evidently thinks there's something to the positive picture, something that explains its hold over us. The tyrant is not a force, but his desire is. Tyrannical desires, like tyrants themselves, see the absence of government as an opportunity, a vacancy, into which they can slip and take over.

8.4.3

Where does Kant stand on this issue? Most of the time Kant seems to regard evil as mere venality or selfishness. As we've already seen, he thinks the bad agent acts on the principle of self-love, which is the principle of following his desires where they lead. Often, though, Kant—a bit inconsistently, I believe—portrays the bad agent as a calculating person, bent on maximizing his pleasures (C2 5:23) or his advantage (C2 5:35). He characterizes the immoral agent as making an exception of himself (G 4:424). His model, when he thinks about evil, seems to be the cheat, the chiseler, the guy who bends the rules in his own favor, not the tyrant or the mafia kingpin, and not the serial sex killer or the addict.

Yet Kant does discuss the existence of the unhealthy, luxurious desires, our potential tyrants, and tells a somewhat different story than Plato does about their origin. In "Conjectures on the Beginning of Human History," Kant links their development quite closely with the development of reason and our original liberation from instinct (6.2.1). As we saw before, self-consciousness leads to new desires, and these are not only desires for things that are not the original objects of instinct. They include desires that go contrary to our instincts. Kant says:

> it is a peculiarity of reason that it is able, with the help of the imagination, to invent desires which not only *lack* any corresponding natural impulse, but which are even *at variance* with the latter. Such desires, which are known primarily as *lasciviousness*, gradually engender a whole host of superfluous or even unnatural inclinations to which the term *luxuriousness* applies. (CBHH 8:111)

For Kant free reason and tyrannical desire are twins, born of our universal mother on the same fateful day.

8.4.4

But if a tyrannical desire unifies the soul, how is it different from aristocratic government? Why doesn't it make effective action possible? Well, first of all, the tyrannical person does not really choose *actions*, in the technical sense I defined in 1.2.5. For the tyrannical person doesn't choose *an act for the sake of an end*, the whole package as something worth doing. There's one end—as in the case of the serial killer, it may be the act itself—one end or act that he's going to pursue or to do *no matter what*, and it rules him. And for him that end makes anything worth doing, anything at all, and that's a fact that is settled in advance of reflection. It is this fact, the fact that he is willing to do certain things *whatever the consequences*, which makes him such an unsettling parody of the just person. Yet our sense that there is something mechanical about him is not accidental. As I imagine the tyrant, his relation to his obsession is like a psychotic's relation to his delusion: he is prepared to organize everything else around it, even at the expense of a loss of his grip on reality, on the world. In fact tyranny is not merely like psychosis; it includes psychosis as one of its components, for as I have tried to emphasize, each principle is paired with a set of incentives, a representation of the world in its terms. The serial killer may actually see his victim as *asking for it*, for example, because he needs to see her that way. And for the addict of course the house is not full of furniture, much less somebody else's furniture, but of things you can sell for the money for the drug. The tyrannical person may be clever, in Aristotle's sense—he may have considerable instrumental intelligence.[10] But he doesn't decide what is worth doing for the sake of what, because for him, that's already settled. That means that he doesn't really choose maxims, and that means that he doesn't make laws for himself, and that means that he isn't autonomous, and that means that he isn't free.

8.4.5

How do I know this? I mean, can I prove *logically* that the tyrant isn't choosing actions? Can I prove that he isn't deciding, separately, each and every time, that doing *this* act for the sake of *this* end is a thing worth doing for its own sake, and it just turns out that the end is always the same? Probably I can't prove that this isn't logically possible. Although if the tyrant's condition depends on his psychosis—if, say, he *has* to see all women as harlots, or all Jews as conspirators, or something like that—then this looks like pretty good evidence that he's crazy and not merely choosing something different than the rest of us would. Remember the so-called rational egoist who decides to pursue subjective satisfaction at all costs (8.3.3)? That's like deciding to be a tyrant, and he turned out to be crazy after all.

But a psychotic view of the world can be more or less complete, so perhaps the tyrant is willing to grant that if he himself were a woman and so a harlot or a Jew and so a conspirator, he would deserve the same fate as he is dishing out to them. In that case, he is willing a universal law, or the semblance of one.

But of course, he doesn't grant that. Oh, he is more than ready to grant that *any* woman or Jew would deserve the fate he reserves for his victims. But he doesn't think there is any content, any content whatever, to the thought that he himself might have been a woman or a Jew. He sees nothing in common with them that would admit of an exchange of positions.[11] He doesn't think he's a person who happens to be a man or a Gentile; he thinks he's the avenger of masculinity or the defender of Aryan purity all the way down.

So why can't he choose actions? Because his condition is both the mirror image and the opposite of the particularistic willer (4.4.3). The particularistic willer, who identifies separately with each of his impulses, can't see himself as anything over and above them, and so shatters into a mere heap. The tyrannized soul can never separate himself from *one* of his impulses, and so consolidates himself into a mere a force of nature, an object, a thing.

---

[10] See my "Aristotle's Function Argument" (CA essay 4), pp. 145–8.   [11] See SN 4.2.11, p. 144.

8.5 Degrees of Action

8.5.1

And that thought—that the tyrant has made himself into a force of nature or a thing—brings us back to a worry that this account of evil naturally evokes. At the beginning of this chapter I claimed that Kant's account of evil as heteronomy wouldn't do, because if an agent's movements are caused from without, then he is not responsible for his actions (8.1.2). But I also said that there is an element of truth in Kant's account of evil as heteronomy (8.1.4). Because to the extent that an agent's legislation fails to unify her, and render her the autonomous and efficacious author of her movements, she is less of an agent, and to the extent that she is less of an agent, the source of her movements must be some force that is working in her or on her. As I have tried to convey, all of this is a matter of degree: the extent to which one is unified, and so is an agent, is a matter of degree. Timocrats, whose problem only emerges in a special kind of circumstance, are pretty well unified; oligarchs, who are divided against themselves, still manage to hold themselves together so long as one part keeps the other firmly repressed; even democrats, who are united only by the principle of being all in pieces, can hang together if they are lucky (or perhaps just conventional) in the contents of their desires. But if tyrants really are tyrannized over by some force within them, whose thing they have become, are they responsible for their condition? And, more importantly, are we to say that the other characters become less responsible to the extent that there is less of agency about them, and more of the operation of some external or internal force?

As far as tyrants are concerned, I'm not sure what to say—but then no one knows for sure what to say about the responsibility of some of the characters I've classified as tyrants—serial killers and addicts, for instance. But to the question whether the others become less responsible as they approach the tyrannical condition, the answer is no. There is no general principle saying that you are responsible to the extent to which you acted. And that is true according to every moral theory, not just the one I am defending here. For every sensible moral theory, like every sensible friend, lover, colleague, family member, and fellow citizen, holds people just as responsible for *omissions* as they do for actions. If you forget to pick the children up to take them home from school, say for a month or two, we are hardly going to say, "well, after all, it wasn't something that he did, only something he omitted." I won't try to specify the rules here for exactly when we are responsible for not doing something, because it's a gigantic topic, but the basic principle is that you can be held responsible for an omission, if the thing you omitted was in some general sense your job.

What is true is that in the sort of theory I am defending, responsibility in general is going to look a lot more like responsibility for omission. What we are going to blame you for is not that other force that was working in you or on you, but for the fact that you let it do that, that you failed to pick up the reins and take control of your own movements. And the reason we are going to do that is that making yourself into an agent, giving yourself an identity, becoming a person, is your *job* (1.4.9).[12]

<h2 style="text-align:center">8.5.2</h2>

All of Plato's intermediate forms of constitution (timocracy, oligarchy, democracy) have an element of aristocracy—for those who have them give themselves laws—and an element of tyranny—for reason itself is not the source of those laws. So in Plato's story, as in Kant's, bad action is action governed by a principle of choice which is not reason's own: a principle of honor (timocracy), prudence (oligarchy), wantonness (democracy), or obsession (tyranny). It is action, because it is chosen in accordance with the exercise of a principle by which the agent rules himself and under whose rule he is—in a sense—constitutionally unified. It is bad, because it is not reason's own principle, it does not rule for the good of the soul as a whole, and therefore the unity it produces—at least in the cases of timocracy, oligarchy, and democracy—is contingent and unstable. The agent's unity is propped, so to speak, by the fact that the circumstances that would reveal the competing factions in his soul and undercut his efficacy don't happen to occur. The timocratic person may lose track of his ends in his efforts to maintain his honor. The oligarchic person is divided, and must repress half of his nature to keep from falling apart. The egoistic person prefers an apparent satisfaction to the very reality needed to make sense of that satisfaction. The democratic person drops his projects in the face of the slightest temptation or distraction. And tyranny, or obsession, finally, is not just a defect but in the most literal sense a perversion of self-rule, the subjection of the self to a single thing inside it.

Reason's own principle, in contrast to all of these, is the principle that truly unifies the soul, and unifies it in a way that makes it capable of effective action.

---

[12] Importantly, I think it is only those who have a stake in your doing that job who have any business holding you responsible, or perhaps I might say only *to the extent* that others have a stake in your doing that job, do they have any business holding you responsible. On this see my "Creating the Kingdom of Ends: Reciprocity and Responsibility in Personal Relations" (CKE essay 7).

And both Plato and Kant think that that principle, the one that really unifies us, and renders us autonomous, is also the principle of the morally good person. According to Plato and Kant, integrity in the metaphysical sense—the unity of agency—and in the moral sense—goodness—are one and the same property. In the next chapter, I will explain why this is so.

9

Integrity and Interaction

9.1 Deciding to be Bad

9.1.1

At the end of the last chapter, I claimed that in the conditions of timocracy, oligarchy, and democracy, your unity and so your capacity for self-government are propped by external circumstances, by the absence of the conditions under which you would fall apart. But what, you might ask, is so bad about that? The defect in these characters is like a geological fault line, a potential for disintegration that does not necessarily show up, and as long as it doesn't, these people have constitutional procedures and so they can act. So why not just go ahead and be, say, oligarchical? You'll hold together most of the time, you'll be able to perform actions, and you'll save all that money besides. If that's what it amounts to, what's so bad about being bad?

9.1.2

There is another way to ask this same question, which is to ask whether Glaucon's famous challenge is not too extreme. Glaucon wants Socrates to tell him what justice and injustice do to the soul. So he sets up the following challenge: take on the one hand a person who has a completely unjust soul, and give him all of the outward benefits of justice, that is, all the benefits that come from people believing that you are just. And take on the other hand a person who has a completely just soul, and give him all of the outward disadvantages of injustice, all the disadvantages that come from people believing that you are unjust (R 360d–361b). In particular the just person who is believed to be unjust will be "whipped, stretched on a rack, chained, blinded with fire, and . . . impaled" (R 361e). Socrates is supposed to show that it is better to be just than unjust *even then*. But isn't that too much to ask?

In the context of the argument of the *Republic*, it is not. For the question of the *Republic* is asked as a *practical* question. It is not merely the question whether the just life is better than the unjust life. It is the question whether the just life is more worthy of *choice*. And if you choose to be a just person, and to live a just life, you are thereby choosing to do the just thing even if it means you will be whipped, stretched on the rack, chained, blinded with fire, and impaled. You can't make a conditional commitment to justice, a commitment to be just unless the going gets rough. Your justice rests in the nature of your commitments, and a commitment like that would not *be* a commitment to justice. So when deciding whether to be a just person, you've got to be convinced in advance that it'll be worth it, even if things do turn out that way.[1]

9.1.3

Suppose—for it's plausible enough—there's a person who lives a just life, is decent and upstanding, always does his share, never takes an unfair advantage, sticks to his word—all of that. But then, one day, he is put on the rack, and under stress of torture he does something unjust. Say he divulges a military secret, or the whereabouts of a fugitive unjustly pursued. Am I saying that this shows that he was never really committed to justice, because his commitment must have been conditional? *Of course not.* What the case shows is that the range of things people can *be* is wider than the range of things they can choose to be, so to speak, *in advance.* This person was committed to keeping his secrets on the rack, but he failed, that's all—and very understandably too. But the fact that you can be a just person who in these kinds of circumstances will fail does not show that you can decide in advance to be a just person who in these kinds of circumstances will fail. That is, it doesn't show that you can make a conditional commitment to justice. For suppose you surprise yourself and you do hold out and you keep the secret even when they put you on the rack. Did you then fail to *keep* your conditional commitment?

So Glaucon's challenge is a fair one. But Plato more than meets it. For he doesn't merely prove that the just life is the one most worthy of choice. He proves that the just life is the only one you can choose.

9.1.4

Consider Plato's account of the principle of just or aristocratic action. Here is what Plato says:

One who is just does not allow any part of himself to do the work of another part or allow the various classes within him to meddle with each other. He regulates well what is really his own and rules himself. He puts himself in order, is his own friend, and harmonizes the three parts of himself like three limiting notes in a musical

---

[1] On this point see also Rawls, *A Theory of Justice*, section 86.

scale—high, low, and middle. He binds together those parts and any others there may be in between, and from having been many things he becomes entirely one, moderate and harmonious. Only then does he act. And when he does anything, whether acquiring wealth, taking care of his body, engaging in politics, or in private contracts—in all of these, he believes that the action is just and fine that preserves this inner harmony and helps achieve it, and calls it so, and regards as wisdom the knowledge that oversees such actions. And he believes that the action that destroys this harmony is unjust, and calls it so, and regards the belief that oversees it as ignorance. (R 443d–444)

The action that the just person calls "just" is the one that maintains his inner harmony. In other words, the principle of justice directs us to perform those actions that establish and maintain our volitional unity. Now we have already seen that according to Plato volitional unity is essential if you are to act as a person, as a single unified agent. So reason's own principle *just is* the principle of acting in a way that constitutes you as a single unified agent. This should not be surprising, because we've also already seen that Kant's categorical imperative is also the principle by means of which we constitute ourselves as unified agents (4.4). When you deliberate in accordance with these principles, you pull yourself together and place yourself, so to speak, *behind* your movement, rendering it an action that can be ascribed to you as a whole.

In fact, deliberative action by its very nature imposes unity on the soul. When you deliberate about what to do and then do it, what you are doing is organizing your appetite, reason, and spirit, into a unified system that yields an action that can be attributed to you as a person. Whatever else you are doing when you choose a deliberative action, you are also unifying yourself into a person. And this means that Plato's principle of justice, reason's own principle, is the *formal* principle of deliberative action.

It is as if Glaucon asked: what condition could this be, that enables the just person to stick to his principles even on the rack? And Plato might reply: don't look for some *further* condition which has that as an *effect*. Justice is not some *other* or *further* condition that enables us to maintain our unity as agents. It is that very condition itself—the condition of being able to maintain our unity as agents.

To see that this is formal, consider the following comparison. One might ask Kant: what principle could this be, that enables the free person to be autonomous, to rule herself? And Kant would reply: don't look for some *further* principle that enables us to rule ourselves and give ourselves laws. The categorical imperative is not some *other* or *further* principle that enables us to rule ourselves. It is that very principle itself, the principle of giving laws to ourselves.

9.1.5

On the one hand, this account of the aristocratic soul shows us why the demands of Platonic justice are so high. On certain occasions, the people with the other constitutions fall apart. For the truly just person, the aristocratic soul, there are no such occasions. Anything could happen to her, anything at all, and she will still follow her own principles—and that is because she has universal principles, principles that can consistently be followed in any kind of case. She is entirely self-governed, so that all of her actions, in every circumstance of her life, are really and fully her own: never merely the manifestations of forces at work in her or on her, but always the expression of her own choice. She is completely self-possessed: not necessarily happy on the rack, but *herself* on the rack, herself even there.

And yet at the same time, Plato's argument shows that this aristocratic constitution is the only one you can choose. For you can't, in the moment of deliberative action, choose to be something less than a single unified agent. And that means you can't exactly choose to act on any principle other than the principle of justice. Timocratic, oligarchic, and democratic souls disintegrate under certain conditions, so deciding to be one would be like making a conditional commitment to your own unity, to your own personhood. And that's not possible. You can be a timocratic, oligarchic, or democratic person, in the same way that you can be a just person who fails on the rack. But you cannot decide in advance that this is what you will be.

Of course this doesn't mean that everyone lives a just life. Rather, as I said earlier, you don't strive to be just, to be good (1.4.9). You strive to be unified, to be whole, to be *someone*. And if you do that well, then you are just. So living an unjust life is not a different activity from living a just one. *It is the same activity*—the activity of self-constitution—*badly done*.

9.2 The Ordinary Cases

9.2.1

But at this point we reach a famous crux, which shows up in both of the arguments. Kant tells us that action requires autonomy and autonomy requires universalizability. Plato tells us that action requires constitutional unity and constitutional unity requires procedural justice in the soul. Both of them then tell us that these properties are only fully realized in the soul of the morally good person. But how do we get from the formal properties that these philosophers have identified as essential to action—from universalizability and from procedural justice—to a commitment to substantive morality?

In Kant's argument, the crux concerns the question whether an action that is autonomous in the formal or procedural sense—in the sense that the agent chooses its maxim for himself—must also be in accord with the categorical imperative in the more substantive sense necessary for morality: a universal law that governs all rational beings, yielding reasons that all of us can share (4.5.5). Why, after all, if the agent is autonomous, should there be any limitation on which maxim he can choose as his law?

And in Plato's argument, the parallel crux comes at a famous or perhaps infamous moment in Book 4. In the text immediately preceding his description of the just person, quoted above, Socrates proposes that he and Glaucon should test his theory by appealing to what he calls the "ordinary cases" (R 442e). Accordingly, he asks Glaucon whether the just person as they have by now described him, the unified person, would embezzle deposits, rob temples, steal, betray his friends or his city, violate his oaths or his other agreements, commit adultery, be disrespectful to his parents, or neglect the gods, to all of which Glaucon in effect says, with a complaisance that is startling to the reader: no, he would not, the just person as we have described him would not do these kinds of things (R 442e–443b). Why, we find ourselves wondering, is the usually skeptical Glaucon so sure?

9.2.2

What is the relationship between maintaining unity in your soul, and doing things like telling the truth, keeping your promises, and respecting people's rights? Here the Constitutional Model again suggests a way to approach the question. When we call a political state "just" or "unjust" there are in fact two different things we might mean. We might mean that the way the government treats the citizens—and so the way the citizens treat each other—is just or unjust. Or we might mean that the state as a whole is just or unjust in its dealings with outsiders—with foreigners, for instance, and, especially, with other states. I will call these things *inward* and *outward* justice. A state or a city-state is *inwardly* unjust if it is racist or sexist or lacks a free press or has an established religion or has a large population of homeless citizens whom it makes no effort to help—things like that. It is *outwardly* unjust if it is imperialistic or violates treaties or has unfair trade laws or secretly meddles in the affairs of other states.

By the analogy then, Socrates has been describing what inward justice is in a person. When he comes to the test of the ordinary cases, though, he is asking whether the person he has described would be outwardly just. It's interesting to note that Socrates proposes this as a *test*, that is, he uses it to *confirm* that his description of inward justice is correct. This shows that Socrates himself takes the connection between inward and outward justice for granted—he assumes that a person who is inwardly just will be outwardly so. But why should this be so obvious?

9.2.3

Well, here's a case for you to think about for starters. Suppose you are a utilitarian. When people ask you questions, your answers are guided, not—or at least not in the first instance—by what you think is the truth, but by what you think it is most useful for those people to believe. Of course you think that *in general* it is most useful for people to believe the truth, so this doesn't have to mean that you go around telling lies to people right and left. Nevertheless, you don't tell people the truth until you have satisfied yourself that it is most useful for them to believe the truth, so when you answer their questions, the first question that you must ask *yourself* is what it is most useful for them to believe. Perhaps, for instance, when they ask you for the time, you always tell them it's a little later, so they'll hurry up and make it to their appointments on time. And there is your outward justice.

And then one day it occurs to you that there is really no reason for you to treat yourself any differently than anybody else. You are just another person, and you don't tell the truth to people until you've satisfied yourself that it is most useful for them to believe the truth, so you shouldn't tell *yourself* the truth until you've satisfied yourself that it is most useful for *you* to believe the truth. So you undertake to believe, not what is true—at least not in the first instance—but what it is most useful for you to believe.

But now you've got a problem. Because before you can allow yourself to believe what is true, you have to satisfy yourself that it is most useful for you to believe what is true. But you can't do that without first satisfying yourself that what you think about *that*—about what it is most useful for you to believe, I mean—is, quite simply, true. That is, when you say to yourself "well in this case, it is most useful for me to believe the truth," or, as it may be, "in this case, it would really be better if I believed something false," you have to be satisfied that those thoughts, the ones I just mentioned, are, quite simply, true.

So you have to try to tell yourself the truth, in the first instance: there is no way around it.[2]

And this is no accident. Thought requires a little more respect for the humanity in your own person than utilitarianism allows. For treating yourself in accordance with the Kantian prohibitions against deception and coercion is a condition of thought, without which thought isn't possible.[3] You can't treat yourself in accordance with the principle of utility while you are thinking. For the principle of utility is a tyranny, while thought, by its very nature, is free.

9.2.4

Let's return to the argument. Do inward and outward justice necessarily go together? Following the rules of Plato's analogy, we might pursue this question by asking whether inward justice and outward justice go together in the case of actual political states. Is a nation's honesty and fairness in its dealings with other nations the natural outward expression or consequence of its honesty and fairness in its dealings with its own citizens? Certainly we can spot, in a general way, pressures and tendencies in this direction, although they may not seem decisive. To start with, there are the simple embarrassments of elementary inconsistency—making a big fuss about human rights at home while trampling on them overseas, say—but there other sorts of pressure as well. It's hard to have a free press and yet lie to the world. So is it hard to have a free *mind* and yet lie to the world? This is a question we will come back to. Here's another case. Let's suppose, as I think we may suppose, that constitutional democracies are inwardly just, and that war is at least usually outwardly unjust. Kant argued that constitutional democracies would not be very likely to go to war, since in a constitutional democracy the citizens have to give their formal consent to a war, and that isn't likely to happen, since it is usually only the rulers, not the citizens, who really want to go to war (PP 8:351). Constitutional democracies, as we have learned since then, do sometimes go to war, but it's one of everyone's favorite observations these days that they don't go to war *with each other.*

---

[2] You may think I could have made my point more simply by insisting that in order to decide whether it is most useful for you to believe what's true, you have to have some conception of what's true, and then *ipso facto* you believe that. But once we have a conception of what it's best for us to believe, there are many ways to trick ourselves into believing it. For instance, there are tardy people who deliberately set their clocks fast in order to help themselves keep their appointments, and though there is a puzzle about how that works, it does seem to. So I prefer to stick with the more complicated point: when setting their clocks, those people *have* to tell themselves the truth about the fact that it is good for them to believe that it is later than it is.

[3] The platinum rule: do unto others as you cannot help but do unto yourself.

9.3 Dealing with the Disunified

9.3.1

And this brings me back to Plato. It's a curious fact that he has little to say about his perfect Republic's practice of outward justice. It's more curious still that the little he does have to say is contained in one of the most sinister moments in a book that, after all, has no shortage of sinister moments. In the passages I have in mind, Adeimantus is wondering how Socrates' ideal Republic will be able to fight wars if, as Socrates has claimed, it is not going to be a wealthy city. Socrates proposes that when the Republic is attacked, it should make an alliance against its enemy with some third city, offering the third city the proceeds of victory as an incentive. That's bad enough, but the passage I have in mind is the one that follows, when Adeimantus complains that if the wealth of all the other cities came to be gathered in a single city, the Republic would be in danger. And Socrates replies:

You're happily innocent if you think that anything other than the kind of city we are founding deserves to be called *a city*. (R 422e)

Adeimantus asks what Socrates means, and Socrates says:

We'll have to find a greater title for the others, because each of them is a great many cities, not *a* city ... At any rate, each of them consists of two cities at war with one another, that of the poor and that of the rich, and each of these contains a great many. If you approach them as one city, you'll be making a big mistake. But if you approach them as many and offer to give to the one city the money, power, and indeed the very inhabitants of the other, you'll always find many allies and few enemies. (R 422e–423a)

Socrates here recommends exploiting your enemy's fundamental weakness, turning its factions against one another, winning the allegiance of the poor by offering them the possessions, and perhaps even the persons, of the rich. Consider what the analogy on the personal level would be to *that*! Appeal to your enemy's worst desires, the ones that will expose the disunity in his soul, foment civil war within him, and you can render him incapable of effective action. Is *this* how the good person is going to deal with his enemies? The essential Kantian commitment to respecting another's humanity, even when that other acts badly, seems a long way away. Of course we are in the territory of non-ideal theory here, for we are talking about war, and even Kant agrees that in the case of war the rules are different (PP 8:355–7). But it's still a little chilling.

9.3.2

Yet Plato has a point. How do you interact with someone who is seriously divided against himself? *If you approach them as one city*, Plato says, *you'll be making a big mistake.* To see the problem, consider one of the stock characters of contemporary moral philosophy, a character who is, in fact, a sort of diachronic version of the disunited city—I mean Derek Parfit's nineteenth-century Russian nobleman.[4] The story goes like this. The nineteenth-century Russian is now, in his youth, a socialist, and he plans to distribute large portions of his inheritance, later, when he comes into it, to the peasants. But he also anticipates that his attitudes will become more conservative as he grows older, and that he may not think that this is the right thing to do when the inheritance is finally his own. So he makes a contract *now*, to distribute the land when he gets it, which can only be revoked with the consent of his wife, and he asks his wife to promise not to revoke it *then*, even if he tells her *then* that he has changed his mind, and that she is released from the promise. Parfit makes it clear that the case is not like that of Ulysses binding himself to the mast to resist the Sirens' song. The young Russian does not anticipate that he is going to become irrational, that his judgment will be clouded, or that the immediate temptation of having the estates will undermine his self-control. He simply believes that when he is older he is going to have different values than the ones he has now. Parfit portrays him as telling his wife that his younger self is his real self, that his ideals are essential to him, and that if he loses those ideals she should regard him as effectively dead. Being dead, he cannot release her from her promise, and if his middle-aged avatar claims to release her, in an effort to keep hold of the estates, she should regard him as someone else, who therefore cannot release her—almost, although Parfit does not put it this way—as a kind of impostor, posing as the continuation of his younger self. If she does make the promise, and it all happens as her husband predicts—when the estates come to him, he wants to keep them after all, and he tries to release her from the promise—then, Parfit says, "It might seem to her as if she has obligations to two different people."[5]

To two different people, it appears, at least one of whom she now *must* wrong. Parfit envisions her deciding to keep her commitment to her husband's younger self, feeling that he is the one she ought to be loyal to, the one that she loves. But staring that fact in the face is an everyday moral reality: she is a married woman, yet now she must set herself up as her husband's

---

[4] Parfit, *Reasons and Persons*, pp. 327–8. I have also discussed this case in "Creating the Kingdom of Ends: Reciprocity and Responsibility in Personal Relations" (CKE essay 7).

[5] Parfit, *Reasons and Persons*, p. 327.

enemy, accuse him of being a kind of impostor, and deny him a voice in the disposition of the estates—and she must do all of this, although he is not, as Parfit has specified the example, in any way irrational or out of control. With what possible right could a wife do this? Don't be blinded by the fact that, substantively speaking, you are probably on the young man's side, and hope that the peasants will get the estates, for there are procedural issues at stake here.

9.3.3

The procedural issues I have in mind spring from the nature of marriage. What is marriage, anyway? This will sound like a digression but you'll see in a moment why I am raising the question. Kant thought that marriage is the solution to a problem. In both the *Lectures on Ethics* and the *Metaphysics of Morals*, Kant claims that there is something morally troublesome, even potentially degrading, about sexual relations (LE 27:384–386; MM 6:278). What bothers him is *not* the conventional notion that in sexual interaction one person is using another person as a mere means to his own pleasure. That's not what Kant thinks, and, in any case, any difficulty about that would, according to Kant's own theory, be alleviated by the other's act of free consent: a person is not using you as a *mere* means if he has your own free consent. What worries Kant is rather that sexual desire takes a *person* for its object. He says: "They themselves, and not their work and services, are its Objects of enjoyment" (LE 27:384). Regarding someone as a sexual object is not like regarding him as an instrument or a tool, but more like regarding him as an aesthetic object, something to enjoy. Only in this case the attitude is not just appreciation but desire (MM 6:426). So viewed through the eyes of sexual desire, another person is seen as something wantable and therefore, inevitably, possessable. To yield to *that* desire, to the extent it is really *that* desire you yield to, is to allow yourself to be possessed—in a way, to be someone's property. The problem is how you can do that in a way that is consistent with respect for your own humanity. And the solution, according to Kant, rests in a complete reciprocity of possession, in which each of you belongs wholly to the other. Kant says:

If, then, one yields one's person, body and soul, for good and ill in every respect, so that the other has complete rights over it, and if the other does not similarly yield himself in return and does not extend in return the same rights and privileges, the arrangement is one-sided. But if I yield myself completely to another and obtain the person of the other in return, I win myself back; I have given myself up as the property of another, but in turn I take that other as my property, and so win myself back again in winning the person whose property I have become. In this way the two persons become *a unity of will.* (LE 27:388; my emphasis)

It actually doesn't matter for my purposes what you think about Kant's view of the problem, as long as you are prepared to believe that he's on to something when he offers the solution: that marriage creates a unity of will. Two people who get married pledge to share one another's lives and possessions; there is therefore a range of decisions that they pledge to make together—decisions about where they will live, decisions about the house, the car, the children, and the money—including the disposition of those inherited estates. Indeed, Kant makes the joint ownership of property one of the necessary conditions of marriage, believing as he does that without equal ownership the absolute equality of power that is necessary for reciprocal possession cannot possibly be maintained (MM 6:278–279). So the Russian nobleman's wife cannot operate as an independent person free to choose now between two loyalties. She has unified her will with that of her husband, and therefore she is committed to making the decision together with him. But how can she do that, when he cannot make the decision together with himself?

9.3.4

And anyway, think about the assumptions behind the young nobleman's original request. The young nobleman asks his wife to commit herself, to make a promise, and to keep her promise in the future. She is to hold him, by holding herself, to giving up the estates. But if she can do this, why can't he? Nietzsche wrote that in order to have "the right to make promises" one must "be able to stand security for her own future" and that this involves having "a real *memory of the will*" (GM 57–8). For, as Nietzsche points out:

between the original "I will," "I shall do this" and the actual discharge of the will, its *act*, a world of strange new things, circumstances, even acts of will may be interposed without breaking this long chain of will. (GM 58)

Nietzsche believed that the achievement of this kind of will, a specifically human achievement, required an enormous overcoming of our distractible, forgetful, animal nature, and that centuries of human cultural evolution, political development, punishment, and with it suffering—and especially suffering—went into the breeding of:

the *sovereign individual* . . . , the person who has her own independent, protracted will and the *right to make promises*—and in her a proud consciousness, quivering in every muscle, of *what* has at length been achieved and become flesh in her, a consciousness of her own power and freedom, a sensation of humanity come to completion. (GM 59)

I've been taking liberties with the translation of the pronouns again, for the Russian nobleman's wife is apparently a creature of this kind, or at least the Russian nobleman relies on the thought that she is, but it is all too evident that no such proud consciousness is quivering in *him*. His only way of keeping his commitment is to get his wife to keep it for him. So what is she supposed to think of his *marriage vows*? Nietzsche recommends that creatures like her "reserve a kick for the feeble windbags who promise without the right to do so" (GM 60). I don't know about *that*, but I think we can agree with Plato here: *if she approaches her husband as one person, she'll be making a big mistake.*

9.3.5

We were looking for the conclusion that someone who is inwardly just will also be outwardly just. Instead, we wandered off into another but related point. People who are not inwardly just are hard to *treat* justly. That's one of the deepest problems of non-ideal theory. Inward justice in the people involved is a necessary condition of outward justice in personal interaction.

9.4 Kant's Theory of Interaction

9.4.1

What is interaction, anyway? Kant's theory of marriage is just one instance of a general theory of personal interaction. Friendship, as Kant understands it, is also the solution to a problem. The problem is how you can devote yourself to the happiness of someone else without losing track of your own. And as in the case of marriage, the solution involves a reciprocal exchange that leads to a unification of the two friends' wills. Kant characterizes friendship in the *Lectures on Ethics* as "the maximum reciprocity of love" (LE 27:423). There he argues that friends *exchange* their private projects of pursuing their own happiness, each undertaking to care for the other's happiness instead of his own. Kant says: "I, from generosity, look after his happiness and he similarly looks after mine; I do not throw away my happiness, but surrender it to his keeping, and he in turn surrenders his into my hands" (LE 27:424). This requires the maximum reciprocity of love because, as Kant says, "if I am to love him as I love myself I must be sure that he will love me as he loves himself, in which case he restores to me that with which I part and I come back to myself again" (LE 27:424). So the structure is just like that of marriage. I pledge myself to pursue my friend's happiness, but her happiness in turn includes my own; she pledges herself to pursue my happiness, but mine now includes hers. So like marriage, the exchange produces something new, a shared object, *our* happiness, which we now pursue together, and make decisions about together, as the object of our unified wills.

9.4.2

Kant's theory of marriage and friendship is based on Rousseau's theory, which Kant basically accepts, of the social contract.[6] Marriages and friendships, like the state, depend on the formation of a General Will. And because marriage and friendship therefore represent, in their way, small societies, it is natural to think they will have constitutions of their own. We could play with this thought. Marriages can come to grief from timocracy just as surely as they can from tyranny, when it seems too dishonorable to forgive and forget. Egoistic friendships, like egoism itself, put you in the way of preferring delusions to reality, like when you enjoy being flattered by someone for whom you have no respect. Adolescent friendships, like adolescents themselves, tend to suffer from democracy, being led by whoever is just now uppermost. And so on . . .

9.4.3

But it is not just these ongoing relationships that according to Kant involve the formation of unified wills. It is everyday interaction itself. For the idea also shows up in Kant's treatment of two closely related issues in the theory of political right. Kant conceives all rights on the model of property rights, and that means that he supposes that when we make someone a promise what we are doing is in effect giving that person a kind of property right in an act of our own. To make a promise is therefore to transfer your right over your choice to perform a certain act to another person. Your action, or at least your choice whether to perform the action, now belongs to the other person and he can claim it. So if I promise you that I will meet you for lunch tomorrow, a certain act of my will—the decision whether to meet you for lunch—now belongs to you and not to me. That is why it is you and only you who can release me from my promise—because the choice now in fact belongs to you (MM 6:273–274).

But there is a problem, as Kant points out, about how this can possibly happen. Here's the problem. Suppose I offer you a promise. Until you accept my promise, I can always take it back—I am not committed until you have accepted. But if in making my offer I have not yet committed myself, then I have not yet promised, and you have nothing to accept. If promises were empirical, this problem would be insoluble, for there is necessarily a temporal

---

[6] I owe the point to Arthur Kuflik.

gap between my offer and your acceptance, and however small the gap is, it prevents the promise from happening. The same problem exists and is even more vivid when what is happening between us is a transfer of an ordinary piece of property rather than of an act of my will. How do I transfer my property to you? It cannot be that I first abandon my property and then you pick it up, for if I abandoned it then during the interval anyone could legitimately pick it up—it would be an unowned object, which anyone may claim. Yet until I have abandoned it, it is mine, so how can it possibly become yours? If you take it when it's still mine, you'll be stealing it. The temporal gap again prevents the transfer. These problems show that promises and transfers cannot be understood as the results of successive acts. Instead they must result from the formation of a single common will, from a moment of unity between us. Promises and transfers involve four acts, Kant says: the empirical offer and the acceptance, which are actually mere preliminaries, and then the two reciprocal acts of will that constitute the unification of our two wills that makes the transfer possible (MM 6:272). You agree to take what I agree to relinquish, I agree to relinquish what you agree to take, and so we form a unified will that the thing in question should be yours and not mine: it all has to happen at once, as a single action, if it is to happen at all. Kant even says that we try to symbolize this unification of our two wills by performing essentially simultaneous empirical acts such as *shaking hands* (MM 6:272).[7]

9.4.4

What does it mean to say that we unify our wills? If you think of the will as a pre-existing entity, rather than as a product of self-constitution, it sounds very mysterious, like some sort of act of ontological fusion. But Kant doesn't mean anything like that. When we interact with each other what we do is deliberate *together*, to arrive at a shared decision. Since the conclusion of a practical syllogism is an action, the result is an action that we perform together, governed by a law we freely choose together. The free choice of this law is an act that constitutes our unified will and makes shared action possible. That, in Kant's view, is what personal interaction is.

Still, there is *something* mysterious about it. For why did I say that, because they cannot consist of successive acts, promises cannot be "empirical"? What I meant was that promises cannot take place under the conditions of space and time. This is too large an issue to go into here, but students of Kant will know what I mean when I say that, as exercises of freedom, choices ultimately

---

[7] These arguments in general are from MM 6:271–276.

take place in the noumenal world. And what Kant means when he denies that promises are empirical is that when I make you a promise, we come together, we *meet*, in the noumenal world.

9.4.5

So the possibility of personal interaction depends on the possibility of shared deliberation. And that possibility in turn depends on a certain conception of reasons. Our reasons must be what I call public reasons, reasons whose normative force can extend across the boundaries between people.[8] Public reasons are roughly the same as what are sometimes called objective, or agent-neutral reasons.[9] They may be contrasted to what I call private reasons—subjective or agent-relative reasons. A private reason is a reason whose normative force is private, in the sense it belongs to only one person.

As many philosophers have pointed out, the privacy of reasons is consistent with a kind of universalizability requirement. If I conceive of reasons as private, and accept a universalizability requirement, I am committed to the view that if I have a reason to do action-A in circumstances-C, then I must be able to grant that you also would have a reason to do action-A were you in circumstances-C. So for instance, if I think that the fact that something will make me happy is a good reason for *me* to do it, then universalizability requires me to think that the fact that something will make you happy is a good reason for *you* to do it. But my happiness is still mine, and yours is still yours; mine is a source of reasons for me, but not for you; yours is a source of reasons for you, but not for me.[10] On the public conception of reasons, by contrast, a universalizability requirement commits me to the view that if I have a reason to do action-A in circumstances-C, I must be able to *will* that you should do action-A in circumstances-C, because your reasons are normative for me.

So on the private conception of reasons, a universalizability requirement leaves us each with our own system of private reasons, which don't have to be consistent with anyone else's. And this can leave us in a condition of essential conflict. For instance, suppose you and I are competing for some object we

---

[8] See also the discussion of public reasons at SN 4.2.1–12, pp. 132–45.

[9] I say roughly the same, because objective or agent-neutral reasons may be understood in either of two ways: on a substantive realist model, as things that exist independently of agents and are grasped and applied by them; or, on the model I am about to describe, as things that emerge in the interaction between people and so are more properly characterized as "intersubjective" than objective. On this see my "The Reasons We Can Share: An Attack on the Distinction between Agent-Relative and Agent-Neutral Values" (CKE essay 10).

[10] A private reason is like a toothbrush. They are all pretty much alike, but we must each have our own.

both want. I think I have a reason to shoot you, so that I can get the object. On the private conception of reasons, universalizability commits me to thinking you also have a reason to shoot me, so that you can get the object. I simply acknowledge that fact, and conclude that the two of us are at war. Since I think you really do have a reason to shoot me, I think I'd better try very hard to shoot you first.

But on the public conception of reasons, we do not get this result. On the public conception I must take your reasons for my own. So if I am to think I have a reason to shoot you, I must be able to *will* that you should shoot me. Since presumably I can't will that, I can't think I have a reason to shoot you. So it is only on the public conception of reasons that a universalizability requirement is going to get us into moral territory.

9.4.6

I just claimed that if personal interaction is to be possible, we must reason together, and this means that I must treat your reasons, as I will put it, *as reasons*, that is, as considerations that have normative force for *me* as well as you, and therefore as public reasons. And to the extent that I must do that, I must also treat you as what Kant called an end in yourself—that is, as a source of reasons, as someone whose will is legislative for me.

To see why, consider a simple coordination problem. Suppose you and I are related as student and teacher, and we are trying to schedule an appointment. "Stop by my office right after class," I say, thinking that that will be convenient for me, and hoping that it will also be convenient for you. It isn't, as it turns out. "I can't," you say, "I have another class right away." So I have to make another proposal. It's important to see why I do have to do this: it's because having the meeting is something that we are going to do together. The time I suggested isn't good for *you*, and therefore it isn't good for *us*, and it follows from that that it isn't after all good for *me*, and so I need to suggest another time. To perform a shared action, each of us has to adopt the other's reasons as her own, that is, as normative considerations with a bearing on her own case. That's why the fact that the time is not good for you *means* that it also is not good for me. So we both keep making suggestions and considering them until we find a time that's good for both of us. The aim of the shared deliberation, the deliberation about when to meet, is to find (or construct) a shared good, the object of our unified will, which we then pursue by a shared action. And it follows from the fact that the action is shared that if either of us fails to show up, we will both have failed to do what we set out to do. Our autonomy and our efficacy stand or fall together.

9.4.7

On the Kantian conception, in other words, an agreement is like an exchange of promises, like a marriage. I give you authority over my will as to whether I will meet you at a certain time, provided that you give me authority over your will as to whether you will meet me at that same time, and in winning authority over the will that has authority over mine, I win myself back. And for the reasons I mentioned earlier, this double exchange has to happen simultaneously, all at once, if it is to happen at all. And the result is the formation of a shared will, that we shall meet at a certain time. So an agreement, like a promise, can't be a merely empirical event. When we make an agreement, we *meet* in the noumenal world.

9.4.8

What's the alternative? Suppose I don't treat your reasons as reasons, as considerations with normative force for me. What does that mean? We might think it means that the discussion will go like this: I ask you to meet me right after class. As before, that isn't possible. "I can't," you say, "I have another class." Perhaps I just look puzzled as if I cannot make out why this is supposed to be relevant and I say something like "well, just skip it." I don't try to work out something that's good for both of us, because your reasons are *nothing* to me, and any objections that might be grounded in your reasons are nothing to me: I can't see why your reasons should count; all that counts is that a certain time is good for me. Obviously, we can't relate at all on those terms. So if that's how it is, no personal interaction is going to be possible.

9.4.9

But of course that is putting it too strongly, for I was imagining that I disregard your reasons altogether, as if they weren't even there. But there is something in between treating someone else's reasons *as reasons*, and disregarding them altogether. I could take your reasons into account, not as public reasons with normative implications for me, but as private ones with normative implications for you, implications that bear on my predictions of how you are going to act. I know that you have certain reasons, and that being rational you are likely to act in accord with them; this fact is one of the facts I have to deal with in planning my own actions. I don't in this case treat your reasons as reasons; instead I treat them as possible tools and obstacles, things that might help me to achieve my ends or get in my way. As I said before, if I treat your reasons *as reasons*, they may change my mind about what counts as the best outcome. Only an appointment time that suits us both is the best outcome, and that is what I am aiming at, since that is what our shared deliberation is aiming at. But if I treat your reasons as tools and obstacles, they will come into my deliberation in a different way—I will see whether I might use them as tools in the pursuit of my own ends, or if not, if they are obstacles, then I will try to determine whether I can remove them from my path.

In my example, your reason not to meet me right after class presents itself to me as an obstacle. So I might try to get rid of it: instead of simply telling you to skip your class, I might try to persuade you to skip it, to talk you out of thinking you really have the reason that is in my way, or that it has as much force as you thought. "Is something *important* happening in your class that day?" I might ask. And even if our reasons concern commensurable things, I can't try to urge that my reason is weightier, as a way of justifying my choice, because by hypothesis, we are private reasoners, and so have no reason to weigh our private reasons against one another's. But I could try to inflate the strength of my reason as a way of influencing *your* predictions of how I am going to behave. "Look," I say, "I'm so busy. There's really no other time I can meet with you." If these techniques don't work, I may change my mind about what is the best possible outcome, the best time to meet. But it won't be like the case in which I treat your reason as a reason, and find that a certain outcome isn't best for me because it isn't best for us. If I change my mind about when to meet because your reasons present me with an obstacle, it will be because, given the obstacles that stand in my path, finding a new time is the best I can do. So if I regard your reasons this way, as tools and obstacles, we will be able to have a *sort* of relationship—for we will be able to fence and negotiate and bargain. Well, isn't that how it is? Certainly it must be admitted that when you are trying to arrange a meeting with someone who cannot meet at any time that is convenient for you this is often *exactly* what it feels like.

But it is one thing to say that it is *work* to overcome the egocentric predicament, and another to say that we can't do it. It is also *work* to overcome the temptation of the moment, and yet sometimes we must, if action is to be possible at all (4.3.3). Is personal interaction really just a matter of negotiating and fencing and bargaining between two private reasoners? Consider—as indeed the example has already made clear—that if reasons are really private, then there is no reason for the sort of negotiation I have been describing to be open and aboveboard. Quite the contrary: insofar as I am a rational private reasoner, I should use force or tricks if I can, because I see your reasons only as obstacles to be defeated, or tools to be used. In effect, this means that our relationship will be a kind of war, or combat. We aren't aiming at constructing shared reasons, so one of us, the one whose private reasons will prevail, will be the victor, and the other will be the vanquished. And in trying to achieve that victory we will rightly use all the arts of war. Of course if neither of us can get the upper hand, we may have to reach a compromise, but we won't think of the compromise as a good thing in itself, because it is something that respects both of our reasons as far as that is possible. Instead we will each think of it, privately, as the best he or she could do under the circumstances.

9.4.10

And this of course is how the Russian nobleman is related to *himself*. He doesn't think of his future reasons as reasons—he thinks of them as facts to contend with, as tools and obstacles, and in his case mainly obstacles—and he is therefore in a condition of war with himself. His efforts as a young man are dedicated to ensuring that his younger self wins, and his older self loses. His soul is therefore characterized by civil war, and that is why he fails as an agent, and his younger self cannot be efficacious without the help of his wife. But for the same reason he, his whole self now, is unable to interact with his wife.

9.4.11

Does the contrast I've been drawing seem too extreme to you? On the one hand, we have the shared deliberations of two public reasoners, sharing each other's reasons, in an effort to construct a shared good, which both of them will acknowledge as the best thing all around. And that, I say, is like a marriage. On the other hand, we have the negotiations of two private reasoners, which I've claimed will rightly be filled with tricks and deception and mutual manipulation. And that, I say, is like a war. Goodness! Isn't there any form of personal interaction between a marriage and a war? Or to put the point more calmly, isn't there such a thing as a fair negotiation, between two parties whose interests are legitimately at odds?

Basically, I want to say there is not, but let me put it in a less paradoxical way. Negotiation is like the advocacy system in the law, or like competition in the market, or in the classroom, or in sports. In all of these cases, at least in theory, that is, in Kantian theory, the goal is a shared good: the conviction of the guilty and the exoneration of the innocent, economic efficiency, a motivated performance from the student, the realization of athletic excellence, or the excitement of the game in the case of sport. It's just that in some kinds of cases, a shared good is, for familiar reasons, best pursued by pitting people against each other, but within the limitations of certain rules.

Consider: if a negotiation ends in such a way that all parties to the dispute are quite delighted with the outcome, then all of the parties, and even the onlookers, are pleased and think it especially successful. If its aim were simply to end the conflict or determine which party wins, that would make no sense at all, for every negotiation that reaches any sort of conclusion does that. So all negotiations are aimed at the construction of a shared good. Those that end with one party feeling disgruntled have just been badly done.

9.4.12

Actually, I've mentioned three possibilities: I treat your reasons as nothing, as irrelevant to our decision; or I treat them as public reasons, with normative force for me; or I treat them as private reasons, with normative force only for you, that I see as tools or obstacles to the pursuit of my own ends. In the *Sources of Normativity*, I argued that in the case of the normativity of *meaning*, this last possibility doesn't exist. Although, as I argued there, it is nearly impossible, I can at least *try* to hear your words as mere noise—and that's the analog to the first possibility, to my treating your reasons as nothing.[11] Or I can hear them as words with public meanings, with the same meanings for me as they have for you, and then what we do when we talk is think together. But if your words have meaning only for you, and mine have meaning only for me, there is no point in talking: if we can't think together, we can't communicate at all.[12]

Still, there is something analogous, in the linguistic case, to the kind of interaction that private reasons produce: it is the manipulative use of speech; it is *spin*. For in a case of spin, instead of thinking together when we talk, I think of the meanings that I know certain words have for you as tools that I can use or obstacles I must contend with in the pursuit of my ends. What I say is determined, not by what I think is true, but by the effects that I want to produce on you, the effects I hope my words will have.

Sidgwick couldn't see the difference between straight talk and spin. Discussing what he called the "Intuitional" view that telling the truth is right regardless of the consequences, he says,

we find that in the common notions of different kinds of actions, a line is actually drawn between the results included in the notion and regarded as forming part of the act, and those considered as its consequences. For example, in speaking truth to a jury, I may possibly foresee that my words, operating along with other statements and indications, will unavoidably lead them to a wrong conclusion as to the guilt

---

[11] SN 4.2.6, pp. 139–40, and 4.2.11, p. 144.

[12] SN 4.2.3–12, pp. 136–45. Many readers have a misimpression about how I intended that argument to go. I did not intend to suggest that the publicity of reason can be *inferred from* the publicity of meanings. I meant rather to be making an argument for the publicity of reason that is analogous to Wittgenstein's argument for the publicity of meaning. Wittgenstein's argument, as I understand it, is intended to show that meaning can't be normative at all—you can't be wrong—unless it is public. My argument was meant to show that reasons cannot be normative at all unless they are public.

or innocence of the accused, as certainly as I foresee that they will produce a right impression as to the particular matter of fact to which I am testifying: still, we should commonly consider the latter foresight or intention to determine the nature of the act as an act of veracity, while the former merely relates to a consequence.[13]

But later, after investigating some troublesome cases, Sidgwick *denies* that we have any adequate notion of which consequences are to count as rendering a communication truthful:

we found no clear agreement as to the fundamental nature of the obligation; or as to its exact scope, i.e. whether it is our actual affirmation as understood by the recipient which we are bound to make correspondent to fact (as far as we can), or whatever inferences we foresee that he is likely to draw from this, or both.[14]

For Sidgwick, talking to someone is always a matter of trying to do things to him, to do things with words, to cause him to have certain ideas. So Sidgwick can't see why we should count the immediate effect of using a word as telling the truth, while the more distant effects of using it—the inferences drawn and so forth—count as further consequences. For Sidgwick, it's *all* just so much spin.

But that can't be right, because as we saw earlier, there are limits on the extent to which you can use spin on yourself (9.2.3). You can't determine your thoughts by determining what would be best for you to think, not all the way down. Thinking, after all, is just talking to yourself. And since meanings are public, talking is just thinking in the company of others. When we talk, like when we make an agreement, we *meet* in the noumenal world.

9.5 My Reasons

9.5.1

Anyway, what could it mean to say that a reason is private, mine, not yours? On a Kantian conception of reasons, the claim will be ambiguous. Every reason arises from the endorsement of a proposal presented by an incentive. When we talk about *my* reasons, we may mean the reasons that I endorse, the ones that I legislate, the ones that I embody in my actions. This notion *is* ineluctably first-personal, and there is nothing wrong with that, for the notion of human action, self-conscious action, is of course a first-personal notion. But the first person doesn't have to be the first person singular: the fact that a reason has to be *mine* in this way doesn't prevent it from being *ours*. So taken in that way, the category of *my reasons* doesn't exclude an identification between my

---

[13] Sidgwick, *The Methods of Ethics*, pp. 96–7.   [14] Ibid., p. 355.

reasons and the reasons of others. I may want to climb a mountain, and you and I may both take that as a reason why I should do so, and act accordingly: I do so by climbing, say, you by dropping me off at the start of the trail.

9.5.2

But as that example suggests, sometimes when we talk about "my" reasons or a person's own reasons, we mean the ones that arise from a particular set of incentives, some set of incentives that is supposed to be in some plain sense "the person's own." If the reason for me to climb a mountain arises from my ambition to do so, then somehow it is more essentially "my reason" than yours, even if you acknowledge and respond to its normative force. The most obvious candidates for this might seem to be the incentives that arise from events in a person's own body—the appetites, pains, and pleasures to which she is necessarily, as an embodied being, subject. Now I think it is true that there is a clear sense in which these incentives are a person's own, for her agency and her embodiment are necessarily related—it is only in so far as a person is in some way continuously embodied that she can act at all.[15] So when she legislates for herself she is legislating for—let me put it this way for the moment—all of the conscious inhabitants of her body, present and future. And although there is room for controversy here, I am prepared to say that as an embodied being she *must* take into account all of the incentives, present and future, to which she will be subject in the natural course of her embodied life: that is part of what Plato means when he talks about willing for the good of the whole.

But we can imagine science-fictional conditions—the literature on personal identity is full of them—in which our continuing embodiment would be managed differently, and in that case, what count as "my incentives," and so as "my reasons," would be different too. For instance, consider Thomas Nagel's concept of a "series-person." Nagel imagines a society in which people are replicated in new matter once every year after they reach the age of 30. This prevents them from aging, and barring accidents and incurable diseases, may even make them immortal.[16] A series-person, who would be able to carry out plans and projects, and have ongoing relations with other people, would be an agent, and presumably would count incentives arising from his subsequent materializations extending into the indefinite future as "his own" in the sense we are considering now.

---

[15] See my "Personal Identity and the Unity of Agency: A Kantian Response to Parfit" (CKE essay 13), especially pp. 372–4.

[16] I borrow the example from Parfit, *Reasons and Persons*, pp. 289–90.

And there's a reason for this flexibility in the concept of "my incentives." For as I explained earlier, I believe that the sources of our incentives are our particular practical identities, the "parts" from which our overall practical identity is constructed (1.4.4). Most of us identify with our own bodies, our own animal nature, perforce—the nature of pleasure and pain make it hard not to—and so we find reasons in our own health and comfort and physical joy for their own sakes. But we must also identify with our bodies because we are embodied beings, and our capacity to be agents and have identities of any kind—physical or otherwise—depends on some sort of continuing embodiment. Now the science fiction examples show that what I regard as "me," and so as "my incentives," can vary with the possibilities of embodiment. But what I regard as "me" and so as "my incentives" can also vary according to what sort of embodiment a particular form of practical identification requires. Someone who values his identity as a scientist or an artist may, in a certain mood, see the tradition in which he works as the embodiment of that identity, and may feel hot under the collar at the thought of restrictions on free speech or free inquiry five hundred years hence, taking it personally as a violation of his own reasons. Someone who deeply identifies with a political movement or a church or a nation regards the interests of that movement or church or nation as among *his own* reasons. What he counts as himself, as his own embodiment, depends on, rather than preceding, the kind of identity that he constructs for himself.

And that is what is important here: as I've been saying all along, we *constitute* our own identities. So what counts as me, my incentives, my reasons, my identity, depends on, rather than precedes, the kinds of choices that I make. So I *can't* just decide I will base my choices only on *my own* reasons: because that category—the category of incentives that counts as mine and from which I construct "my reasons"—gets its ultimate shape from the choices that I make.[17]

9.5.3

So to say that *only* the incentives that arise directly in me in the course of my individual embodied existence can be the source of "my reasons" is

---

[17] Of course, I could, logically speaking, identify the person I am now in some other way, and decide to attend only to her reasons. Suppose I call my body "Korsgaard" and I decide that I am going to attend only to the reasons arising directly from Korsgaard's thoughts and experiences, or something along those lines. That seems possible. But then I would have to be prepared to will it as a universal law that I should attend only to those reasons even if I turned out not to be Korsgaard, say because some science-fictional event separated me from my body, or perhaps just because I was curiously deluded about which body was mine.

simply to beg the question against the possibility of personal interaction. I *must* interact with the conscious inhabitants of my body, because I must act with my body. But I *may* also interact with other people, and when I do, then their reasons, as well as my own, become as it were incentives in the deliberative process that we undertake together, resources for the construction of our shared reasons. Indeed, in one of the cases I mentioned above—the case of someone who sees himself as the representative of a tradition—those two things are indistinguishable, because the actions of a tradition depend on the interactions of its members. So taken in that way, the category of *my* reasons doesn't exclude an identification between my reasons and the reasons of others. I need not legislate alone, and that being so, I need not regard the incentives that arise in the natural course of my individual embodied life as the only possible sources of reasons for me.

9.6 Deciding to Treat Someone as an End in Himself

9.6.1

So interaction as Kant envisions it is certainly possible: we can share our reasons, and in normal personal interaction—in making agreements and promises and exchanges—that is what we do. And as I have said already, that means that in normal personal interaction, we are committed to treating one another as ends in ourselves. But the defender of private reasons will claim that I have said nothing so far that he needs to deny. For of course the private reasoner will say that he can choose whether to interact, in the Kantian sense, with other people or not. He can decide he will engage in shared deliberation, with certain other people, for various private reasons of his own. But until this decision is made he has no reason to accord normative force to the reasons of other people.

9.6.2

So what are these private reasons for personal interaction going to look like? Perhaps in view of certain ends that he and another person share, he thinks that the other person would serve well as an ally: they both can improve their efficiency by pursuing these ends together. Perhaps he and another person have made an agreement to take each other's reasons into account, as a kind of truce or social contract. Or perhaps he simply cares about some other people—he loves or respects them—and taking their reasons to be normative for him is part of what it means to care in this way.

It's hard to see how the first of those reasons, sameness of purpose, could launch the private reasoner out of his solitary stance by itself. Suppose we both have a certain purpose; we each have private reasons to pursue a certain end. As I mentioned earlier, if we are aware of the private reasons of others, we can predict their behavior, and so use their reasons as tools for our own ends. So if your purpose coincides with mine, then you and your reasons are usable as tools for me, and I and my reasons are usable as tools for you, and our awareness of this may give us a sort of reason to act together. But it does not really give me a reason to accord your reasons any normative standing of their own, although it may give me a reason to pretend to, in order to keep you on my side. Both of our farms are threatened by the fire, and we can fight it more effectively together. So we join forces, and fight the fire together. But have I thereby accorded normative force to *your* reason for fighting the fire? Suppose that, as it happens, my farm is saved but yours is not. Psychologically, I may be inclined to grieve for you, but am I logically committed to doing so? A reason for cooperating with someone is not in itself a reason for treating his reasons as reasons, that is, as considerations with normative force for you. Mutual use is use all the same.

Well, suppose then we move to option two, and we make an agreement—an explicit agreement to accord one another's reasons normative force. We agree to pursue our shared end together, and we therefore agree that when we deliberate about how to pursue it, we will give each other a vote, so to speak, in the deliberative process. So here a private reason gives each of us a reason for treating the other's reasons as normative considerations, and for treating our reasons, yours and mine, as reasons that are public between us. But there are problems with this proposal. For one thing, if we make the agreement for some specific purpose, and that purpose is achieved, then we seem to run into Hobbesian problems: why shouldn't I free ride on the agreement, for whatever private reason drove me into it in the first place? And why shouldn't you? And if I know that, why should I trust you? and so on and so on . . . by now we all know how *this* goes. It is the familiar stuff of the crime caper—once the robbery is successful and the spoils are in our hands then our previous agreement about the division of the spoils is up for grabs again.

And anyway, if Kant is right about the nature of agreement, how do we make this agreement? If Kant is right, we have to treat our reasons as shareable in the first place, in order to make an agreement. So we can't make an agreement to treat our reasons as shareable, and it would be superfluous if we could.

So long as I treat your reasons as having normative force only because it somehow serve my interests to do so, I am not really treating them as reasons after all, because if my stance towards them is instrumental I am necessarily regarding them as tools. In order to treat your reasons as having authentic normative standing I must treat them as having normative standing simply because they *are* your reasons, I must respect them for their own sake, out of some sort of attitude of love or respect that I have towards you, and for no other reason than that.

So this brings us to the third option, that you can decide to interact in Kantian fashion with some people because you care about them. But it doesn't work that way: it is not that I *decide* that because I love or respect someone I will accord normative force to his reasons. It's rather that finding myself loving or respecting someone, I simply do accord normative force to his reasons. The interactive attitude may be called forth in us by something about a person or about our relationship to a person. But it is not, therefore, something chosen.

9.6.3

We can't choose to treat someone's reasons as reasons, as considerations with normative force for us. We can't decide to treat someone as an end in himself. So am I saying we are all locked away from each other, in our own little system of private reasons? No, just the opposite. I am saying that responding to another's reasons as normative is the default position—just like hearing another's words as meaningful is the default position. It takes work to ignore someone else's reasons; it's nearly as hard to be bad as it is to be good. And that's because reasons are public.

But for now, leave all those arguments aside. Let's suppose that you can just decide to treat someone's reasons as reasons, with normative implications for you, but that you need not do that unless you choose to. Would that show that morality is optional, depending as it does on whether you have any private reasons that favor personal interaction? It is not that simple, for there is one person with whom even the most determined private reasoner must interact in the way that Kant's theory requires. And that is himself.

9.7 Interacting with Yourself

9.7.1

Personal interaction, I have argued, is quite literally acting with others. But for a creature who must constitute her own identity, it is equally true that acting is quite literally interacting with yourself. The requirements for unifying your agency internally are the same as the requirements for unifying your agency with that of others. Constituting your own agency is a matter of choosing only those reasons you can share with yourself. That's why you have to will universally, because the reason you act on now, the law you make for yourself *now*, must be one you can will to act on again *later*, come what may, unless you come to see that there's a good reason to change it. This is what Plato means—and he means it literally—when he says that a good person is his own friend, and legislates for the good of his soul as a whole.

The Russian nobleman fails as an agent because he doesn't do this, because he doesn't will a law that he thinks he can commit himself to acting again later on, come what may. In fact he has what in 4.4 I called a particularistic will, for he expects to change his mind without a reason. And if you expect to change your mind without a reason, then you are not willing your maxim as a universal law, not even a provisionally universal law (4.4.2). And if you aren't willing your maxim as a universal law, then you lack self-respect. More precisely, that fact is the same as the fact that you lack self-respect, for you aren't governing yourself by the law of your own will.

9.7.2

In saying this, I don't exactly mean to imply that the younger Russian nobleman has to respect his older, future self, the older Russian nobleman, or at least I don't mean that he has to respect the older Russian nobleman's *verdict* about the proper disposition of the estates. However, that's certainly one way that he could go about re-establishing his unity. That is, the younger Russian nobleman could take the attitude that the older Russian nobleman, in making the predicted decision that he has a reason to keep the estates, is making a claim with normative standing. And the younger Russian nobleman could conclude that if he and his future self are to act together he must take that claim into account. He, the younger Russian nobleman, could decide that he cannot now make a promise to give up the estates, or perhaps not all of them, without a manifest failure to will for the good of his future self, and so for the good of the whole. Ordinary prudence with respect to an overly enthusiastic charitable impulse might look like that.

But we don't have to saddle the young Russian nobleman, or ourselves, with some dreary piece of ordinary prudence in order to make the case here, for, as I said, his respect for his future self is not what is at stake here. This isn't because his future self has no standing, but rather because his future self is just himself. He can decide to disagree with his own future attitude. But *unless* he is then also prepared to regard his own future attitude as one of weakness or irrationality, he is not according the reason he himself proposes to act on *right now* as having normative standing. For he is not making a law for himself unless he thinks of his future attitude as a violation of that law, and if he does not think he can make laws for himself then he lacks self-respect. So his problem is not his disunity with his future self, but his disunity with himself here and now. And his problem is not disrespect for his future self, but disrespect for himself here and now.

9.7.3

I have suggested that the conditions for successful personal interaction are the joint conditions of respect for the other's humanity, and the treatment of her reasons as considerations with public normative standing: when we interact, we legislate together, and act together, for the good of the whole we in this way create. But action is simply interaction with the self. If this is so, then respect for the humanity in one's own person, and the consequent treatment of one's own reasons as considerations with public normative standing, are the conditions that make unified agency possible. Without respect for the humanity in your own person, it is impossible to will the laws of your own causality, to make something of yourself, to be a person; and unless you make something of yourself, unless you constitute yourself as a person, it will be impossible for you to act at all.

9.7.4

At the beginning of Chapter 2, I said that, on the conception of normativity that I believe common to Plato, Aristotle, and Kant, normative principles are in general principles of the unification of manifolds, multiplicities, or, in Aristotle's phrase, *mere heaps*, into objects of particular kinds (M 8.6 1045a10). What I've just argued is that the reasons embodied in those principles must be public if they are to do that job. Shared normative force is the glue that holds an agent together.[18] The argument from particularistic willing shows why the young Russian nobleman must will his maxim as a universal law, for if he does not, he will be a mere heap of unrelated impulses. The argument I just gave shows that he must will it as a public law, with normative force for his later self. For if he does not, he will just be a mere heap of private reasons, and that is no better, and really no different, from having a particularistic will.

But couldn't he still will it as a public law only for himself, binding together only the parts—parts of the soul, or time slices, or whatever they might be—that are parts of himself? Couldn't he, that is, decide to respect only his own humanity? This is an ill-formed question. What is your own, in the individual sense of your own, is not your humanity but what you make of it, your practical identity, and the existence of that *depends* on your respect for humanity in general. And besides—or maybe this is the same point—to

---

[18] See also SN 4.2.4, p. 139 n. 12.

respect your own humanity is to respect your own reasons, and we have already seen in 9.5 that the category of "my own reasons" cannot be fully identified in advance of choice.

9.7.5

In *Ethics and the Limits of Philosophy*, Bernard Williams argues that there is a disanalogy between theoretical and practical reason. Theoretical reasons are, in my language, public, because theoretical reasoning is about a world that exists independently of yourself and is shared by other theoretical reasoners, while practical reasoning is first-personal and essentially private and therefore not committed to "a harmony of everyone's deliberations."[19] In contrast, I've claimed that we are committed to deliberating together with others, and so that both kinds of reasons are public. But do I think they are public for completely different reasons, or that the explanation of why they must be public is entirely different in the two cases?

No, I don't, because I don't think Williams has the story about theoretical reasons exactly right. Obviously, this is a big topic, so I can only sketch in a general way how I think that story should go. It's the story I think we find in Kant, and in Plato's *Theaetetus*, although I won't try to defend those claims here. If the role of practical reasons is to hold an agent together in one piece, and they have to be public to do that, then the role of theoretical reasons is to hold the world as an object of knowledge together in one piece, and they have to be public to do that. It's not that we know in advance that there is one world out there, and we are the knowers of it. Rather, in order to conceive of ourselves as knowers, we have to conceive of the world as one public object; we have to *construct* our conception of it that way. If I am to think of my experience as perception of an object, and perception as a way of knowing that object, then I have to think that, suitably situated, you would be having that experience too. But couldn't I just construct a world that was my world, which only existed for me and nobody else? No, because if I am to think of my experience as perception of an object, and perception as a way of knowing that object, then I have to think that were I to come back here tomorrow, and everything else was equal, I would have the same experience again. And that is the same thought as the thought that if you were suitably situated, you would have the same experience: both, after all, just involve a change of position. And if I can't have that thought—that if I come back tomorrow I will have the same experience again, if everything else is equal—then I can't think of

---

[19] Williams, *Ethics and the Limits of Philosophy*, p. 69. The general discussion is at pp. 65–9.

my experience as perception of an object, and of myself as the knower of that object, and my mind shatters into a *mere heap* of unrelated experiences. The argument is the same here (or would be, if I were competent to make it): calling a reason "mine" is just a claim about position. Unless reasons are public, they cannot do their job.[20] The publicity of theoretical reason holds the mind and its object, reciprocally, together; just as the publicity of practical reason holds an agent and her interactors, reciprocally, together—into a Kingdom of Ends.

9.7.6

If the argument of this chapter is correct, respect for humanity is a necessary condition of effective action. It enables you to legislate a law under which you can be genuinely unified, and it is only to the extent that you are genuinely unified that your movements can be attributable to you, rather than to forces working in you or on you, and so can be actions. So the moral law is the law of the unified constitution, the law of the person who really can be said to legislate for himself because he is the person who really has a self. It is the law of successful self-constitution. So the basic insight behind Plato and Kant's confidence here is not really anything surprising or paradoxical. It is simply that every person interacts with others as he interacts with himself, and in this the good person is no different. A person who cannot keep a promise to himself cannot keep a promise to another. A person who is prepared to sell himself for a little money is prepared to sell others as well. A servile person lacks respect for his own rights and so for the rights of others. Inward and outward justice go together. Earlier I suggested that it is hard for a state to have a free press, and yet lie to the world. So is it hard to have a free mind and yet lie to the world? The answer of course is yes. For when the good person thinks, she tries to tell herself the truth, and when she talks, she is just thinking in the company of others. And more generally, for a creature who has to constitute herself—to make up her mind and her will—acting is simply interacting with the self, just as interacting is simply acting with others. It is this that made Plato and Kant so confident that the inwardly just person will also be outwardly just; or to put it Kant's way, that legislating for oneself, and legislating for the Kingdom of Ends, are one and the same thing.

---

[20] For a longer version of this argument, see my "The Activity of Reason."

10

How to be a Person

10.1 What's Left of Me?

10.1.1

If all this is true, you now want to ask, what's left of the individual? I started by saying that we construct ourselves from our choices, from our actions, from the reasons that we legislate. But if all reasons, once we legislate them, are public, then it seems as if *none* of them are *mine*. Everybody's reasons seem to belong equally to everyone, that is, they have normative force for everyone, and so apparently I have just as much reason to carry out your projects as my own. How is that supposed to leave me with a practical identity that is my own and no one else's?

This kind of worry is familiar to us from criticisms of utilitarianism, especially those of Bernard Williams.[1] According to Williams, utilitarianism deprives the moral agent of her integrity or individual character, because it does not allow her actions to be guided by commitments to a set of people and projects that are distinctively her own. But these are the very commitments that make us who we are as individuals and give us reasons for caring about our own lives: in my own language, they give us our practical identities. A person may surely find that some project or person is the most important thing in the world *to her* without having to suppose that it is the most important thing in the world *absolutely*. But if reasons are public, how is that possible? And if everyone's reasons are reasons for everyone, how can we ever decide what to do?

10.1.2

On the weighing model, we settle this question by weighing up all these reasons, and deciding where the balance of reasons lies (3.2.2). But I don't believe that reasons can be added and subtracted, except when we are actually dealing with commensurable things. So whatever we are going to do with all

---

[1] See J. J. C. Smart and Bernard Williams, *Utilitarianism For and Against*, pp. 108–18; and Williams, *Moral Luck*, pp. 1–19.

these reasons, we are not going to add them all up and discover that everyone in America and Western Europe is under a moral obligation to sell three-fourths of their resources and send all the proceeds to Oxfam. That's not to say we shouldn't do that—only that if we should, it's not going to be because that's where the "balance of reasons," in some simple weighing sense, lies. But since I have claimed that all reasons are public, I do want to say something about how we are related, in my view, to our own projects and loved ones, and to our own practical identities more generally.

10.1.3

The kind of worry I am talking about here—the worry about what's left of the individual—moved Thomas Nagel, in *The View from Nowhere*, to reverse his own earlier defense of the publicity of reason, and to argue that *some* kinds of reasons are private or agent-relative after all.[2] An agent has a special relationship to his own projects and own loved ones, and Nagel argued that, because of that relationship, the agent's desires to engage in those projects and to promote the happiness of his loved ones are sources of reasons for him but not necessarily for anybody else. If you have a desire to climb to the top of Mt. Kilimanjaro, for example, that could give you a good reason to make the climb, without giving others any reason to help you to make it.[3] Or it might be the most important thing in the world *to you* that your child be successful or happy, so that you are willing to sacrifice a great deal for that end. You can surely have this attitude without supposing that your child is objectively any more important than any other child, and without supposing that everyone should be willing to sacrifice as much as you are for the sake of your child, or that you should be willing to sacrifice as much for any other child. So your reasons for climbing the mountain, or making the sacrifice, must be private reasons.

10.1.4

What this analysis leaves out, I believe, is the fact that most people do not regard the value of their projects (or of course of the happiness of their loved ones) as resting merely in their own desires.[4] Some philosophers would say this is because their desires are responses to reasons, reasons that exist independently of the desires themselves, but I have to put this point a little more carefully.

---

[2] Nagel, *The View from Nowhere*, pp. 164–74. In his previous book, *The Possibility of Altruism*, Nagel argued that all reasons are public, or as he called them there, objective.

[3] Nagel, *The View from Nowhere*, p. 167.

[4] On this point see also Stephen Darwall, *Impartial Reason* (Ithaca, NY: Cornell University Press), p. 139.

I believe that all values and reasons are human creations, and that the materials from which they are created are things like our desires (6.3). When I will a certain maxim as a universal law, when I will to perform a certain act for the sake of a certain end, I am also willing a value, for I am declaring this action to be worth doing for its own sake. But in the normal course of things, when what inspires me to perform the action is my desire for the end, that goes along with my setting a value on the end itself. A value, like everything else, is a form in a matter. In the case of value, the form is the form of universal law, and the matter comes from human psychology: some desire, interest, or taste. In that sense, we can see our values as depending on our desires: the objects of desire, ultimately, provide the matter for our values. But it is only the most primitive and basic of our desires that we regard as mere brute likings and dislikings. Values are human creations, but they are not created *ex nihilo* with every action. When we create values, we invite others to share them, not just in the sense of helping us to promote them, but in the sense of interesting themselves in the valued object too. And, because we share a nature, the invitation is often accepted, and then people begin to explore the possibilities, and a tradition begins to take hold. A certain way of painting pictures or cooking food or telling stories is found stimulating or satisfying by a number of people, and they develop it, and work up standards for doing it well or badly, and teach it to their children. The standards don't have to be arbitrary; they either come from our nature, as in the aesthetic and gustatory cases, or from the nature of the valued activity itself. Science and philosophy get their value from the human desire to understand our situation, but the standards for doing them well or badly come in part from what it is we are trying to do, although partly too from traditions of doing it a certain way. And we all live inside of such traditions of value, traditions of value that we hope and expect others around us to share. It is only, so to speak, at the outer fringes of the world of value that values are a *raw* creation. All of that is by way of explaining why even a philosopher like me, who thinks that values are created, can say that most of us see our desires as responses to value.

10.1.5

And that makes a difference to the way we understand our relationship to the projects that are grounded in these values. Suppose it is my ambition to write a book about Kant's ethics that will be required reading in all ethics classes.[5] Nagel might say that this ambition is private or agent-relative, since it gives

---

[5] This example and the discussion are lifted from my "The Reasons We Can Share" (CKE essay 10), pp. 287–8.

me a reason to try to bring it about that my book is required reading, but it doesn't give anyone else a reason to require my book. This seems to fit, for surely no reason for anyone to require my book could spring from the bare fact that I *want* it that way. The only conceivable reason for anyone to require my book would be that it was a good book. So I have a reason to bring it about that my book is required reading, and since nobody else seems to have that reason, the reason must be private.

But this way of describing the situation suggests a strange description of my own attitude. It suggests that my desire to have my book required is a product of raw vanity, and that if I want to write a good book, this is merely as a means to getting it required. And that doesn't correctly reflect the structure of most people's ambitions. Part of the reason that I want to write a book on Kant's ethics good enough to be required reading in all ethics classes is that I think that such a book would be a good thing, and my ambition is not conceivable without that thought. It is an ambition *to do something good*, and it would not be served by people's requiring my book regardless of whether it was good. For now, let us describe this by saying that I think *someone* should write a book on Kant's ethics good enough that it will be required reading. I think that this is something for which there is public reason.

This doesn't, however, mean that my ambition is just a disinterested response to that public reason. It is essential not to sanitize the phenomena here, or we shall go wrong. I may be interested in personal adulation, I may really like the idea of my book's being required reading, and I may even harbor competitive feelings towards others who are engaged in similar projects. I don't just want it to be the case that someone writes the book. I want to *be the someone* who writes that book. That element in my ambition is ineliminably agent-relative or private; no one else, except possibly my friends, has a reason to care whether I write the book in question or someone else does.

So the structure of this ambition is not:

(1) I want my book to be required reading (where that gives me a private reason).
(2) therefore: I shall write a good book (as a means to that end).

but rather:

(1) Someone should write a book on Kant good enough that it will be required reading (I will that as public reason).
(2) I want to be that someone (and that's private).

In other words, to have a personal project or ambition is not to desire a special object that you think is good for you privately, but rather to want to stand in a special relationship to something you think is good publicly.

10.1.6

A personal project so characterized clearly does have a private component: you want to stand in a special relationship to something that is good. Is this component the source of private reasons for action? On the one hand, the private component does seem to *motivate* me to do a lot of work I would not otherwise do. It is often true that without the personal element in ambition, people would not be able to bring themselves to carry out arduous tasks. There are therefore public reasons for encouraging the personal desires associated with ambitions of this kind. But should the agent herself treat these personal desires as the sources of reasons? If I took it seriously that my desire that *I* should be the one to write the book was a reason for action, then I would have a reason to prevent one of the other Kant scholars from writing *her* book. But in fact, neither I nor anybody else thinks I have a reason to do this, even if in competitive moments I am tempted to feel it. This is not an expression of ambition, but rather a very familiar perversion of it.

And of course it's even clearer in the case of your relationship to your loved ones. Although I may not suppose that the happiness of my loved ones is objectively more important than that of anyone else, I certainly do suppose that their happiness is something for which there is public reason. So the structure of reasons arising from love is similar to the structure I have proposed for the case of reasons of personal ambition. I think that someone should make my darling happy, and I want very much to *be that someone*. And others may have good reason to encourage me in this. But if I try to prevent someone else from making my darling happy or if I suppose that my darling's happiness has no value unless it is produced by me, that is no longer an expression of love. Again, it is a very familiar perversion of it.

10.1.7

That, I want to say, is the relationship in which we should stand to our practical identities. In 1.4.7, I rehearsed an argument I used in *The Sources of Normativity* to establish that we have to value ourselves as human, as rational beings. I argued that the value of our contingent forms of identity depends on the value of our human identity, which gives us a reason for having those contingent forms of identity. So if we do continue to maintain them—as we must, in order to have reasons—then we act in a way that expresses the value we set on our human identity.

Part of what I am saying now is that when you come to see that your contingent practical identities are normative for you only insofar as they are endorsable from the point of view of your human identity, you also come to have a new attitude towards your contingent practical identities. You come to see them as various realizations of *human possibility* and *human value*, and to see your own life that way: as one possible embodiment of the human. Your life fits into the general human story, and is a part of the general human activity of the creation and pursuit of value. It matters to you both that it is a particular part—*your own part*—and that it is a *part of the larger human story*. What you want is not merely to be me-in-particular nor of course is it just to be a generic human being—what you want is to be a *someone*, a particular instance of humanity. So it's like this: in being the author of your own actions, you are also a co-author of the human story, our collective, public, story. As a person, who has to make himself into a particular person, you get to write one of the parts in the general human story, to create the role of one of the people you think it would be good to have in that story. And then—at least if you manage to maintain your integrity—you get to play the part.[6]

10.2 Conclusion

10.2.1

Let's take it from the top. A non-human animal acts on what I called "instinct." Her instincts are her principles, and they constitute her will. They work by structuring her perceptions. Because of her instincts, she perceives the world in a certain way, a normatively loaded way: as inhabited by things *to-be-eaten*, *to-be-fled*, *to-be-mated with*, *to-be-cared for*, and so on. Those perceptions are grounds of her actions. Because she sees the world that way, with the reasons already loaded into it, she nearly always already knows what to do.

10.2.2

You are not so lucky. As a rational agent, you are aware of the grounds of your beliefs and actions—or, I should say, the potential grounds. For

---

[6] I am not the first to propose such an attitude. I think it may have been part of what Marx, following Feuerbach, meant by "species-being": that we see ourselves, identify ourselves, as instances of the human. In the third part of *A Theory of Justice*, Rawls argues that citizenship in a just society fosters an attitude of vicarious participation of the citizens in each other's activities, so that they see themselves as members of a community with a common culture in which they each do their part. I am suggesting that membership in the Kingdom of Ends makes us regard ourselves as parts of a common humanity in the same way.

being aware of them gives you some distance from them, and puts you in control. Self-consciousness divides you into two parts, or three, or any number of parts you like: the main thing is that it separates your perceptions from their automatic normative force. The object may still look threatening, like a *thing to-be-fled*, but you must make a choice about whether you should run. On the one side, there is the threateningness of the object, and we call your perception of that threateningness a desire to run. And on the other side, there is the part of you that will make the decision whether to run, and we call that reason. Now you are divided into parts, and must pull yourself together by making a choice. And in order to make that choice, reason needs a principle—not one imposed on it from outside, for it has no reason to accept such a principle, but one that is its own.

10.2.3

So you are called on to act, in that specifically human way, to make a choice, and you can't escape it. So you need a principle. Where are you to find it? It is implicit in the demands of your agency itself.

What is an agent? An agent is the autonomous and efficacious cause of her own movements. In order to be an agent, you have to be autonomous, because the movements you make have to be your own, they have to be under your own control. And in order to be an agent, you have to be efficacious, because your movements are the way in which you make things happen in the world. So the constitutive standards of action are autonomy and efficacy, and the constitutive principles of action are the categorical and hypothetical imperatives.

It's also true that in order to be autonomous, it is essential that your movements be caused by you, by you operating as unit, not by some force that is working in you or on you. So in order to be an agent, you need to be unified—you need to put your whole self, so to speak, behind your movements. That's what deliberation is: an attempt to reunite yourself behind some set of movements that will count as your own. And in order to reunite, you have to have a constitution, and your movements have to issue from your constitutional rule over yourself. So the constitutive principle of action is also Platonic justice. This isn't different from claiming that the categorical imperative is the constitutive principle of action, for as we saw in 4.4.4, in order to have a unified will, you must will in accordance with a universal law. Otherwise, you are just a mere heap of impulses, and not an agent after all.

10.2.4

So every rational agent must will in accordance with a universal law, because it is the task of every rational agent to constitute his agency. And the law ranges over all rational beings, that is, it commands you to act in a way that *any* rational being could act, because you could find yourself in anybody's shoes, anybody's at all, and the law has to be one that would enable you to maintain your integrity, in any situation, come what may. And the reasons that you legislate when you will the law have to be public, that is, have to have normative force that can be shared by all rational beings, because acting is interacting with yourself—yourself at other times or in other possible situations. You have to make laws for yourself. And unless the laws that you make now bind you at other times and in other situations, and unless the laws that you know you would make at other times and in other situations bind you now, they won't hold you together into a unit after all. And in order to do that, the reasons that you legislate must be public. So the laws have to be laws for *every* rational being, laws whose normative force can be shared.

10.2.5

And in the course of this process, of falling apart and pulling yourself back together, you create something new, you constitute something new: yourself. For the way to make yourself into an agent, a person, is to make yourself into a particular person, with a practical identity of your own. And the way to make yourself into a particular person, who can interact well with herself and others, is to be consistent and unified and whole—to have integrity. And if you constitute yourself well, if you are good at being a person, then you'll be a good person. The moral law is the law of self-constitution.

Bibliography

Aristotle. *The Complete Works of Aristotle: The Revised Oxford Translation.* Edited by Jonathan Barnes. Princeton: Princeton University Press, 1984. *NOTE: In quoting from this edition, I have deviated from the translation in two ways: I have always translated "ergon" as "function" rather than "work," and I have always translated "arete" as "virtue" rather than "excellence."*

Austen, Jane. *Emma.* Oxford: Oxford University Press, 1990.

Bentham, Jeremy. *A Fragment on Government; with An Introduction to the Principles of Morals and Legislation* (1776; 1789). Edited by Wilfrid Harrison. Oxford: Basil Blackwell, 1948.

Blackburn, Simon. *Ruling Passions: A Theory of Practical Reason.* Oxford: Clarendon Press, 1998.

Broome, John. "Normative Requirements," *Ratio* 12 (1999): 398–419. Reprinted in *Normativity.* Edited by Jonathan Dancy. Oxford: Blackwell, 2000.

——— "Practical Reasoning," in *Reason and Nature: Essays in the Theory of Rationality.* Edited by José Bermùdez and Alan Millar, pp. 85–111. Oxford: Oxford University Press, 2002.

Brown, Charlotte. "Is Hume an Internalist?," *Journal of the History of Philosophy* 25 (1988): 69–87.

Butler, Joseph. *Fifteen Sermons Preached at the Rolls Chapel* (1726). The most influential of these are collected in Butler, *Five Sermons Preached at the Rolls Chapel and a Dissertation upon the Nature of Virtue.* Edited by Stephen Darwall. Indianapolis: Hackett Publishing Company 1983.

Clarke, Samuel. *A Discourse Concerning the Unchangeable Obligations of Natural Religion, and the Truth and Certainty of the Christian Revelation,* Boyle Lectures, 1705. Selections in *British Moralists 1650–1800.* Edited by D. D. Raphael. Indianapolis: Hackett Publishing Company 1991.

Darwall, Stephen. *Impartial Reason.* Ithaca, NY: Cornell University Press, 1983.

Hume, David. *A Treatise of Human Nature.* Second edition edited by L. A. Selby-Bigge and revised by P. H. Nidditch. Oxford: Clarendon Press, 1978.

Hutcheson, Francis. *Illustrations on the Moral Sense.* (Part II of *An Essay on the Nature and Conduct of the Passions and Affections with Illustrations on the Moral Sense* (1728).) Edited by Bernard Peach. Cambridge, Mass.: Harvard University Press, 1971. Selections from this work may also be found in *British Moralists 1650–1800.*

Kant, Immanuel. *Anthropology from a Pragmatic Point of View.* Translated by Mary Gregor. The Hague: Martinus Nijhoff, 1974.

Kant, Immanuel. "Conjectures on the Beginning of Human History," in *Kant's Political Writings*. Second edition translated by H. B. Nisbet. Edited by Hans Reiss. Cambridge: Cambridge University Press, 1991.

_____ *Critique of Judgment*. Translated by Werner S. Pluhar. Indianapolis: Hackett Publishing Company, 1987.

_____ *Critique of Practical Reason* (Cambridge Texts in the History of Philosophy). Translated and edited by Mary Gregor with an Introduction by Andrews Reath. Cambridge: Cambridge University Press, 1997.

_____ *Critique of Pure Reason*. Translated by Norman Kemp Smith. New York: Macmillan, St Martin's Press, 1965.

_____ *Groundwork of the Metaphysics of Morals* (Cambridge Texts in the History of Philosophy). Translated and edited by Mary Gregor with an Introduction by Christine M. Korsgaard. Cambridge: Cambridge University Press, 1998.

_____ "Idea for a Universal History with a Cosmopolitan Purpose," in *Kant's Political Writings*. Second edition translated by H. B. Nisbet. Edited by Hans Reiss. Cambridge: Cambridge University Press, 1991.

_____ *Lectures on Ethics*. Translated by Louis Infeld. Indianapolis: Hackett Publishing Company, 1980.

_____ *Perpetual Peace: A Philosophical Sketch*, in *Kant's Political Writings*. Second edition translated by H. B. Nisbet. Edited by Hans Reiss. Cambridge: Cambridge University Press, 1991.

_____ *Religion within the Limits of Reason Alone*. Translated and edited by Theodore M. Greene and Hoyt H. Hudson with an Introduction by John R. Silber. New York: Harper Torchbooks, 1960.

_____ *The Metaphysics of Morals* (Cambridge Texts in the History of Philosophy). Translated and edited by Mary Gregor with an Introduction by Roger J. Sullivan. Cambridge: Cambridge University Press, 1996.

Korsgaard, Christine M. *Creating the Kingdom of Ends*. New York: Cambridge University Press, 1996.

_____ "Fellow Creatures: Kantian Ethics and Our Duties to Animals," in *The Tanner Lectures on Human Values*. Edited by Grethe B. Peterson, Volume 25/26. Salt Lake City: University of Utah Press, 2004; and on the Tanner Lecture website at <www.TannerLectures.utah.edu>.

_____ "Morality and the Distinctiveness of Human Action," in Frans de Waal, with commentary by Robert Wright, Christine M. Korsgaard, Philip Kitcher, and Peter Singer, *Primates and Philosophers: How Morality Evolved*. Edited by Stephen Macedo and Josiah Ober. Princeton: Princeton University Press, 2006.

_____ "The Activity of Reason." *The Proceedings and Addresses of the American Philosophical Association*, Volume 82, Number 2, November 2009.

_____ *The Constitution of Agency: Essays on Practical Reason and Moral Psychology*. Oxford: Oxford University Press, 2008.

_____ *The Sources of Normativity*. Cambridge: Cambridge University Press, 1996.

Locke, John. *The Second Treatise of Government: An Essay Concerning the Original, Extent, and End of Civil Government.* Edited by C. B. Macpherson. Indianapolis: Hackett Publishing Co., 1980.

Mackie, John. *Ethics: Inventing Right and Wrong.* Harmondsworth: Penguin, 1977.

Mill, John Stuart. *Utilitarianism.* Edited by George Sher. Indianapolis: Hackett Publishing Company, 1979.

Mineka, Francis E., and Dwight N. Lindley, editors. *The Later Letters of John Stuart Mill, 1849–1873.* Toronto: University of Toronto Press, 1972.

Nagel, Thomas, *The Possibility of Altruism.* Oxford: Clarendon Press, 1970. Reprinted in Princeton: Princeton University Press, 1978.

____ *The View from Nowhere.* New York: Oxford University Press, 1986.

Nietzsche, Friedrich. *On the Genealogy of Morals.* Translated by Walter Kaufmann and R. J. Hollingdale. In *On the Genealogy of Morals and Ecce Homo.* Edited by Walter Kaufmann. New York: Random House, 1967.

Nozick, Robert. *Anarchy, State, and Utopia.* New York: Basic Books, 1974.

Parfit, Derek. *Reasons and Persons.* Oxford: Clarendon Press, 1984.

Pepperberg, Irene Maxine. *The Alex Studies: Cognitive and Communicative Abilities of Grey Parrots.* Cambridge, MA: Harvard University Press, 1999.

Plato. *Plato: Complete Works.* Edited by John M. Cooper. Indianapolis: Hackett Publishing Company, 1997.

Price, Richard. *A Review of the Principal Questions and Difficulties in Morals.* Selections in *British Moralists 1650–1800.* Edited by D. D. Raphael. Indianapolis: Hackett Publishing Company, 1991.

Raphael, D. D., editor. *British Moralists 1650–1800.* Indianapolis: Hackett Publishing Company, 1991.

Rawls, John. *A Theory of Justice.* Cambridge, MA: Harvard University Press, 1971; second edition, 1999.

____ *Political Liberalism.* New York: Columbia University Press, 1993.

Raz, Joseph. *Engaging Reason.* Oxford: Oxford University Press, 1999.

____ "The Myth of Instrumental Rationality," *Journal of Ethics and Social Philosophy* 1/1 (Apr. 2005), 1–28.

Ross, W. D. *The Right and the Good.* Oxford: Oxford University Press, 1930.

Rousseau, Jean-Jacques. *On the Social Contract,* in *The Basic Political Writings of Jean-Jacques Rousseau.* Translated by D. A. Cress. Indianapolis: Hackett Publishing Co., 1987.

Sandel, Michael J. *Liberalism and the Limits of Justice.* Cambridge: Cambridge University Press, 1982.

Scanlon, T. M. *What We Owe to Each Other.* Cambridge, MA: Harvard University Press, 1998.

Scheffler, Samuel. *The Rejection of Consequentialism.* Oxford: Clarendon Press, 1982.

Sidgwick, Henry. *The Methods of Ethics* (7th edition). Indianapolis: Hackett Publishing Co., 1981.

Smart, J. J. C., and Bernard Williams. *Utilitarianism For and Against.* Cambridge: Cambridge University Press, 1973.

Strawson, Peter. *Freedom and Resentment and Other Essays.* London: Methuen, 1974.

Wallace, R. Jay. *Normativity and the Will.* Oxford: Clarendon Press, 2006.

Williams, Bernard. *Ethics and the Limits of Philosophy.* Cambridge, MA: Harvard University Press, 1985.

———— *Making Sense of Humanity and Other Philosophical Papers.* Cambridge: Cambridge University Press, 1995.

———— *Moral Luck.* Cambridge: Cambridge University Press, 1981.

Index

24552177R00139

Printed in Poland
by Amazon Fulfillment
Poland Sp. z o.o., Wrocław